Distant Son *An Alabama Boyhood*

Distant Son
An Alabama Boyhood

Norman McMillan

Except for family, all names have been changed to protect the privacy of individuals written about in this memoir.

Grateful acknowledgment is made to Dougie MacLean for permission to quote from "Distant Son," Riof, © 1997 Dunkeld Records, published by Limetree Arts and Music.

Jacket and interior designed by Lucinda Taylor.

LIBRARY OF CONGRESS CONTROL NUMBER: 2002102047

ISBN 0-9711913-1-X

First edition

Cahaba Trace Commission
13728 Montevallo Road
Brierfield, Alabama 35035

FOR JOAN

Acknowledgments

Like me, the writing of this book began in Hale County, Alabama. To be more precise, it began in 1997 at the Hale County Library in Greensboro, where I went to conduct some writing seminars as part of the *Reading Our Lives: Southern Biography* program, sponsored by the Auburn Center for the Arts and Humanities. The enthusiasm the participants had for writing their own life stories inspired me to write along with them, and I was greatly encouraged when they seemed to like what I was producing. Subsequently, I obtained a sabbatical at the University of Montevallo and began this book.

Although much of this memoir has its genesis in my own experience, it also contains family stories I heard throughout my childhood and adolescence. While working on the book, I spent many hours talking with my sisters and brothers—Bill, Elizabeth, Marcille, Donald, Julia, and Kenneth—and they reminded me of many details long forgotten or, in some cases, never known. I simply could not have done this book without them. Early on, Julia and Kenneth, my younger sister and brother, read the manuscript and offered much good advice.

My friends, colleague Sarah Palmer and writer Randall Curb, read new drafts as I produced them, and their sage advice helped me immensely. Jimmy Vines also made a very thoughtful response to an early draft, helping me see important ways to revise. Later Scotty Merrill and Lulu and Shelley Richardson read it and were greatly encouraging. Marty and Sandra Everse have been staunch supporters all through this process.

Besides those I've mentioned, I have received the encouragement and assistance of many others, including Bill and Loretta Cobb, Sandra and Pat Conroy, Jeanie Thompson, Jay Lamar, Scott Brunner, Lex Wiliford, Virginia Howard, Andrew Hudgins, Julyan and Madeleine

Davis, Mary Ann Shirley, Jim and Melissa Garrett, Mike Mahan, Helen Praytor, Betty May, Ed and Mary Ann Avery, Lib Bird, Lee Otts, Avery Vise, Roger Vise, Clay Swanzy, and Frances and Clyde Phillips. Special thanks also go to the board of the Cahaba Trace Commission.

Finally, I do not have sufficient thanks for my wife Joan, to whom this book is dedicated, and for my children Sally and John, whose abiding good will and support have been sustaining.

Norman McMillan
Montevallo, Alabama

My Family

Daddy: Albert Avery Becton McMillan *(1902-1981)*
Mama: Annie Lucille Goodson McMillan *(1905-1979)*

Brothers and sisters in order of birth:

Evelyn *(1926-1992)*
Buddy *(1928-1932)*
Sarah Alice *(1929-1976)*
Bill *(b. 1931)*
Elizabeth *(b. 1933)*
Marcille *(b. 1936)*
Donald *(b. 1938)*
Norman *(b. 1942)*
Julia *(b. 1944)*
Kenneth *(b. 1946)*

I have been strengthened
me your distant son
You fill my sails with winds to move me on
And on the swell of the great Atlantic sea
I find forgotten roots to steady me

Dougie MacLean

My birthplace at Mount Hermon (photo taken in early 1980s)

PART 1

The Beginning

It is Friday, August 13, 1942—a typical dog day in Hale County, Alabama. Even though the sun hasn't been up long, the bedroom of the little farm house in Mount Hermon is already warm. No air seems to be circulating. Outside the window on the limb of a chinaberry tree a cardinal chants a desperate "bree bree," and, lying uncovered on a low iron bed, the blond woman named Lucille looks over at her newest child, her eighth, an hour-old baby boy whose unwrinkled, shiny head protrudes from his baby blanket.

Turning to her oldest living son, a carrot-haired boy standing in the doorway, Lucille asks weakly, "Bill would you go kill a couple of chickens? We've got to feed Doctor Norman."

At ten years of age, Bill is slightly embarrassed about the preceding night's gynecological event he listened to from the adjacent bedroom, and he darts out, relieved.

"And would you go help him dress them, Evelyn?" Lucille asks her oldest daughter, a thin girl of sixteen with close-cropped dark brown hair who is standing next to the open window. Evelyn nods and eases into the kitchen, where she builds a fire in the cook stove to boil water to scald the chickens with.

Lucille looks over at her second oldest daughter, Sarah, who is sitting in a straight chair next to her bed. Sarah is the prettiest of her daughters, she thinks, with a milky complexion like her own and shiny blond curls hanging down her back. Although she is only thirteen, Sarah has remained at her mother's side all through the difficult night, comforting her and bringing hot water and towels to Doctor Norman, who is now on the front steps smoking a cigarette.

"Sarah, honey," she says, "Would you fry some chicken for Doctor Norman and make him some biscuits and gravy? We just can't let him go back to Greensboro hungry."

"Sure," Sarah answers, and as she leaves she pauses in the doorway and says, "Doctor Norman says to tell you that he'll let Daddy know."

Albert, the baby's father, is fifty miles away in Tuscaloosa working as a nurse's aide at Northington General Hospital, where he is particularly effective at dislodging the compacted bowels of the bedridden veterans treated there. The absence of her husband does not bother Lucille particularly because she has long since given up on counting on Albert McMillan for moral support.

Lucille shifts in the bed to try to become more comfortable, and soon she drifts off into a shallow sleep. Almost immediately she is dreaming of Buddy, her first-born son who died at the age of four. In the dream she seems to feel him in her arms, hot and listless. She is wiping his face with a wet wash rag, but he is so hot that she has to dip the rag repeatedly in the pan of cool water. Buddy is gasping for breath. If only Albert would return with Doctor Norman, she is thinking.

In a while she dreams that the boy's body becomes calm, she sees the breathing stop, and then she knows she is holding a dead baby. But she does not get up. She sits there waiting. She feels numb.

She dreams that Albert brings in Doctor Norman, who leans over the child and questions her. He straightens up and says, "It's acidosis. I feel sure it's acidosis. Too bad you didn't get to me earlier. I could have saved him." He shook his head. "It's too late now." She sees him take the baby from her and gently lay him out on the bed.

In her dream Lucille stares at her empty arms. Tears will not come.

Albert, who has been crying softly with his face to the wall, comes to her and kisses her, but she is not consoled.

Lucille is startled awake by her youngest daughters Elizabeth and Marcille, aged nine and seven, who have just entered the room and are shaking her arm and smiling broadly. Donald, a skinny boy of four and the baby until an hour ago, hangs back, rubbing sleep from his eyes.

"Is it a boy or a girl?" Elizabeth asks.

"A boy."

"Can we kiss it?" Marcille asks.

"You certainly can," Lucille says. She watches the girls crawl up on the bed and kiss the baby's cheek. Then she says to Donald, who is still hanging back, "You can kiss him too."

When Donald does not respond, Elizabeth and Marcille try to pull him to the bed. But he breaks loose, hollering, "I don't want to kiss that ugly thing."

"Do you think he's ugly, Mama?" Marcille asks.

"I certainly do not think he's ugly. I think he's the best looking baby I've ever seen."

Evelyn, who has returned to the doorway going into the kitchen, says flatly, "She says that about all of them." She then returns to the stove and picks up the pot of boiling water and goes into the back yard, leaving Sarah Alice rolling out biscuits on a marble slab.

"What's his name?" asks Marcille, her eyes large as she peers at her new brother.

Lucille pauses a moment. "Why, he's going to be named Norman Robert, and we'll call him Norman."

"You named him for Doctor Norman then," Elizabeth says.

The tone of Lucille's voice becomes stern. "No," she says, "I did not name him for Doctor Norman. I have told you before that it is *common* to name children for the doctors who deliver them. Only *common* people do that." She pauses a minute to catch her breath. "I admired the name long before I even met Doctor Norman, and Norman's what he'll be called." Then she adds, "The Robert is of course for your daddy's uncle, the one who died in the Civil War."

Lucille, fatigued and aching sharply between her legs, feels herself drifting off again, but soon she is awakened by the clattering of dishes in the kitchen. She looks up to see Sarah bringing her a plate of chicken and biscuits. "I was going to bring you the pulley bone to make a wish with, Mama," Sarah is saying, "but Evelyn didn't cut pulley bones. So I gave you and Doctor Norman the breast pieces."

"Not the whole piece, honey," Lucille says. "Go cut mine in half and eat one part yourself. And would you see that the others get something?"

Sarah goes back to the kitchen and cuts off a piece of the breast and takes the plate back to Lucille. As she passes the kitchen table she looks resentfully at Evelyn, who has taken a place across from Doctor Norman and is breaking the tiny bones from the chicken's back and stripping the meager meat from them with her teeth. She is talking to Doctor Norman about what to do for a dog with the running sickness. "Shoot him," Doctor Norman says.

Bill comes in and takes a chicken leg and biscuit off the stove and goes back out in the yard without bothering to get a plate. Sarah helps the little ones get their food, and she takes them to the back porch where they sit on the steps and eat. The sun is high by now, and everybody is sweating.

Albert leaves Tuscaloosa so fast that he forgets his straw hat. He is anxious to see what the baby looks like and to find out firsthand how Lucille is doing. By the time he gets to Mount Hermon it is nine o'clock that night, and the house is quite dark.

"Wake up, everybody, I'm home," he yells, feeling his way to the kerosene lamp in the main bedroom. He takes a match from the box on the sideboard, strikes it on the wooden floor, and lights the wick. He takes the light to the bed where the baby is sleeping with its mother, and when Lucille opens her eyes he kisses her. Then he puts the lamp near the baby's face so that he can see it clearly. "That is one more good looking baby, Lucille," he says.

The rest of the children drift into the room. Albert feels around in his overnight bag and pulls out a white paper sack, which the children know will be filled with lemon drops. He hands the bag to Elizabeth and says, "Why don't you divide them up this time."

Evelyn goes into the kitchen and lights another lamp. "Bring that candy in here," she shouts, and her brothers and sisters obey.

Albert closes the door and blows out the lamp. He climbs in beside the baby, then cautiously reaches over its head and pats Lucille's shoulder, but she does not respond.

I am the baby in the bed. Because my eyes do not see far, I am largely oblivious to what has been happening. I do not understand that the figure lying next to me is my mother, although I know instinctively that she will put some sweet liquid in my mouth if I cry just a little bit. I do not know that the other big form stretching himself out on the bed and yawning is my father or that the happy voices in the kitchen belong to my brothers and sisters. I do not know that it is hot, that the house smells bad, or that the world is at war. All told, I feel pretty good.

Mount Hermon Methodist Church

PART 2

Mount Hermon

Nobody got to be a baby long in the McMillan family, but for two years I enjoyed constant attention from Mama and my older two brothers and four sisters. Daddy was off in Tuscaloosa much of the time, and I have no recollection of him at all in those years. Then my baby sister Julia was born, and they told me that I wasn't the lap baby any longer. I was the knee baby now, and I'd have to learn to be a big boy. No longer would I be able to sleep in the bed with Mama and with Daddy when he was there on week-ends. I was exiled to the boys' room, sleeping between Bill and Donald.

Our four-room house at Mount Hermon, constructed of unpainted pine, was surrounded by acres of cotton fields. In the front yard were two chinaberry trees planted by my grandfather McMillan and a few clumps of privet hedge next to the porch, and in the back there were barns and a smokehouse, a tool shed, and a good outdoor toilet sitting on a concrete slab, compliments I was later told of the U. S. Farm Securities Administration. We got our water from a spring behind the house, and when I went there with Bill and Donald they would show me tadpoles and wiggletails swimming in the water and tell me that if I swallowed one I'd die.

It was late fall when I was almost three, and we were all in my parents' bedroom taking the warmth of a small fire that sputtered and flickered in the late afternoon. This bedroom had our best furniture, a cherry sideboard that belonged to my father's grandparents and Evelyn's Duncan Phyffe mahogany table with the folding top, a gift from our grandmother. On the walls were oil paintings and pastel drawings done by Daddy's mother and aunt. Their gilt frames glittered in the firelight.

Mama, reading a folded copy of the *Reader's Digest* she held in one hand and cradling her baby daughter Julia with her other arm, sat in one of two ladder-backed chairs made by slaves on my great-grandfather's place. Elizabeth sat in the other chair, reading. Mama looked up when Bill came into the room carrying several logs for the fire, and she gave him a dirty look when he dropped them loudly to the hearth. He ignored her.

I was sitting beside Marcille on the iron bed watching Sarah, who was painting her fingernails a shiny red. In the corner, Donald, sitting atop Mama's shiny metal trunk, the hope chest she brought to her marriage, was making cups and saucers and Jacob's ladders with a piece of string.

The trunk Donald was sitting on had almost nothing in it associated with Mama's family, but there was a stack of old photographs of my father's family, some of them tintypes, and various old papers. There were some love letters from Daddy, written in the months before their marriage, that Mama had saved, tied together now with a faded pink grosgrain ribbon.

Daddy never seemed interested in the contents of the trunk, not even the family photographs. He kept whatever papers were important to him in a Prince Edward cigar box on the mantel, and occasionally we would see him take the box down, spread the contents on the bed, and look at them carefully.

I came to look forward to the visits of the policy man, who arrived weekly to collect money for our burial policies. Daddy or Mama would take the yellowed payment sheets from the cigar box, and the skinny man in a shiny felt hat and a dirty tie would put a check mark on each policy with a stubby pencil after he took the money. I later learned that my policy cost twelve cents a week and that eventually I would have a $300 funeral.

I was not thinking about a $300 funeral this afternoon. I was watching Sarah blowing on her nails to dry the polish when I heard Marcille say, "Emma Lee Webb said we had too many children for one family."

"Well, I suppose Emma Lee is entitled to her opinion," Mama said, putting the *Reader's Digest* on the floor. "But I do not happen to agree." By the look on her face, I could tell Mama didn't like what Emma Lee said at all. After a moment she added, "I cannot claim that all of my children were sent for, but I can tell you that they are all welcome." Whatever Mama said, she said with such finality that we never doubted her.

"Was I sent for?" Marcille whined. I liked the way she said it, and I whined too, "Was I sent for?" Everybody laughed.

"I will make no distinctions between those sent for and those not sent for," Mama said. "I have told you. You are *all* welcome." I felt welcome, and, being among the youngest, much later I came to feel especially lucky that Mama and Daddy were so ignorant about birth control.

Late that afternoon, just as darkness was beginning to steal into the house Mama lit the kerosene lamp and set it on the dining table in the kitchen and told us it was time to eat. I liked mealtimes more than anything, sitting on my knees in my chair to Mama's left and looking back and forth at my brothers and sisters and Mama. I began to eat my corn bread and dried butter beans from a saucer, glancing over at Evelyn, who had just come back inside from working in the garden. She was not sitting at the table like everybody else. Because Elizabeth had broken a plate washing dishes the day before, Evelyn volunteered to eat her meal from the iron top of a boiler, and she stood next to the stove with her supper.

"This is far preferable to a plate," she announced to us all. "The handle on the bottom makes it easy to eat while standing up, and the pot liquor follows the pull of gravity and goes right down into the center of the lid. That way the juice doesn't run through your other food. See," she said, holding out the lid toward the table to demonstrate.

"Barbarian," Sarah Alice said, sitting primly with her left arm in her lap, the way she was taught.

In the quiet that followed, Marcille said weakly, "Emma Lee Webb made me cry at school today. She was climbing a tree, and she told me that if I brought her shoes to her she wouldn't ever call me a chip owl again. But she did. As soon as I gave her her shoes she called me a chip owl."

Bill, who normally leaned over his food and ate as fast as he could, lifted his head and said, "Called you a what?"

"A chip owl. She keeps on calling me a chip owl."

Bill thought for a minute, then said, "You dumb girl. Don't you know she called you a shitass?"

"Ah-um," Marcille said gravely, looking down, but everybody else except Mama started laughing. I laughed too and beat my spoon on the table. "Shitass," I said. Everybody but Mama laughed louder, and I said it again: "Shitass."

Mama, looking serious, said to me, "Norman baby, I don't ever want to hear you say that again. That's a baaad word."

I clouded up because I didn't want to do anything to upset Mama. When she saw I was about to cry, Mama patted my arm and said, "You didn't know any better, honey." Then she turned to Bill and said, "But you did. Can't you ever behave at the supper table?"

"I wasn't the one who said shitass. Emma Lee Webb was. If there's any complaining to do, complain to her," he said, and I thought Mama would probably send him away from the table for that.

But Mama must have been too worn out to deal with him, and she let it pass. Instead, she reached in her pocket and pulled out a letter. "This is from your Daddy," she said. "He says he's coming home. He misses you too much to stay away."

"Oh goody," said Elizabeth.

"Hmm," Evelyn said.

Everybody else was quiet.

When Daddy quit his job in Tuscaloosa in the early spring, he came home and threw himself into his farming. I wouldn't see him until lunch time every day because he was in the fields at sunup. I learned that he actually got up every morning about three o'clock to read for a couple of hours by the kerosene lamp in the kitchen. "These kids worry the life out of my body," he would say. "The only time I can get any peace and quiet is when they're asleep."

Evelyn was puzzled by Daddy's taste in reading. "He'll read a Zane Grey western one day and a Faulkner novel the next," she noted, "and he doesn't seem to be able to tell a damn bit of difference." His lack of judgment was actually a good thing because he never bought books himself, but was supplied with them by his sister and some of the neighbors.

Besides reading, Daddy had few other pleasures. He did love his Brown Mule chewing tobacco, which he kept in his pocket, carving off a thin piece with his pocket knife several times a day. And every day he would take down the brown jar of Brewton snuff from the mantel and fill the tiny nickel-plated can from which he tapped a dip into his lower lip every once in a while. In retrospect, one would have to assume that he also got some pleasure from sex. Otherwise, why did the string of children keep coming.

Daddy had two sharecropping families on the place, but he worked right alongside of them. We always knew when he was plowing because we could hear him all the way from the field. A mule seemed to unleash some pent-up rage inside him, and we could hear him screaming, "Get back in that goddamn furrow, you goddamn son of a bitch." The first time I saw him cursing the mule, I was scared he was going to die. His face was almost purple, and the leaders on the side of his neck were throbbing in anger.

Carter Rollins, one of our black sharecroppers, said to Bill one day, "Yo daddy can outcuss any white man I ever knowed. But somebody mention pussy or something like that around him and he be so got away with he'll walk off." He was right. Profanity Daddy cultivated with pleasure, but sexual and scatological references or any other off-color remark embarrassed him greatly, especially in the presence of women.

Anytime Daddy started cursing and somebody was around, I made myself scarce, but Mama would simply pretend it was not happening. One day a music teacher from Greensboro, a Miss Sadie Christenberry, came out to look at a walnut bedstead she was interested in buying, and we could hear Daddy in a nearby field cursing away. Mama sat there, her head lifted in studied serenity, while Miss Sadie looked down at her lap. I ran out in the yard.

The other kids were practicing a song, and they marched to the open window of the bedroom where Mama and Miss Sadie were sitting and sang the words loudly to the tune of the National Anthem:

Oh Sadie, can you see
Any red bugs on me.
If you do, pick a few,
And we'll have red bug stew.

Mama did not acknowledge the song at the time, pretending, as she did with Daddy's cursing, that it was not happening. But when Miss Sadie left, she came to the back yard, her eyes narrow and her jaw set. "I am too tired to whip you now," she said, "but you're going to get it. That was a refined lady in there. First it's your daddy, and then y'all have to act like barbarians."

Mama wanted desperately for us to behave in front of people, and, for the most part, haloes might have been seen hovering above our heads when we were out in public or when someone was visiting us. But when nobody was visiting, we knew Mama had her limits and that she would resort to spankings when we went too far. Most often, though, she drew on her powers of speech and her sense of moral superiority to keep us in line. She was a master at putting guilt trips on her children, and Bill, especially, seemed to be the object of her constant berating.

They told Bill when Daddy left to work in Tuscaloosa that he, as the oldest son, would have to be head of the family, but he knew better. All they wanted, he said, was a workhorse to cut stove wood, tote water from the spring, carry trash to the gully, and milk the cow. If he balked, Mama told him that the Bible said for children to obey their parents and that if they didn't do so they were in danger of hell fire.

The room would still be dark when Mama came into the bedroom and roused Bill to do the morning's milking, and I'd hear him complaining as he got out of bed. As he sat beside the cow, pulling at her udders, the cow would swish her tail, which was covered over with cockle burs and matted dung, sometimes hitting him in the face. He would begin to cry and think, "I'm getting out of this damn place as soon as I can."

Most often, however, it was Daddy, not her children, who bore the brunt of Mama's tongue lashings. Daddy drank, not all of the time but in binges every month or two, bringing home paper sacks holding bottles of bonded bourbon or jars of white lightning. When he was not drinking, liquor still loomed large in our consciousness. We constantly dreaded the next spree, knowing it was bound to come.

From our hiding place behind the toilet, we watched Daddy uncork the pint bottle of whiskey. Even though he was behind the smokehouse, he looked around him to make sure no one was watching, then lifted the bottle to his lips and took long rolling swallows until the bottle was empty. He made a sour face and ejected air from his mouth with a "hah." He eased the bottle to the ground, wiped his mouth with the back of his hand, then went around to the front of the house.

Donald went over and picked up the bottle. I followed him. Donald smelled of it and I did too, deciding that I would never drink anything that smelled that bad. "He doesn't even like it," I said. "You saw the face he made."

Donald spit on the ground and said, "It ain't the taste he's after, son. It ain't the taste." Donald was nine years old, and he sounded like an old man already, explaining things to me as if I were the biggest fool in creation.

"Why does he do it then?" I asked.

"It's the effect. He likes to get drunk."

"Why does he want to get drunk?"

"So he can forget where he is." Donald looked at the label on the bottle and added, "That part I can sort of understand." He tossed the bottle into a clump of sumac.

"Well I don't like it, and I'm gonna go tell Mama."

"Help yourself, son. Help yourself," Donald said in a bored voice.

I ran to the kitchen where Mama was boiling peas and potatoes for dinner. "Mama, Mama. Daddy drank whiskey. Me and Donald saw him."

She hardly looked up from her cooking.

We heard Daddy coming in the front door. "I'm hungry," he yelled. "When are we going to eat?"

"Eat?" Mama said, without looking at him. "I didn't think you were interested in *eating*. I thought all you cared about was drinking."

"You can cut the sarcasm," he said. He leaned against the door facing and stared at her. "Can't a civil word ever come out of your mouth, woman?" he finally asked.

"Civil actions provoke civil words," she said, smugly, then looked at him straight in the eye to deliver the crushing blow. "You are the sorriest excuse for a human being I ever saw when you start in on that stuff."

"Don't push me too far," Daddy said, grinding his jaw, but he didn't leave his place in the door. I wished he would just go on and pass out. He always would, but invariably there would be a period beforehand when anything could happen. Some of the other children came into the room to watch because they, like me, sensed something was about to happen.

"Why don't you go on out on the front porch and make a spectacle of yourself in front of the neighbors?" Mama said to Daddy, lifting out a piece of potato from the boiling water with a long spoon.

"I said don't push me, goddamnit," he said, moving toward her, his face becoming increasingly red. "You are the meanest goddamn woman in Hale County. You can't be happy unless you are running me down, and I'm not gonna take it any goddamn more. I'm telling you, you better take these children and get out of my sight before I do something you'll regret."

Mama was not the least bit scared of him. She got right up in his face and said in her most sarcastic voice, "Oh, you are a Mister Big Ike, aren't you? That booze really makes you a big, strong man, doesn't it? Big enough to bully a woman and defenseless children."

This made Daddy so mad that he was incapable of articulate sound, and he grit his teeth and drew back his fist and punched at her. He hardly connected at all, and I couldn't tell whether Mama was just too fast for him or whether he really didn't want to hit her. But Mama knew that she'd better get out of his way for the time being. She pushed the pots of vegetables to the back of the stove and shooed us children into the boys' bedroom, coming quickly in behind us and thumb bolting the door to keep him out. He beat on the door and screamed, "Open this goddamn door before I blow it off its hinges."

Mama knew that Daddy had a loaded twelve-gauge shotgun in their bedroom, but she seemed to have no fear of his using it. In fact, she lay on the bed quite serenely as we children huddled around her. Julia was crying, and I whimpered a little.

Daddy kept on raging outside the door for a while, but after a bit it sounded like he had passed out, probably on his and Mama's bed. We listened for a while before getting up and going to the kitchen to eat. As we passed by his bed, we could see he was dead to the world.

Mama never learned to deal with Daddy's drinking, but she never gave up on her attempts to reform him. She was in the weirdest way an optimist, so sure she was of the correctness of her position. She believed in the corrective power of shame, and she would scheme up ways to embarrass him out of drinking. Once I saw Mama in the kitchen grimly pouring water in an empty whiskey bottle and coloring it with vanilla flavoring. She then took a deep breath and staggered into the room where Daddy was sitting, feeling the first effects of the pint of whiskey he had drunk.

She took a big swig from the bottle and said in a voice that was meant to mimic Daddy's drinking voice, "I just love this old whiskey. It makes me sooo smart, it makes me sooo charming and sooo articulate." She took another swallow. "People are really impressed with me when I'm drinking this stuff. I don't think they notice that I can't feed my children."

Daddy, too far gone now for rage, just sneered at her and never said a word, his head wobbling slightly left and right.

Once when Daddy started to walk down the road to the bootleggers, Mama tromped a few paces behind him, chanting in cadence to her heavy footsteps, "Your children are starving, but drink, drink. Your children are starving, but drink, drink." This attempt, like all others, failed to reform him, but it made a real impression on me, cutting to the core. For years I could not bear to recall the scene. Her statement was not much of an exaggeration. We were not starving, but we were often underfed or poorly fed.

My older brothers and sisters told me about the most extreme step ever used to reform Daddy, and this wasn't Mama's doing. By the late thirties Daddy had gotten to drinking so bad that his father and sister, my Aunt Elizabeth, had him committed to Bryce State Insane Asylum in Tuscaloosa, where he stayed for six months.

Daddy was in Bryce's at Christmas time. Nobody had seen him for a few months when a cousin drove Mama and my older brothers and sisters for a visit. They told me that they all sat stiffly in the visiting parlor waiting for him to be brought in. The room, they said, was decorated with a lopsided Christmas tree covered with large glowing lights and angel hair. When a male nurse brought Daddy in, everyone got up, Mama standing austerely behind her children.

Daddy, wearing a khaki shirt and pants and looking fatter, appeared a little sheepish, especially when he kissed Mama, but he smiled when all of the kids handed him the Christmas cards they had made out of paper sacks and on which they had written messages saying how much they missed him. When he looked at the card drawn by Elizabeth, which depicted one vacant seat at the head of a dinner table at which a woman and some children were eating, they said it looked for a second like he might cry.

Afterwards, he sat there awkwardly, asking about people from Mount Hermon, asking about Mama's mother, saying that he expected to be out in time to get a cotton crop put in in the spring. He had little to say about life in the hospital, but all in all he seemed pretty contented. Mama showed little emotion throughout the proceeding.

Bryce Hospital was supposed to cure Daddy of his addiction to alcohol, but in those days there was no counseling or therapy for the disease, at least not at Bryce's. Abstinence was of course enforced, and the doctors, concluding that he had no chemical dependency, proclaimed him cured and sent him home. There he almost immediately began to drink again.

Daddy had great trouble making cotton farming pay. He worked from sunup to sunset along with the tenant farmers on the place, but farming was a rough life, and he could never seem to earn enough from his cotton to keep things together. He constantly had to borrow money from the bank to put in the crop or to pay the workers or to tide everybody over during the winter. Things got especially bad in the winter, and for long stretches we went on a steady diet of dried peas, collards, and sweet potatoes, along with cornbread and biscuit.

To get himself out of financial crises, Daddy began to sell off much of the stuff he'd been given by his family. Slowly the acreage surrounding our house at Mount Hermon shrunk around us, and prized furniture inherited from his mother's family was sold off, piece by piece.

One bright Sunday morning in June Donald and I spotted Daddy in the passenger seat of a blue International pickup which was entering the front yard. The driver turned the truck and backed it up to the front steps, and Daddy slowly got out, cradling a brown paper sack under his arm. A strange tall man wearing a double-breasted black suit and a striped wide tie emerged from the other side and leaned against the cab.

Daddy needed a shave, and one side of his shirt was not tucked in. He looked at Donald and me standing nervously on the front porch, freshly scrubbed and dressed for Sunday School. "Tell your mama to come out here for a minute," he said to us.

Daddy was not talking right. He slurred his words, and one of his eyelids was drooping. Something bad was going to happen, I thought, as I ran inside. Mama was standing at the dresser putting on rouge, and I pulled on her dress tail and said breathlessly, "He's drinking again."

Donald said, "He says he wants you to come out there."

The look on Mama's face was not new. It was not just disgust; it was determination too. She picked up the brush and ran it slowly through her hair, and as she moved to the porch you could see her getting steelier and steelier, her back ramrod straight.

First she nodded at the man, and he tipped his hat and looked down at the ground. She then turned to my father and stared at him, placing her hands at her waist. She did not speak immediately, and when she did she merely said, "Yes?"

Daddy looked over at the man quickly, then set his jaw to get out the words: "Lucille, I need you to clean out that sideboard."

"Oh, Albert, you didn't sell your grandmother's sideboard." She closed her eyes and put her head down for a moment. I wanted to pat her on the back, but I kept my place.

Daddy said in a thick-tongued voice tinged with defensiveness and defiance, "I sold it because we need the money, Lucille, so will you please just go on and clean it out." I didn't like to hear him talk that way in front of the strange man.

Mama pointed at Daddy's sack and gave him a cutting look. "Yes, I see *we* need the money." She turned to go back in the house and said calmly, "The children and I are leaving for church, and for your information I will not be cleaning out any sideboard."

She went inside, and, when she came back out carrying Julia, she had put on a black hat with a black veil an inch or two down her forehead. As she walked out in the yard with us behind her, she nodded once more at the man in the suit. He nodded back. But she walked right by Daddy as if he were no more human than the chinaberry tree he was standing next to.

As we followed Mama down the dirt road to Mount Hermon Methodist Church, Donald and I could not help but look back, and we saw Daddy and the man entering the house. A few minutes later as we threaded our way through the cars and trucks in the church yard, I saw the International truck go by with the sideboard sitting in its bed. Mama and Elizabeth and Marcille did not even look in that direction.

Inside the small church we took our usual seats. Mama handed the baby to Elizabeth and walked erectly up the aisle, nodding at people as she made her way. I thought she looked like a queen, and I was proud of her. She stood next to the piano, which was played thunderously by

Mrs. Inell Crumb, and she announced the hymns with great dignity. She was definitely in charge. She fanned her right hand back and forth as mechanically as a metronome and sang in a voice that was a match for the entire congregation:

Jesus, Jesus, Jesus,
Sweetest name I know,
Fills my every longing,
Keeps me singing as I go.

Later, when the preacher called for the responsive reading, you could hear Mama's voice above everyone else's, setting the pace at which the reading was to proceed. I couldn't tell that she was thinking about Daddy at all. "How could she not be?" I asked myself. I knew I was.

I was so worried that I couldn't listen to the preacher, who said everything in a high twangy voice he reserved for the pulpit. He was talking about a lost sheep, but I was not interested. I thought of Daddy taking swigs from the tall bottle and hiding what was left in the barn.

When we got home Donald and I would find the hammer and go looking for the whiskey. I would sing "Onward Christian Soldiers" as we searched, and when we found the bottle we would break the neck off and pour the stinking whiskey on the ground. When he discovered it, Daddy would curse us for it and threaten to beat us, but it would be worth it because we were Mama's little soldiers fighting a religious battle and she would be proud of us.

Back home from church, we found Daddy, as expected, passed out on the front porch, his chin resting on his chest, a big slobber stain on his shirt front. No one wanted to rouse him. Mama certainly was not going to waste any words on him now. She went in the house to find something to cook for us, her jaw set in anger, and I figured she was running over the words she would use when she let that man on the front porch know that she thought he had sunk to a new low this time. She was probably thinking, "This is the last straw." That is what she usually said.

As for myself, I lingered in the doorway and peered at Daddy. His skin was a sweaty red, his eyes were closed, and a slimy drool came from the corner of his mouth. I felt no attachment at all to him at that moment. He might as well have been someone from Mars. But I was profoundly embarrassed that he was out on the front porch where anybody driving or walking by could see him. How could he do this to us? I thought. How could he do this to Mama?

I knew that when Daddy came to, he and Mama would begin the constant bickering that filled our house at Mount Hermon. Bill wondered how two people who were fighting when they went to bed and fighting when they got up could continue to have so many children, but apparently there was a truce in the dark. There were always arguments going on among the children too. I often found myself taking sides, especially in the disputes between my two oldest sisters, Evelyn and Sarah.

It didn't take me long to realize how different Evelyn and Sarah were. While Evelyn was tough and talked tough, choosing to work in the fields, Sarah liked staying close to Mama and was always trying to be a lady. Everybody said Sarah was Mama's favorite girl, as they would say later on that I was Mama's favorite boy. Sarah was unquestionably my own favorite when I was a child.

Like everybody else, I was scared of Evelyn. She liked to pretend she was spastic, or she would walk sideways toward you shaking her hands like a person with palsy and making hideous faces. She thought it was fun to hear babies howl in fear, and I seldom disappointed her.

Sarah Alice, on the other hand, was like a second mother. When I was a baby she would feed me and change my diapers, and when I got older she would ride me around in the kiddie coop, an ancient perambulator that had belonged to my great-grandmother. Covered with screen wire, this contraption looked like an oversized bassinet on wheels. Family folklore claimed that thousands of Confederate dollars had been found under its mattress long after the Civil War, but southern families generally had their Confederate money stories, most of which were as fictional as the accounts of the sterling silver the southern ladies were supposed to have buried to keep the Yankee soldiers from getting it. Nobody ever seemed to be able to find where it was buried.

One hot Saturday afternoon when I was three or four Mama and Daddy had gone into Greensboro. Sarah was pushing me around the front yard in the kiddie koop when Evelyn came up, saying, "I'm bored as hell. I've decided we need to catch one of the mules and ride him."

"Well, let's ride right now. We don't want Daddy to come home and catch us," Sarah said, pushing me up next to the front steps and following Evelyn around back. A few minutes later they came back leading our big dumb-looking mule Daddy named Archibald for an uncle of mine.

I watched as Evelyn got up on the porch and eased onto Archibald's back, riding off down the path toward the dirt road and then out of sight. A little later we saw her coming back. She was kicking Archibald's sides and yelling at him, "Get up there, sir," but he still stumbled along at his own pace. "The bastard won't run," she called out fiercely as she stopped him and jumped to the ground. "That's no fun."

Sarah was ready for her turn, and as she led him up to the porch to get on him I noticed Evelyn going over to the privet hedge and breaking off a keen switch. As soon as Sarah was mounted, Evelyn ran at Archibald and began to switch him as hard as she could on the flanks. He was too stunned to move for a second, but then he exploded, running around the side of the house. Then he came flying wildly around the other side, with Sarah hanging onto his neck and riding off balance. Evelyn began laughing, and when she ran at Archibald to switch him some more, the mule bucked to get out of the way, throwing Sarah off. She hit the ground solidly, lying there still, unable to catch her breath. I began to cry, but Evelyn turned to me and said real mean, "Shut up, you, she'll be okay."

Evelyn pulled Sarah to her feet and began beating her hard on the back. "There. See. There's nothing wrong with you," she said. Then she began laughing again. "You ought to have seen your eyes just before you hit the ground."

Sarah's breath came back slowly. Her face was red. She whimpered and whined in jerks. Then when her sobs became more regular she dusted herself off and checked her arms and legs for cuts and scratches. She limped over to the kiddie coop and lifted me out, taking me up the steps and sitting down in the rocking chair. By now Evelyn was bent double laughing. "It hurts, you old shitass," Sarah hollered, cradling me in her arms and sobbing. That just made Evelyn laugh harder.

"That is the meanest white person I ever knew," Sarah said to me, and I figured she was right. I longed to let her know how much I sympathized, but I lacked the words.

I could tell that Evelyn commanded a lot of respect, if not fear, from everybody in the family and out. She was smart and mean. She seemed to know everything. Sarah always said that if Evelyn hadn't done it she had read a book about it, and that was not far from the truth. Her smartness was confirmed by her being double promoted twice and being named valedictorian of her senior class in Greensboro.

Despite Evelyn's superiority in school, she did not excel in home economics, a course required of all girls in that day. It was assumed that most of the girls would marry and become homemakers and that they should take the latest scientific knowledge to that pursuit. Evelyn naturally felt above such things, and she turned it all into a joke.

Evelyn's major project for the course was to make a dress, and she chose to make a two-pieced one. When she finished, neither piece fit her, but the top fit Sarah and the bottom fit Mama perfectly. The class ended with a big fashion show in the school auditorium in which the students would model their creations before their families and friends. The teacher, a woman with dyed red hair who was rumored to drink bourbon during the day from a thermos on her desk, called Evelyn to the front and said in a hushed voice, "Evelyn, you don't have to model your dress if you don't want to. You've got a good strong speaking voice and real good grammar so I'm gonna make you the mistress of ceremonies. Now, how does that suit you?"

"That's fine," Evelyn answered, but finding herself embarrassed at feeling flattered by the invitation, she told the woman mischievously, "If you want me to, I can get my mama and sister to model the two parts of my dress."

"I don't think that will be necessary," the teacher answered dryly, pouring some liquid into the thermos top.

If Evelyn was undervalued for her home ec skills, she was prized in her other courses, particularly in senior English, taught by a trim, chic woman named Mrs. Weathers, who drew Evelyn into her confidence and spoke to her more as an equal than as a student. In the class Evelyn took from her, there were twins, one bright and one dumb. Of the dumb one, Mrs. Weathers commented to Evelyn, "That girl's got an IQ about room temperature." And whenever Mrs. Weathers mentioned the twins to Evelyn thereafter she called them plus and minus. Evelyn idolized Mrs. Weathers, deciding she wanted to be an English teacher just like her.

Mrs. Weathers found out about a new state-wide Phi Beta Kappa essay contest, the winner of which would be given a scholarship to Birmingham-Southern College, and she thought Evelyn had a good shot at it. Uninspired by and uninformed on the required topic, "War Efforts in My Community," Evelyn made up a bunch of stuff in her essay, and Mrs. Weathers sent it in.

A few weeks later a large black sedan, covered with a film of road dust, slowly entered the yard at Mount Hermon. Evelyn, dressed in overalls and her short hair uncombed, looked up from the chop block where she was splitting kindling. Two men emerged slowly from the car, looking around quickly at the unpainted house and the grassless yard. They were dressed identically in pinstriped suits and striped ties and had golden straw hats on their heads. One of the men, the taller one, straightened his tie a little and addressed Evelyn: "Is this the McMillan residence? We're looking for a Miss Evelyn McMillan."

Evelyn looked down at her bare feet for a minute, then said, "Just come up here and have a seat on the porch, please, and I'll go get her for you." She went inside the house and hurriedly slipped into her best blouse and skirt. She lightly applied some lipstick and ran a comb through her hair. Then she rummaged around in the corner for her loafers, scooted her feet into them, and went back out to the men, who were sitting side by side on the porch, their hats resting on their laps. They rose.

"Hello," she said, extending her hand to one of the men and then the other. "I'm Evelyn McMillan. My brother said you wanted to see me."

The taller one looked at her rather hard, then said, "Miss McMillan, we are from Birmingham-Southern College and we've driven down to bring you some very good news. You have been selected by the judges as the first recipient of the Phi Beta Kappa scholarship."

The other one picked it up, "Out of literally hundreds, your essay was selected as the best."

The other: "Congratulations are certainly in order. And here's an

Mama (upper right), about 1920. Her sister Gussie is to her right, and the three children from left to right are her nieces, Fannie George, Helen, and Hazel Hurtt.

envelope that explains everything thoroughly."

Evelyn wanted to jump up and down, but she remained calm. "I thank you very much," she said as she moved to the front door and called, "Mama, can you come out here a minute."

Mama came out holding my hand. Donald, Marcille, and Elizabeth followed us. After the men explained again why they had come, Mama shook their hands graciously like some society lady, not giving the least suggestion that she was surprised that Evelyn had won. She said slowly and very formally, "It is so very kind of you gentlemen to come all of this way down here to bring such good news to Evelyn. I want you to know that we appreciate your generosity more than we can express, and I assure you that Evelyn will not disappoint you."

The men got to their feet exactly at the same time, put on their hats, and dusted off the seats of their pants. They looked once more around the bare yard. The tall one said, "Mrs. McMillan, you have an exceptional daughter—an exceptional daughter, indeed—and Birmingham-Southern and Phi Beta Kappa want to play a significant role in helping her realize her potential."

"We appreciate that very much, sir," Mama said, and the two men walked to the car and drove away.

Evelyn turned to the others and made a "who, me?" face. Then she said, "This exceptional daughter has got to go change clothes. I've got to split the rest of that kindling."

Deep inside, however, Evelyn was thrilled, and, whether or not she would admit it, she was most pleased that Mama seemed genuinely proud of her.

Mama was an imposing, strong woman—smarter and stronger, I thought, than anyone I knew, even Evelyn. I was as proud of her as I was ashamed of Daddy. She had first arrived in Hale County in the fall of 1923 when she came to a little red clay community just north of Greensboro to teach fifth grade at Valley School. Born about 150 miles to the north in Attalla, Alabama, she had attended nearby Jacksonville State Teachers' College for two years, after which she was certified to teach grade school. Her students seemed surprised when she told them, "You may call me Miss Goodson," because—had she followed the accepted practice at Valley School—she would have been Miss Lucille.

Daddy, who had spent most of his life in the nearby community of Mount Hermon, was greatly attracted to this shapely honey blond with bee stung lips. She was intelligent and self-confident and made a great splash at parties wearing a King Tut gown. He came on strong, a handsome man with abundant inky black hair, dark eyebrows and lashes, and very dark skin. He was also said to be very good in the romantic line, and he was willing to vie with all suitors.

As a part of Daddy's courting strategy, he had a two-pound box of Whitman's Sampler candy delivered to Mama at school every week. One week when the drugstore was out of two-pound boxes he had them send two one-pound boxes. Mama was not pleased. "Albert," she told him frankly, "that was a gauche thing to do. Send one box or nothing."

A worse lapse on Daddy's part occurred a little later when he kissed her "in too familiar a way"—as she vaguely put it—in the presence of her colleagues. Whether his sin had to do with duration or penetration was never clear, but she was shocked and angry. "You are just about to blow it, mister," she told him privately. "I have a reputation to protect."

He begged forgiveness, and she granted it. The truth was, she liked him. In fact, she believed she loved him. He was good looking, he came from a good, prominent family, and he owned land and stood to inherit lots more. His worst attributes he had managed to keep covered up quite well during the courtship. So when he proposed to her, she accepted. Shortly afterwards, she left the classroom, never to return.

During the period when Mama returned to Attalla to plan the wedding, Daddy wrote her rambling letters that revealed his joyous anticipation of the marriage as well as a hypochondriacal nature that marked him for life. On April 15, 1925, he wrote to her:

At home
Monday night
My dearest one,

This has sure been a long lonesome day, but the twenty seventh is one day nearer. It looks very much like rain today. Sugar nearly every body I have seen today has congratulated me and told me how lucky I was. Sweet Heart, Mother has been telling me what different ones were going to give us, most of them are going to give Silver ware such as knives forks and spoons. I guess I will feel better now that I have been taking some medicine. I guess I will get a letter from you tomorrow.

Sweet Heart if you drive the car any do be careful for you don't know what time you will meet some drunk person. Sweet Heart don't forget to write every day, and remember I love you with all my heart.

I am yours forever
Albert

The wedding was small, just close family, taking place in the living room of Mama's parents' house. The couple stood before the Baptist preacher to whom Mama's Daddy had paid five dollars to perform the ceremony and promised to do all the normal things, Mama even saying she would obey, a pledge she was constitutionally unable to fulfill. But her intentions were good, as were Daddy's, and they vowed themselves to each other forever.

Forever is a long, long time, but—despite the rough and often unhappy life they lived in the years that followed—Daddy did belong to Lucille and Lucille belonged to him. By all the evidence we had, he never cheated on Mama. She herself felt so secure when it came to that issue that she once told somebody that she would rather that Albert ran around on her than to be a drunkard.

It appears that Mama never considered divorcing Daddy. It was rare for good Christian women at that time and place, and Mama's natural tendency toward martyrdom worked against it. Plus she thought adversity was beneficial for all, put there to anneal the flabbiness of our characters into a steely firmness. She also had such an unswerving faith in the righteousness of her convictions that it never occurred to her that she would not eventually be able to mold Albert into the man that she wanted him to be.

Daddy probably never thought of leaving Mama either, no matter how miserable she might have made life for him at times. In his marriage as in the other aspects of his life, he demonstrated an almost Dostoevskian will to suffer. It was as if he deserved whatever adversity he met in life, and he embraced it like a lover.

It didn't take long after the happy couple returned to Greensboro from the honeymoon that the joy began to fade. Mama didn't find Mount Hermon very hospitable to her intellectual interests, as most of the people were hard working country people who might read at most the *Greensboro Watchman* or the *Farmer's Almanac.* She wasn't cut out to be a farm wife. She didn't garden, she didn't can food, and she certainly wasn't suited for field work of any kind. The first year they were married, she begged Daddy repeatedly to let her try her hand at picking cotton, as did some of the other farm wives, and he finally gave in. She picked pretty much all day, though she did interrupt her work fairly often to chat with the other pickers, and at weighing up time she discovered that she had picked merely twenty-nine pounds. The least anybody else had picked was 110, and that was by a frail old grandmother. She was so disappointed she cried, and Daddy ordered her never to set foot in field or garden ever again. For once, she obeyed.

Mama's adjustment to her new life also had another downside. Very quickly she began to see in Albert some of his less flattering traits. Daddy had been greatly spoiled by his parents, perhaps because they had lost a boy to pneumonia before he was born, and they, like his maiden aunts and bachelor uncles, doted on him, thinking him the best looking boy in Hale County. All of them gave him things—land and houses and furniture and automobiles, expecting nothing in return. Though he tried to make use of the gifts wisely, working hard at whatever he did, he didn't seem to know how to make a living any more than a bird dog would.

Daddy also had blown his opportunity to get a good education. After he finished the eight grades of public school in Greensboro, his parents, not wanting too much space between them and their son, talked him into going to Marion Military Institute in a nearby town, but he lasted only two weeks there. He wrote his parents, "This place is hell and the commandant is the devil, and I'm not staying." There was not a whisper of protest from his parents, and he returned home, for the next decade piddling around doing various jobs in Greensboro.

Daddy's mother was fond of saying that she thought her children were made out of a little bit better clay than most people's, and, while she said it as a joke, no one doubted that she believed it. Apparently, all of her family, the Averys, were proud. As a child I was taught to admire them, mainly by my mother, who took immense pride—more than Daddy did—in this family she had married into. Very early she made it quite clear that I had a responsibility to live up to the Avery blood that coursed through my veins. The most she could do from her own side of the family was to say that the Goodsons were descended from Robert E. Lee and Zachary Taylor, but all she had to prove it was a mass-manufactured family tree, yellowed with age, an actual tree with thousands of names printed on its trunk and branches.

From a young age I began to get a picture of the Averys as an exalted tribe who had come to Alabama from North Carolina in the early nineteenth century. When I was in grade school my aunt read aloud to me a letter written to my great-grandfather David Avery from his brother who preceded him to Alabama. Even though the words were strange, I could feel the excitement my great-grandfather must have felt when, at eighteen years of age, he looked down at the familiar ornate hand of his brother:

Perry County, Alabama
September 6, 1830

My dear brother David

Of all my kin I long for you the most. Accordingly, I must prevail upon you to come west at your earliest convenience. Carolina has grown to be so crowded that the land is about worn out with too much planting. Here in Alabama the land is abundant and rich, with fields of cotton growing almost as high as a grown man's shoulders, and there are nearby rivers to transport it easily to market. As the demand for cotton so greatly exceeds our capabilities to produce it, premium prices are to be gained for it. And David, best of all, I have begun the manufacture of cotton gins, and this, God willing, will make our fortune. It is for this enterprise that I most desire your presence.

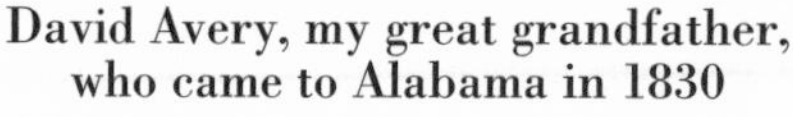

David Avery, my great grandfather, who came to Alabama in 1830

Elizabeth Williams Avery, my great grandmother

Though you be but eighteen, dear David, plead with our father to stake you and hurry here at once, for certainly with your earnest work and that of the negro labour and with the abettance of almighty God your future is certain.

Your loving older brother,
Bryant

David did secure his father's blessing, I learned, and in 1831 he began his journey with some acquaintances down the Federal Road in the direction of Alabama. He was said to have traveled light, on horseback, carrying a rucksack containing some clothes, a couple of hundred dollars in gold certificates pressed between the pages of a Bible, and a copy of *Pilgrim's Progress*.

Settling eight miles east of Greensboro on Brush Creek, David found a hilly country with sandy soil and clay subsoil, a country sparsely populated at the time. He moved in with his brother and joined him in manufacturing horse-drawn gins. More ambitious and energetic than his brother, he soon took over the operation and successfully marketed his gins as far away as Texas. He ordered his metal from England and cleared lands of the giant hardwoods he needed to make his gins. He planted cotton and other crops on the cleared land.

At the same time he began to buy slaves and acquire rich bottom acreage in the western part of the county, which was better for cotton growing, and in 1839 David felt sufficiently established to marry Elizabeth Williams, a darkly handsome woman from the neighborhood. They began a family, which at last numbered ten children.

Alabama was turning out to be the promised land for David, but the War Between the States changed everything. Family members died in the war and others were maimed, and much of David's fortune was swept away, casting a shadow over his spirits from which he was said never to have recovered. My Aunt Elizabeth showed me a sheet on which David had vented his indignation about the Emancipation Proclamation. On it he had written at the top: "Property of which I have been deprived of by the United States," and below he had painstakingly written out a list of his emancipated slaves. By their names he wrote their ages and occupations: "Pressley, 28 years, valuable mechanic; George Mitchell, 48 years, faithful laborer; Parlor, 38 years, cook. . . ."

"Slavery was wrong, no doubt about it," Aunt Elizabeth commented, "but the change was just too quick. It upset everything." But even as a young boy, I had an uneasy feeling about my great-grandfather, unable to resolve the image of a worthy man I was to look up to and that of an angry man supporting the institution of slavery.

David's children were spoken of in proportion to their success in life. I picked up early on the omission of details about two unmarried alcoholic sons who, despite good educations, got up every morning, dressed themselves in suits and ties, and never turned their hands to do a thing. Nor did I hear much of the unmarried sister DoDo, who was college-educated but never worked. I did once hear that she complained, "Saturdays are really hard on me. The washerwoman brings back the laundry, and I have to put it up."

I did hear about Uncle Robert, from whom I got my middle name, but there was little to say of him beyond recounting the tragic tale of

My great uncle, Albert Monroe Avery

how when he was nineteen he dropped his studies at Southern University and marched off in May of 1861 to Richmond as a private in the Greensboro Guards, Company D, 5th Alabama Regiment. In Richmond a measles epidemic broke out, and he fell victim to the disease before he fought a single battle.

The two Averys that I heard the most about were my great-uncle Albert and my great-aunt Sallie. Both were held up to all of us as models worthy of emulation. Both had been scholars, I was told, attending first the Greensprings School in Havana, just north of Greensboro, an academy patterned after Rugby which was operated by the prominent educator, Dr. Henry Tutwiler. Later both had gone on to college, he at the University of Alabama and she to Judson College.

In our trunk was a sepia-toned photograph of Albert wearing the full dress captain's uniform of the 20th Alabama Regiment, CSA, staring out imperiously and clasping a sword. I thought he looked exactly like an Avery should look, proud and strong. At Vicksburg, he was wounded and taken prisoner, but he managed finally to get back to Alabama, where he became a gentleman farmer in Havana and, for a couple of

My great aunt, Sarah Jane (Sallie) Avery

years, the registrar of the federal land office in Huntsville under President Grover Cleveland. He also represented Hale County in the Alabama legislature for a while. When I was taken to the family graveyard on a high hill above Mount Hermon Church, I would admire the tall obelisk marking his grave. It towered above all the other markers.

Daddy was named for his Uncle Albert, probably with the hope that he too would so distinguish himself. At some point he was given Uncle Albert's oil portrait, which also depicted him in his Confederate uniform. After a few years the canvas broke loose from the frame, and the portrait was placed under a bed. One day Mama walked into the room to discover one of my older sisters calmly cutting up the portrait to make doll furniture. For my sisters, as for everyone else in the family, such things as portraits were luxuries that easily yielded themselves over to practical demands.

Daddy was horrified about the portrait being ruined, not so much because he mourned the loss of the portrait itself, but because he feared the reaction of family members who had coveted the portrait. In time, when no one seemed to notice its being missing, he settled down.

Sallie Avery was probably held up as a model even more than Albert was because she had overcome the disadvantages of her sex to become distinguished as a scholar and teacher, or so we were told. Evelyn said she was a bluestocking, which she told us meant a lady scholar, and I never looked at her photograph without wondering if her legs, which were not in view, were covered with blue stockings. Her parents realized her ability and ambition early on, and so they took the unusual step they didn't for any other of their girls. They sent her in the 1860s to Greensprings School, where she, as one of seven females, studied the exact same curriculum as the sixty-six male students. On one of her report cards, Dr. Tutwiler recorded that on a field trip in surveying, "Sallie was the best man I had."

Later, after she graduated from Judson College and had studied math at Peabody College and the University of Chicago, she became a protégé of the prominent educator Miss Julia Tutwiler, the daughter of the headmaster at Greensprings School, who was President of Livingston Normal School. There Sallie became the principal teacher, offering courses in Latin, French, English, photography, and mathematics. In 1893, when Miss Julia sent the first group of girls to enter the University of Alabama, she sent Sallie as their chaperon and tutor. At that time many people thought that young ladies' heads were too soft to take in math, which was required in the University of Alabama curriculum, and math tutoring occupied much of Sally's time.

After retirement Sallie pursued her interest in painting, favoring bucolic scenes, especially English landscapes. Although she had never been to England, she painted Windsor Castle as viewed from across the Thames as easily she did an Alabama landscape. She also spent her time with genealogical investigation. She discovered that my great-great-great-grandfather, a Revolutionary War veteran, had died in 1828 on a Christmas visit to Alabama from North Carolina, and she found his grave in northern Hale County. That got her and a whole host of others into the Daughters of the American Revolution.

It was said of Sallie that when in her genealogical investigations she came upon an Avery that had not done so well in life she would say, "Now, this is where the family tree branches off," and she would banish the person to genealogical oblivion.

My grandmother, Emma Fredonia Avery McMillan

Thus did I fall heir to a nicely polled family tree, enabling me to feel by early grade school that I was a scion of one of God's chosen tribes. Later, I would learn that my great-grandfather's brother Bryant Avery had fathered several mulatto children by a black house slave, but by and large that detail was pushed back somewhere and ignored. But Evelyn did say on a number of occasions that you could tell the black Averys from the white ones. They were the good-looking ones.

I never saw my father's mother, and I never had a name to call her. But when the Avery pictures came out of Mama's trunk I would stare at the photograph of the mannish-looking woman with dark complexion and close-cropped dark hair. "It doesn't look like a woman to me," I would say.

"It is a woman, Norman. It is your grandmother Emma," Mama would say. "She was a fine lady. She was refined and cultured. She studied painting at Tuscaloosa Female College under Hercule Hamilton."

In fact, the only real attachment I felt to Emma Avery was through her paintings. When we went to Greensboro to visit my Aunt Elizabeth,

My grandfather, William Oliver McMillan

I would stand in the hall mesmerized before a large painting of Charlotte Corday in prison, her hands grasping the bars lightly. At the time I had no idea who Charlotte Corday was, but I felt sorry for her languishing in jail. The painting actually belonged to us, but we had no walls large enough to display it.

Another painting of hers that we did keep fell off a truck when we were moving one time and got run over by a car following us, so it was probably just as well that Aunt Elizabeth kept Charlotte Corday for us.

The main impression I was given of my grandmother was that she was a great hypochondriac, spending her days in the sitting room wearing high-necked white linen dresses that reached the floor or starched all-black frocks. According to all I heard speak of her, she never turned her hand to do any work. She is reported to have once said, "I stay out of the kitchen because if you are wearing black you get flour on you and if you are wearing white you get smut on you."

Earlier, however, she had taught school for a period, and there one of her first students had been my grandfather, William Oliver McMillan, an earnest young man who impressed her with his maturity.

At eleven he had seen his father stabbed to death by a man who wanted to renege on a horse-trading deal, and, as the oldest surviving son in a family of seven, William had had to shoulder a great deal of responsibility, running the family farm. Emma was impressed.

After William finished school, he began courting Emma, little bothered that she was fourteen years his senior. As his teacher, she had been Miss Emma to him, and as her suitor, he continued to call her that. They decided to marry, and, although she was thirty-nine years old, he thought it necessary to go to her father David to ask the old man for her hand.

William was not at all sure Emma's father would give his blessing. He knew that some people were whispering that Emma was being courted by a man far beneath her. He knew that the Averys had more money, had a higher social standing, and were better educated than the McMillans. He knew that their history in America was certainly more prestigious, the first Averys, from Devon, England, having arrived in 1630 on the *Arabella* and having settled in Gloucester, Massachusetts, where they became prominent citizens. The first McMillans, on the other hand, had emigrated from Cornworth, Scotland, in about 1765, settling as yeoman farmers in Robeson County, North Carolina. But neither he nor Emma counted these as irresolvable differences.

When William went to David, he discovered that the old man had something other than social class or age on his mind. He said, "Now, my Emma has very weak eyes, and we have never required her to do any housework. The only way I can agree to this marriage is if you will give your word that Emma will never be expected to do such work."

"I give you my word," William said, offering his hand, and so much was he taken to be a man of integrity that David gave his blessing. Down to Emma's death in 1928, William kept this vow, doing the cooking and cleaning himself when he couldn't get outside help. And he called her Miss Emma until the day she died.

Although Miss Emma had long been dead when I was born, PaPa, as we called my grandfather, lived on until I was five years old. I was always glad when this short, dapper man with a large, well-shaped mustache arrived. Speaking little and in a whispery voice, he would sit for hours on the porch, rolling Great Northern State tobacco into cigarettes and smoking them.

My grandmother Fannie Skelton Goodson (in long coat) with her daughter Aouda and family. My sister Evelyn, a student at Birmingham Southern in the 1940s, is at the far right.

PaPa was a man of decided opinions, feeling especially that women should comport themselves with the greatest decorum. He deplored a woman whistling or wearing trousers, and when Evelyn took to doing both he was appalled. About the whistling he would only shake his head, but he would occasionally announce gravely, "When a woman puts on trousers, she is a woman no more."

A few years before he died, PaPa was run over by a car in Greensboro, and thereafter had to use a wheel chair. I really remember the wheel chair better than I remember him, but I was sorry when he died. He was the first person in the family to die after I paid attention to such things, and I was quite eager to attend his funeral, but only the older kids got to go. I felt deprived.

I never saw my mother's father, who was the bookkeeper for a mine in Attalla, but her mother was a great favorite of us children, and we longed for her infrequent visits. Although she died when I was eight, I remember her well, a small, bent woman with a happy smile, apparently as different from my other grandmother as a collie from a Rottweiler.

I remember one visit distinctly. "Grandma Goodson is here," Julia and I yelled, jumping up and down as we saw her get out of the black pickup truck her granddaughter had brought her down from Birmingham in. She came toward the porch, a paper sack in one hand and a seat cushion in the other. Her granddaughter removed a striped suitcase from the back of the truck and followed her.

Everybody crowded around, and she kissed all of us children and called us by name. She then kissed Mama and Daddy. She opened her paper sack and took out packs of Juicy Fruit gum and handed each of us one. "Now don't throw it away when the sweet gets out of it," she said. "It's better when it's old. I once kept a wad going for two years until the girls made me throw it away." She laughed loudly.

I took my package to the doorway and unwrapped all five sticks and crammed them in my mouth. "Look at what Norman did," Marcille said as I tried to chew the mouthful of gum, sweet saliva coming from both sides of my mouth. Everybody laughed and I was embarrassed. I noticed that Donald had not even opened his pack. He would ration his out over several days, and I would envy his having it.

"How long are you going to stay with us?" asked Elizabeth.

"Two weeks," Grandma said, and Mama and Daddy gave each other knowing looks. She had never stayed out her visit. They knew that after about four or five days she would start sending for her granddaughter to come get her. When we asked her why she had to leave early, she would answer, "I don't want to get too far from my burying ground. I'm an old woman and my time is nigh."

We would get serious and crowd around.

"Do you know how you can tell if your time is nigh?" she'd ask. "Look." She would take the loose skin on the top of her hand and pinch it up. "See how slow that skin's going back down? That's a sign your time is nigh."

We'd all pinch our skin to check. Once, lifting my hand to her, I asked, "Is my time nigh, Grandma?"

"No, Norman," she answered, "you'll live one hundred years. I guarantee."

On this day, after Mama had gone to the kitchen and Daddy to work in the garden, we took Grandma to the wing chair in their room. She put her cushion in it and took her seat.

"Tell us a joke," we begged.

"Okay," she said. "Do you know why the little moron buried his mother under the front porch?"

"So he'd have a stepmother," Donald said. "I heard that at school. Tell us another one."

"Okay. Let's see. Do you know who wrote the book, *The Yellow Stream*?"

We didn't know.

Grandma looked to make sure our parents were out of earshot, and she said in a hushed, confidential voice, "I. P. Freely." She put her hand over her mouth and laughed hard.

I didn't get it, but I laughed anyway.

"Who wrote *Spots on the Wall*?" she asked.

No answer.

"*Spots on the Wall* was written by the famous Chinese author, Hu Flung Dung." She laughed again, and we did too. I was going to have to ask Elizabeth to explain these jokes.

"What about *Under the Grandstand*?" She waited. "You don't know, huh?" Do you give?"

"We give," we said.

"Okay, then, it's Seymour Butts."

Grandma Goodson seemed irresistible to everyone. Even Daddy, who didn't like many people at that time, was crazy about her. She had always demonstrated a marvelous zest for life and was full of small charities. During the Great Depression, hobos from all over the nation knew that they could come to her house for food in exchange for some small chore. She well knew that her house was marked by a pointing hand on a nearby utility pole, but she never made any effort to remove it.

Grandma also headed up projects at church to provide food and clothes for the needy. It was whispered in the family that she had joined the Ku Klux Klan auxiliary when she was a young married woman and had delivered Christmas baskets for the organization. I was always told that her involvement had nothing to do with race, but that she thought the Klan was concerned with the falling morals in her town and she felt they did the right thing in giving warnings to loose women and reprobate men.

When Grandma Goodson died, I didn't get to go to the funeral. It didn't even register with me where she was being buried. But at an early age I knew intuitively and by observation that my mother inherited a great deal of her own mother's vitality, creativity, and optimism. Both of Mama's parents had encouraged her to do her best. That was more than I could say for Daddy's parents, who seemed utterly incapable of instilling in him a determination to succeed.

Mount Hermon remained my home for about five years. It was a tiny community, but I found a lot to look at and listen to. Faces, black and white, entered my world and I was fascinated.

I knew the black faces were different from ours. I wasn't color blind. And I knew from a very early age that being white was infinitely more desirable than being black. Even though I knew he was joking, when Daddy told us that if we drank coffee we'd turn black too, I looked at the resulting blackness with horror. What a curse, I thought, to be trapped inside black skin, and sometimes as I looked at a black face I was grateful to have escaped the curse.

Watching black faces actually became a sort of obsession. Every day during the summer I would watch the glistening face of a black man named Sidney Hilliard as he drove by in his cart pulled by a giant ox named Lamb. He worked a patch of land he rented from us, and each day after eating jelly biscuits he took from a syrup can, he lay down under a water oak tree, took off his felt hat and placed it over his face, and proceeded to take a three-hour nap. Donald and I would hide and watch him sleep.

My mother said that Sidney was in love with Viney, a young black woman who lived down the road, but that Viney would have nothing to do with him. She told Mama, "I hope Sidney Hilliard don't pour no love powders around my house cause I can't stand to be in love with that nigger."

Viney went on to marry a man named Sam, but Sam was not a good husband. He was always running around on her, as Viney angrily put it. One day Viney came running up to the house and said to Mama, "I guess I'm gonna have to kill Sam. I promised God on bended knee that I'd do it." Mama told her that she thought God would forgive her for breaking that promise.

Another black face I watched belonged to Roselle, who lived in a little house next to Viney's. When she had a baby, she named him for my Cousin Albert Fagan, a well-to-do man who lived part of the year in a house he owned in Mount Hermon. Cousin Albert had never had anybody named for him, and he was so flattered by the gesture that he would often buy small presents for the little boy and take them to him. One day he took a shiny yoyo down to their house, and while he was there the little boy crawled up on the kitchen table. Roselle said hotly, "Get down off that table, Joe Louis Albert Fagan."

Cousin Albert was incensed. He said to Roselle, "Well, if that's the way it is, Joe Louis can provide him with his gifts from now on." Mama and Daddy would tell this story to people and everybody would laugh, no matter how many times they had heard it.

Another black face lived down the road. Mama said he had dementia praecox, and I said he had it too, but I didn't know exactly what that meant. I knew he was crazy because in those rare instances that a plane would come by he would get up on a shed behind his house, flail his arms about, and yell, "Japanese air monsters, come down." All us younger kids would get up on top of the barn, wave our arms, and shout the same thing until Evelyn or somebody would call out, "Get down from there, or you're gonna get dementia praecox."

We did not often get to see another important black face, a woman named Aunt Jennie, who had taken care of my oldest brother and sister when they were small. She had moved to a neighborhood seven miles away, but she would return for an unannounced visit a couple of times a year. The first person to see her would holler, "Here comes Aunt

Jennie," and we'd all run down the path to meet her. In her hand would be a bouquet of wildflowers or leaves, which she would present to Mama as she entered the house. Mama would say, "How thoughtful of you, Jenny" as she put the arrangement in a quart fruit jar and added a dipper of water.

Then Aunt Jennie would go to the kitchen table and empty her pockets of all the things she had collected on her long journey: apples, pears, peaches, quinces, chinquapins, hickory nuts, chestnuts, black walnuts—whatever was in season. "These are for those sweet chillun," she would say, and Mama would give each of us some of the treasure.

But the thing about Aunt Jennie that made her most interesting to us all was her air of mystery. Mama would say to her, "Aunt Jennie, you are very different from most nigrahs. You hate watermelon, you don't like bright colors, you say you can't dance. Why is that?"

Aunt Jennie would look at her gravely and say firmly, "I am not of the nation." That ended the conversation. Daddy would sometimes say that Aunt Jenny didn't want to get piled in with all the shiftless nigrahs, but the way she said it, even we children sort of intuitively knew that there was more to it than that.

Aunt Jennie would be given lunch, but it was unthinkable that she would have eaten with us at the table. While we ate, she sat on the back steps with her plate. Afterwards she would come in and offer to wash the dishes, but Mama wouldn't let her. "You need to rest. You've got a seven-mile walk home later this afternoon."

And shortly thereafter she would walk off slowly as we children stood in the yard and watched until she went out of sight.

Commanding most of our attention the years we lived in Mount Hermon was the Webb family, a white family that lived just down the road. They were common, Mama said, and she often used them as negative examples when she was teaching us proper behavior. But we weren't supposed to talk about them outside the house, she said, and we were never ever to call them by the vulgar name of white trash.

Ernest Webb was from a family long known in the Mount Hermon area as being somewhat on the uncouth side. A bachelor cousin of ours decided that he would try to civilize Ernest and his brothers and sisters when they were young by reading Shakespeare to them on Sunday afternoons. As he would drone on and on with passages from *Hamlet* or some other play, the children would stare blankly at him. When he finished, he would give them each a shiny dime and they would file grimly out without a word.

No one ever figured out how, but Ernest somehow gained the hand of the daughter of one of the most prominent citizens in Mount Hermon, saw-mill operator Thomas King. He became an expert sawyer in his father-in-law's operation, and he felt like he was a hotshot. A raw-boned man with blue-black hair he always kept oiled, Ernest would recite vulgar poems or sing suggestive songs on the job. One of his favorites was:

My girl went up the winding stair
And I walked up behind her.
When she stooped down to tie her shoe,
I saw her sausage grinder.

Or he would sing a song like

Daddy's got a meatskin hid away
To grease his wooden leg with every day.

Things rocked along fine for Ernest for a while. He and his wife had three daughters, Mary Eloise, Katherine King, and Martha Olivia. But his life changed suddenly when his wife caught pneumonia and died. "I got her some sulfur drugs," Ernest told my parents, "but she up and died anyway."

Ernest needed a wife, but there were few prospects. That changed, however, when he happened to be at our house the day Carrie Mae Pinkin, whose family had just moved to the area, appeared on our place asking to pick cotton. A squatty woman in her late teens with a face as flat as if she had been hit with a water dipper, she had the passive expression of a Guernsey cow. Wearing a pink organdy dress you could see her arms through and a matching hat with bright colored flowers around the band, she was definitely more dressed for courting than for cotton picking.

"I ain't wild about picking cotton," she said, "but I ain't been prepared to do nothing else." She turned to Mama and said, "I quit school in the fifth because I had this hateful teacher who went and told my Mama I was mental minded. I told my Mama I thought the teacher was mental minded, but it hurt my feelings anyway and I quit." She paused a bit before adding, "I wish I had me a good education like you do, Mrs. McMillan."

That day while Carrie Mae was picking, Ernest came back around. He winked at her, and she smiled bashfully. He needed help raising his daughters, and she would have to do, he thought. He was fifteen years older than she was, so he knew he'd have to teach her what she needed to know. But it would be worth it, he thought. Two weeks later he took her before the probate judge in Greensboro, and they returned home a married couple. She got pregnant right away.

Carrie Mae was such a step down from the first wife that the King family wanted nothing to do with her. "Don't you bring that trash into my house," Mrs. King, Ernest's former mother-in-law, was reported to have said. "My grandchildren can come because that's my obligation, but not Carrie Mae nor any children the two of you may have."

Mrs. King did not offer to take in her grandchildren, and so they were trapped with Carrie Mae, to whom they immediately took a disliking. They called her frog face and other names and bossed her around all the time. They also didn't care for the babies that Carrie Mae delivered, and when one would cry, the oldest daughter, Mary Louise, would order the stepmother, "Take the baby out under the oak tree." Carrie Mae would do so without protest.

Ernest began to treat Carrie Mae bad too, making her stay at home most of the time. She would beg to go to town, but he would tell her that Greensboro was not open to women because a rare form of smallpox that affected only women had hit there and a deputy sheriff stood at the city limits sign and turned all females back.

Although Carrie Mae had few clothes, Ernest forbade her to wear his first wife's clothes, which were hanging in a chifferobe. And he joined his oldest daughters in making fun of her.

I was sitting one day in the front yard digging in the dirt with a sterling silver spoon on which was written EAM, my grandmother's initials, when I spotted Carrie Mae walking up the road to our house. I heard Mama saying to the kids on the porch, "This is going to be an ordeal, but y'all treat Carrie Mae nice. She's a pathetic thing, and the least we can do is not add to her problems."

Carrie Mae was wearing a huge dingy shift and was barefooted. Her thin lips were stained with snuff. She was pregnant, but she was carrying a child less than a year old on her hip and a little girl toddled along beside her.

"Come on up here and sit down, Carrie Mae," Mama shouted to her, pointing at a rocker. "Elizabeth, get her a glass of water. It's too hot to live today."

Carrie came up the steps saying, "Hit sure is hot, Mrs. McMillan. I tell you the inside of my house is like a oven. I almost fainted over my breakfast."

Mama leaned over and looked at the baby. "Your baby looks so sweet. How old is he now?"

Carrie Mae didn't answer immediately, but she looked like she was thinking about it as she took a bottle of warm milk out of her pocket and poked it in the grim-looking baby's mouth. Her little girl, wearing a loose printed dress made out of a flour sack, stood close by her chair, and I came up to the edge of the porch and peered at the baby.

"Well, let me see," Carrie Mae said, "the old muley-headed cow calved on October the tenth so this here baby would have to of been born on the seventeenth cause hit was one week later to the day."

I could tell Mama was a little puzzled, but she concealed it. "When is the next one due?"

"Sometime early next year, I think. I ought to go to a doctor, but Ernest ain't had no time to take me."

Elizabeth handed Carrie Mae the water and she drained the glass in several large gulps. "Obliged," she said. Then she turned to Mama. "We are so hoping for a boy, me and Ernest, but I just can't figure out what to name him, Mrs. McMillan. What would you say—would you name him Ernest, Junior, or Junior Ernest?"

"I think Ernest, Junior, is nice," Mama said, and when Elizabeth grinned, Mama stiffened and gave her a stern look.

Carrie Mae stayed all day. Mama fed her and the kids lunch, and it was almost sunset before Carrie Mae made a move to head home. Mama had become more and more fatigued as the day drug on, as there was little to talk to Carrie Mae about, and Mama couldn't abide silences. Somebody had to be talking, and generally she was that somebody. Carrie Mae, who did not mind silences at all, could have rocked for hours without a word.

As Carrie Mae and the children walked slowly down the path, Mama said, "I've got to take a B. C. powder and go to bed. I've got a headache you wouldn't believe. Y'all are going to have to make do with tomatoes and cold biscuits for supper."

One morning in 1947, Ernest Webb appeared at the sheriff's office in Greensboro, pale and shaking. "She has done done it," he said. "Carrie Mae has done gone and kilt herself."

"Who is Carrie Mae and what did she do it with?" the deputy, who barely knew Ernest, calmly asked.

"My second wife, Carrie Mae Webb, has done shot herself with my shotgun. She shot herself in bed."

"Well, let's go take a look," the deputy said. He called to another deputy resting in the next room. "Percy, I got a suicide to investigate. Get up and man the radio, if you don't mind."

The deputy followed Ernest's dirty log truck down the narrow road to Mount Hermon. They pulled up in the red clay yard at the Webb house and went in. "Anybody but the victim here?" the deputy asked.

Ernest looked around a little and said, "Look like they done all run off."

"Escort me to the scene," the deputy said, and Ernest pointed to the next room, making no move to go in with the deputy.

The deputy went into the bedroom, where he found the corpse, her body caked with blood and her face with a look of grim surprise on it. Then he saw a baby lying next to the corpse on the bloody bed. He looked closely at its face, all splattered with brownish blood, then down at its little chest, which was moving up and down as he slept. He yelled in irritation to Ernest, "Hey, come in here and remove this infant," and Ernest came in and grabbed Ernest, Junior, and ran back out.

Then the deputy spotted the weapon propped next to the bed. He studied it a minute, scratching his head before walking slowly out to the patrol car and getting a tape measure. When he came back to the death scene, he put the tape methodically to Carrie Mae's arm and measured shoulder to fingertips: twenty-eight inches. Then he measured the shotgun barrel: thirty-six inches. He nodded his head.

"Would you come in here a minute, sir?" he called to Ernest. Ernest came in with the baby in his arms, his eyes very wide. "I want you to explain something to me if you can, please. How could a woman with arms twenty-eight inches long shoot herself in the chest with a shotgun that's got a thirty-six inch barrel?"

Ernest's eager face collapsed. "I knowed you'd git me," he said. "I knowed there wasn't no need to try and pin it on her. I knowed I wasn't gonna git away with it." He paused a moment and looked at the baby. "Let me take this here baby over to my neighbor's, if you don't mind, and then you can take me in."

The deputy looked satisfied. "And if you don't mind me asking, why did you perpetrate this act?"

"I just couldn't take her frog face no more," Ernest said, shaking his head. "She didn't have walking around sense, and I couldn't take it no more."

"If everybody in Hale County who didn't have walking around sense was shot for it, the population of this county would be a lot less than it is," the deputy said, without a trace of humor. "Let's us go."

Ernest pled guilty by reason of insanity, but the jury didn't buy it and sentenced him to the electric chair. He remained in the Greensboro jail for a year while his case went through the automatic appeals. The Alabama Supreme Court finally ruled the first trial invalid and called for a second trial.

At this trial Ernest pled guilty by reason of insanity again, but this time the defense was ready. They paraded a long string of the extended Webb family members before the jury, trying their best to show a dried-up gene pool. One of them, a middle-aged man with the demeanor of a boy, had a shaven head, around which he continuously ran a long rat-tailed comb. The defense attorney pointed at him and said to the jury, "This is the kind of family Ernest Webb comes from," and the man himself smiled proudly and nodded several times at the jury members.

The defense attorney had instructed Ernest to stare up continuously at a particular point on the ceiling and never ever to remove his eyes from that spot, no matter what went on in the courtroom. Ernest, who'd do anything to avoid the electric chair, followed his directions completely. For hours he never shifted his gaze whatsoever.

Ernest's sister, a stooped woman with a soft voice, was sworn in to testify. The prosecutor asked her whether there was any documentation of the alleged mental problems, and in answering, the woman paid no attention to him, but addressed all of her remarks to the judge. "Ernest wasn't never right, your honor," she said slowly, stretching out the syllables and making her statements sound like questions. "Why, when Ernest was just a little old boy, he used to strip off all his clothes and go and hide way up under the house." Ernest kept his eyes on the point on the ceiling. "Mama, she was afraid that he would take off to the fields and live with the sheep," the woman continued, "so she would get the rest of us childern to make a circle around the house, and you ain't gonna believe this but she'd take and boil a kittle of water, and when she found exactly where he was under the house she would pour that hot water real slow through the cracks in the floor." Several groans were heard from people in the gallery.

"And ever time she done that, your honor, Ernest yonder would come tearing nekkid out from under that house. He'd be squalling more or less like a tomcat. Then me and my brothers and sisters'd catch him and Mama'd make him go inside, and he'd go in real nice like and put on his clothes." She paused a bit before adding, "He wasn't never burnt bad, your honor."

As she finished her testimony, the observers in the courtroom broke into nervous laughter, and the judge glared at them, beating his gavel a couple of times and threatening, "I'll have the bailiff clear this courtroom if you can't maintain more decorum."

The sister seemed rather proud of the response to her testimony.

Before leaving the witness stand, she pointed at her brother and said to the judge, "Ernest, he weren't never right, your honor. He may be my brother, but he weren't right and he still ain't right. Just look at him." Ernest never stopped looking at the point on the ceiling.

Ernest was convicted again, but this time to life in prison. He was said to be a model prisoner, working in the shop that made car tags.

A lot of what happened at Mount Hermon happened at the small two-room schoolhouse about a half-mile down the road from our house, a school I never attended. As my brothers and sisters walked off to school each day, I envied them their books and pencils and theme paper and *Weekly Readers*, and I would beg them to teach me my letters and numbers and to read to me from their readers. I would practice my ABCs carefully with the oversized pencil with an eraser shaped like a dog that my aunt had given me, and I would sing the songs from school they taught me, making them laugh when I sang, "My Bonnet Lies Over the Ocean." They taught me games like "May I?" and "Geese-geese," which they played at school, but, best of all, every day when they came in, Mama would grill them on everything that happened at school that day, and I would listen, enthralled by every word.

Mama did not even have to ask what happened the first day of school after Christmas vacation one year because Elizabeth came in the door crying. "Mama, Mama," she said, "I lost my sweater Aunt Elizabeth gave me for Christmas." She had dressed that morning in a new pair of corduroy overalls, over which she had worn the new pink pullover American Beauty sweater with a white line around the neck.

"Lost your sweater? Where on earth did you lose it?" Mama asked.

"In the toilet. I lost it in the toilet," she said, tears rolling from her eyes.

"Now, try to calm down, Elizabeth, and tell me what happened."

"I asked Mrs. Gravlee if I could be excused cause I needed to peepee. She said okay, and when I went down to the toilet I had to take off my sweater to undo my overall straps." She sobbed a while, then continued. "I was holding the sweater, and when I started undoing the straps. . . .” She cried more, then blurted out, “I dropped my sweater in the toilet hole.”

Mama didn’t seem too upset by the news, I thought. She made no move to comfort Elizabeth.

“I looked down, and it was in there with all that doodoo, and I ran back up to Mrs. Gravlee and told her. ‘I lost my sweater. I lost my sweater. I dropped it in the toilet.’ She said, ‘Well let’s go try to get it out,’ but I knew it wasn’t any use.”

“What did she do?” asked Bill, who had come in and caught the drift of the story.

“She went to the cloak room and got a broom.”

“My gosh, a broom,” Bill said and started to laugh.

“It’s not funny, Bill,” Mama said.

Elizabeth continued, “Everybody followed us out, the boys too, and I was embarrassed. ‘We’re going to try to fish that lovely sweater out,’ Mrs. Gravlee said, and I wanted to draw up into a little knot. We followed her to the girls’ toilet, and the girls crowded in the doorway, watching as Mrs. Gravlee poked the broom down into the toilet and stirred it round and round.

“Then Mary Eloise Webb said what I was thinking. ‘I wouldn’t wear the thing even if you could get it out,’ she said.”

“Amen,” said Bill.

“Mrs. Gravlee got mad at Mary Eloise for saying that. She said, ‘Mary Eloise Webb, you just shut up. You would never have had such a nice sweater in the first place.’

“Then Mary Eloise said, ‘No, I ain’t got no rich aunt from Greensboro who gives me nice things.’”

Elizabeth was getting back her composure. “I was so glad when Mrs. Gravlee finally said, ‘Well, that’s one sweater that’s long gone” and took us back to the schoolhouse. But when we got back at our desks that mean old Harold Thomas leaned over and whispered to me, ‘Elizabeth McMillan’s sweater is swimming in shit,’ and I started crying again. Mrs. Gravlee said the next one who mentioned my sweater was gonna get a spanking, and nobody said anything else. But, Mama, I still can’t help crying.”

Mama said, “Well, look on the bright side, Elizabeth. Lots of little girls don't get to wear a nice a sweater like that for even half a day."

"How consoling," said Bill, who picked up words like that from all the books he read.

Marcille's worst experience at Mount Hermon School came because she was so scared of dying. She had good reason for this fear because when she was two she had actually died and had come back to life. She'd had a terrible case of pneumonia, her rattling breath becoming weaker and weaker until it stopped altogether.

Almost as soon as Mama had the body covered with a sheet, she'd seen it move, just barely. Quickly grabbing up Marcille and shaking her, but getting no visible response, in panic Mama had stuck her finger down Marcille's throat and removed a long, thick string of phlegm. The raling sound of labored breathing then began again, and Marcille was snatched from death's hold.

It was not surprising, then, that Marcille panicked one day at Mount Hermon School during an episode that started when Mrs. Gravlee caught Emma Lee Webb biting her fingernails. "Don't do that, Emma Lee. It's dangerous," she said sternly.

Emma Lee gave Mrs. Gravlee a "Who says?" look.

Mrs. Gravlee, quite used to that look, decided she was going to make a believer out of Emma Lee. "Did you hear about the little girl from Tuscaloosa who was about your age and what happened to her?" she began.

Emma Lee did not answer, but looked out the window. Marcille was sitting next to her and was embarrassed to see her ignore the teacher.

"Well, this little girl from Tuscaloosa was about your exact age, and she was real bad about chewing her fingernails. No matter how often they told her not to, she kept right on chewing them. Then one day the little girl swallowed a nail and she got very, very sick."

Mrs. Gravlee's tone was serious, and Marcille got caught up in the story. Without realizing it, she began to chew on her own fingernails.

Mrs. Gravlee continued, "They took the little girl to the Druid City Hospital, and don't you know when they opened her up they found a double handful of fingernails inside her. Well, there was just nothing they could do at that point but sew her back up."

Emma Lee looked impassive, but Marcille, more and more absorbed by the details, suddenly realized that she had just swallowed a fingernail. The color drained from her face, and she felt like she was going to throw up. Her eyes widened in terror as she thought she could feel her body shutting down.

Trembling, she walked to the front of the room. "Mrs. Gravlee," she said weakly, "I'm sick, and I've got to go home." She was too shocked to cry.

"Go home?" Mrs. Gravlee asked. "You're not that sick are you, Marcille? Why don't you go over and get your pallet and lie down a little. Then I'm sure you'll feel just fine."

Marcille knew better. She would never get any better. She was going to die. She began to cry, and she rolled back and forth on the pallet. Finally, Mrs. Gravlee decided there was nothing to do but go to the next room to get Bill to take her home.

Even though he was glad enough to have an excuse to leave school for a while, Bill gruffly asked Marcille what did she think was wrong with her as he led her down the front steps.

"I'm dying," she said, trembling.

"Dying, hell. You wouldn't be walking if you were dying."

At home, Mama rocked Marcille and told her she wasn't going to die. The stove was still hot from lunch so she went in the kitchen and fried her a sugar pie. As Marcille ate it slowly, she began to feel that she might live after all.

Our life at Mount Hermon had begun with promise. When he moved there, Daddy was thirty-four, he had four children, 200 acres of land, a car, a wagon, two mules, five cows, eight hogs, fifty chickens, and a well-furnished house with barns and sheds. When he left at age forty-two, he had eight living children and one dead, a rough set of furniture, and a ground slide.

One day Daddy came in and told Mama out of the blue, "I've sold the house and land." Holding out a wad of bills, he said, "Four thousand in cash. Pretty good, huh?"

Mama took the bills and stared at them. "Sold the house? What in the world do you mean, Albert?"

"I'm sick of this place. I can't make ends meet, and we need a new start. Maybe I'll just move us to Ohio or somewhere like that. I've heard there are a lot of good jobs there."

I came in to see what was happening, and Daddy turned to me and said, "The only thing is that y'all children will have to get used to going to school with colored children. You know, they actually let them in with the white folks up there?" He mused on the fact, then said, "It's no wonder Yankees are as dumb as they are."

We did not go north. Mama took over the proceeds from the house, and Daddy didn't even argue. She would stretch that money out over a couple of years. Daddy started immediately searching for a sharecropping job. Up until that point we had had people sharecropping on *our* place. "Now we'll become the niggers and see how it feels," Evelyn said.

We sharecropped off and on for six years, living in five different houses, all called by names other than our own: the Walker place, the Marion Highway Place, the Earley place, the Lyons place, and the Rhodes place. In the Lyons place you could see the stars at night through the roof, and the other houses were not much better. The best thing was that we stayed nowhere for long. "We're moving," Daddy would come in one day and announce, and we would happily load our furniture onto somebody's truck and climb in on top of it. Every time we thought things could not get any worse. But they did.

Mount Carmel Methodist Church

PART 3

Marion Highway and Bucksnort

The truck was moving down a gravel road taking us to the Walker Place, the first of the succession of tenant houses we would live in. Julia and I were sitting in the cab with Mama and the driver, a grim looking man who was smacking on bubblegum. I liked being up front where I could see. Daddy and the older kids were riding on the back of the big truck, fitted in among our furniture.

When we turned a bend, suddenly in the middle of the road there was a tall black boy of sixteen or seventeen in a fancy blue and white uniform with gold fringe on the shoulders and a double row of bright gold buttons making a V down the front. He had on a high black hat bordered with fur and a strap under the chin, and he was vigorously pumping a tall baton back and forth in his right hand. He didn't seem to try to jump out of the way at all when he met us, and the driver, who was forced to steer sharply to the right, screamed out the window, "Get out of the way, nigger, or you're gonna get yourself run over."

"My goodness," Mama said. "That was a close call. I wonder who that was."

"That's Allen Peck," the driver said. "He's the prissiest nigger you ever seen. He's the drum major over there at the nigger training school, and he practices out here all the time. One day he's gonna get hisself killed." He pointed to a house we were passing. "That's where he lives," he said.

It was a neat house covered with brick-patterned tar paper. A blue Chevrolet coupe sat in the yard under a water oak, and there was watermelon red crape myrtle blooming all around the house. When we pulled up to our new house, I couldn't help noticing that it was not as nice as Allen Peck's house, and I thought something surely was wrong about that.

The new house was unpainted, like the one at Mount Hermon, but it was a little bit bigger. And it would have to fit two less people into it than our house at Mount Hermon. Evelyn was at college at Birmingham-Southern, and Sarah had just entered the University of Alabama in Tuscaloosa, sponsored by a well-to-do cousin in Newbern with whom she had lived for a while. Bill was supposed to be living at home, but many nights he did not come home, staying in Greensboro with relatives or sleeping on a cot in the fellowship hall of the First Methodist Church.

The wooden front steps of the Walker Place shook under our footsteps. Inside, the floors were unpainted, though long ago the wooden walls had been painted a powder blue. Now they were darkened with grime, and nails were driven here and there. In the kitchen where the stove would go there was a thick circle of soot.

"Bill," Daddy said, "see if you can find the water bucket out there on the truck and draw us a bucket of water. And be fast about it. That driver hasn't got all day." Then he turned to Elizabeth and said, "Would you go find the mop and soap powders? We got to scour this place down before we move any of the furniture in."

Mama had already found the broom and was sweeping out the kitchen. A thick cloud of soot rose. "Stay out of the way," she said to me and Donald, "or you'll turn into little nigrah children." We fled outside and played in a huge stand of kudzu, from which we watched Daddy and Bill unload the furniture. They put Evelyn's table in Mama and Daddy's room, along with the trunk and the slave chairs and an old sofa Aunt Elizabeth had passed on to us. Later when I saw Daddy go to the trunk and take out his Prince Edward cigar box and put it on the mantel, I felt right at home.

Although we had not moved far from Mount Hermon, my older brothers and sisters now began attending school in Greensboro. I still was too young to go, and Julia and I stayed home with Mama. While we were living at the Walker Place, a circular came through the mail warning that rabid foxes were on the loose in Hale County. Small children, it said, should not be allowed to play outside unattended, and older children and adults should be very careful when outdoors. A grown man had died, it said, and several other close calls had been reported. I asked Mama to read it a second time, and I was even more frightened when she did.

The next day Mama called me and Julia into her bedroom. "I've got to go down and get the mail," she said. "Now I want y'all to be good children and stay in this room until I get back." She looked at me directly and said, "Do what I say, Norman. I don't want you outside at all. I don't want a big mad fox to eat you up."

I felt myself shaking. The mailbox was about a quarter of a mile down the driveway, and I could see the fox in my mind, a huge red figure with long yellow fangs, lurking in the bushes. "Don't go," I begged. "Please, Mama. A big mad fox will get you."

Julia began to cry. "Don't go," she pleaded.

"Don't worry about me," she said. "If a grown person stays out of Mr. Fox's way, Mr. Fox will stay out of your way."

We heard Mama's departing footsteps, and I was convinced that we would never see her again. I could not even contemplate what the loss would mean. We counted on her for everything. She was the one who traced the shape of our feet on paper to take to town to buy our shoes. When there was no food in the house, she was the one who wrote a note and sent it to a neighbor to borrow flour or cornmeal.

"I'm scared," Julia said, crying harder.

"I am too," I said and hugged Julia to me. Then we went to the win-

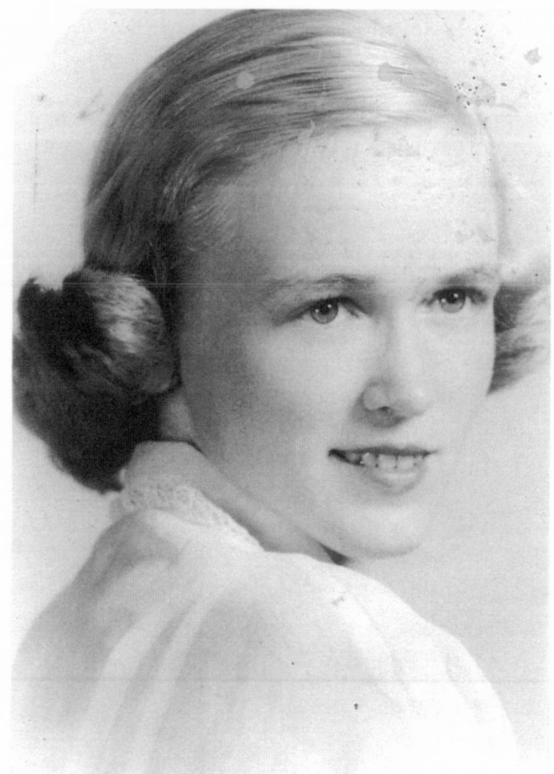

Sarah Alice

dow to look out, but we could not see the driveway. Finally, we heard the familiar footsteps coming up the back steps and across the porch, and we rushed to the door and grabbed Mama's arms.

"Home again, home again jiggedy jig," Mama said happily, unaware of the misery we had been through. And I realized again how strong and brave my mother was.

"Guess what, Norman, you have some mail," she said, handing me a little molded red plastic car attached to a chain with my name printed on a mailing label.

"I bet it's from Sarah," I said, my heart pounding as I looked at the first mail I had ever received.

It was a miracle, Mama said, that Sarah had been able to enroll in the

University of Alabama as a new freshman, but, as she always said, "The Lord will provide." Cousin Albert, who provided the money for her tuition and room and board, also provided her with a little spending money, from which she bought small gifts for the younger children from time to time.

Sarah also wrote us letters regularly. Mama read aloud the one that had arrived today:

Dear Mama,

This is a busy time, but I wanted to write. I'm fine. The classes are interesting. I wrote an English paper about you and I got an A on it. My teacher says I should write for the student magazine, and I may.

I shouldn't tell this on myself, but I will. Last Friday afternoon late this boy in my English class called up and said that he needed a date for a dance. He said—honestly he did—that I just had to go out with him because he had made out a long list of girls to ask and frankly I was at the bottom of the list. But I was so excited to be asked I didn't feel insulted at all. It turned out he was awfully immature though and acted like a fool at the party, even dancing by himself. I asked him to take me back to the dorm at ten o'clock.

Tell Norman I am sending him a little something in the mail. It's not much. My allowance from Cousin Albert doesn't go far. But it will let him know I miss him and will see him soon.

I hope everybody else is well. Tell Elizabeth and Marcille I'll give them a permanent when I come home.

Love,
Sarah Alice

"Read it again," I said, and Mama read back through it. I looked at the stationery, wishing that I could read the cursive writing for myself.

When Mama finished the letter, I looked down at my little plastic car with the tag that had my name on it, and, turning it over and over in my hand, I smelled of it deeply. I then took it over to the sofa. The upholstery would change colors when you rubbed it, and I moved my hand back and forth, making little roads for the car. I pretended I was driving to Tuscaloosa to see Sarah, and I imagined that she asked me to live with her there. I played until everybody got back from school. They didn't seem much interested in my treasure, but they all took turns reading Sarah's letter.

Moving as we did in those years from one tenant place to another, we had some very interesting neighbors, many of whom, according to Mama, were beneath us. As a rule, however, we practiced a strange sort of noblesse oblige, treating our inferiors with courtesy. It didn't matter that most of them were far better off than we were; we were still better. Although we would never imply straight to their faces that we thought them unacceptable in any way, in the privacy of our house we laughed at some of our neighbors' absurd behavior, their faulty grammar, and their general ignorance.

One set of neighbors, the Harlesses, was the only white family who lived near us. Although Allen Peck and his family lived nearby, Daddy said for us to stay away from them. It seemed to be less a matter of their being black than it was his mistrust of Allen. "That Allen Peck is a peculiar nigrah. He's too uppity," he said, "and I don't want y'all messing with him." After a while if any of us got a little prissy or too big for our britches he would say, "All right, Allen Peck, that will be enough."

R. L. Harless lived with his wife Sarah Lena, a slow-talking harassed woman with a number of children, in a little clapboard house with a swept front yard, around which lay eight or ten lazy bluetick hounds. When you walked by the house, the dogs would lift their heads up and look at you for a minute, then flop them back down on the ground. Sometimes when you went by you could hear the incongruous tinny sound of big band music issuing from the windup victrola in the front room.

In almost no time, Daddy took to drinking whiskey with R. L., a lanky man of many moods. Daddy was on the whole quiet when he was drunk, but with R. L. he too would even get a little animated. Mama would usually wind up locking them out of the house, and R. L. would summons all his charm to try to get her to let them back in. Once he sang loudly and earnestly the old hymn, "There's a stranger at your door. Let Him in." He rapped firmly on the door the whole time, but Mama didn't fall for it.

R. L. had fought as a private in France and Germany during World War I, and he was very proud of having been involved in the big conflict. He claimed to have learned German while he was over there, and when he was drinking he would throw in German phrases to try to impress us. One phrase, which sounded like "Fotcha me my gullases," he said meant bring me my galoshes. I liked to hear him say the strange words, but I wondered why, out of all the things he might have learned to say, he learned that.

R. L. was usually happy when he'd had a drink, but occasionally he could turn mean. One afternoon, R. L.'s son had put Bill up to hiding himself in a tree in order to scare R. L. when he came in drunk. When R. L. got just under the tree, Bill hollered out real loud just like a screech owl, causing R. L. himself to holler and rush toward his porch. Then Bill started laughing and jumped to the ground. When R. L. saw him, he ran to the woodpile and grabbed up an ax, lifting it over his head and running at Bill, who took out for the woods and hid. Because he didn't want to take any chances with R. L. while he was so upset and because he knew no way home except past his house, Bill waited until dark to go home.

That night as Bill passed the Harless house, he could see light coming out of the open windows and he could hear the metallic sound of the victrola. Impulsively, he picked up a handful of rocks, walked over, and threw them in as hard as he could through the unscreened window of the main room. Having had his fun, he went home in a hurry, quite satisfied.

The next day there was an all-day singing and dinner on the ground at Mount Carmel Methodist Church, which we attended, and Bill had dressed up in a tie for the occasion. As all of us came out on the porch to leave for church, R. L. drove up in his old flatbed truck. He walked towards us rather calmly, but when he got next to Bill he jumped at him and grabbed his tie.

"I'm gonna kill you, you son-of-a-bitch," he said, pulling the tie tight and trying to choke Bill. Bill struggled and broke loose, running into the house and getting his twenty-two rifle. He came back out and leveled it at R. L., shouting, "I'll kill you if you don't get off this place before I can count to ten." All of us children sort of backed up. Then Daddy, who normally was not very heroic, came running out with a claw hammer in his hand. He lifted it and hollered, "Leave that boy alone or I'll kill you, goddamnit."

R. L. backed out to his truck, trembling all over, and he drove away. The next day he acted as if nothing had even happened.

R. L.'s nickname for his wife was Monkey, and when he spoke of Sarah Lena to others, she was always "My Monkey." One day when he was drinking heavily, he tried to get his monkey to have sex with him, but she would have none of it. "Not while you're drunk, you ain't," she said. That incensed R. L. because about the only time he wanted her was when he was drunk.

"Come on, Monkey, now," he said urgently. "I just gotta have some." But Sarah Lena only shook her head. The more he begged the more she refused, and he finally got so mad he decided to get even. "I'm gonna fix your twat good," he hollered back over his shoulder as he staggered out of the room.

Sarah Lena wondered what was on his mind, but she didn't know of anything to do but wait and see. He returned holding a length of rope in his hand, and he rushed at her and wrestled her to the floor. He hastily tied her up, not uttering a word. She thought of telling him that he could do whatever he wanted to with her if he'd just untie her, but it looked like he was going to do what he liked anyway.

R. L. went out and returned again carrying a kerosene can. Without uttering a word, he doused her all over. Sarah Lena decided that if there was ever a time to pray it was now. "Oh, Jesus," she moaned loudly, "help me. Save me, sweet Jesus, save me."

Sarah Lena would always believe that Jesus heard her prayer because when R. L. went into the kitchen for the matches, he couldn't find any. He looked at Sarah Lena. "Goddamnit," he said, "I'll be back, and your ass is gonna be fried."

Sarah Lena figured he was going to our house to get matches so she had to move fast. Slick from the kerosene, she managed to wriggle herself loose from the poorly tied rope. By the time R. L. returned, Sarah Lena had fled, eventually making her way secretly to the safety of her sister's house in Limestone County.

R. L., when he sobered up, was appalled at what he had done. People said he had to have been temporarily insane to make such an attempt on Sarah Lena's life, but he acted even loonier after she was gone. He realized how much he loved Sarah Lena, he said, and he told everybody, "My heart is as big as a dish pan, I miss that woman so much. I got to find her."

In his bad condition, he somehow got it into his head that Sarah Lena could be found on the West Alabama Express bus that came down the Marion Highway twice a day, and he would flag down the bus repeatedly and ask the driver in a mournful voice, "Is my Monkey on here?"

"No, she still ain't," the driver would reply wearily, staring at the ceiling of the bus.

"I'm obliged," R. L. would say and return to his house to grieve. Eventually he found out where his Monkey was, and he drove to Limestone County in his flatbed truck to get her back. "Please, please come back to me," he begged.

"You promise you ain't never gonna tie me up no more," Sarah Lena said rather coyly.

"Sweetheart, I swear before God I ain't," he said, taking her in his arms and planting tiny kisses all over her face.

"I reckon I'll go then," she said. "I really don't like Limestone County that much."

Our closest neighbors on the Marion Highway were a childless couple, Mr. Grover and Miss Eva Arnold. We didn't like them much because he was a blowhard and she was mean. One day Mr. Grover, who always talked with something like a smirk on his face, came by and announced to us, "Me and Eva done got ourselves a icebox. It's a Kelvinator, twelve cubic feet, and it makes some of the hardest ice you ever seen. We got six trays."

"That's nice," Mama said.

Our own icebox was made of wood and lined with zinc. It had never had a block of ice in it since I was born, and we used it to store junk in.

"And that icebox makes the ice so fast," Mr. Grover said proudly. "Me and Eva unplug it every night to save electricity and plug it in first thing in the morning, and by lunch everyday all six trays are solid as rocks. I think I'll go home and get me a glass of ice tea right now." I wished we had a new icebox so we could have iced tea too.

Miss Eva was active in the Mount Carmel Methodist, which we attended, and when the regular pianist had to be absent, she and Mama together would play the clangy old upright piano for church services. Because neither could read music well enough to play with both hands, Miss Eva, her stern face bowed over the keys, would play the lower notes while Mama would cheerfully take the upper ones. Sitting side by side on the spindly piano bench, they looked comical, and they were never exactly together, causing the congregation at times to start snickering. Not over four or five people in the entire congregation would even attempt to sing when they were playing.

At that time, Miss Eva's brother, who also lived in the community, sent off for a mail order bride, and when she came from the state of Utah she was pretty as she could be. But the brochure had failed to mention one detail about her: she was stone deaf. The first Sunday he brought her to church, Mama and Miss Eva were doing piano duty, and as they broke into their rendition of *Rock of Ages* Miss Eva whispered to Mama, "This is one day that woman ought to be glad she's deaf." Mama got so tickled she lost her place, but no one could tell it.

Mount Carmel Methodist would have a carnival every now and then to make money for the church. Although Mama was not sure she believed in carnivals because she thought that a church should be supported by gifts freely given, when Miss Eva volunteered her house for a carnival she took all of us to it.

For the event, Miss Eva baked a prize four-layer chocolate cake in which she placed a secret item. "Guess the secret item and you win it," she announced to the assembled group in her living room. "It only costs a dime per guess."

An old lady named Miss Ernestine who had buck teeth took a dull-looking dime from her coin purse and handed it to Miss Eva. "Say, is it a hair pin?" she asked in a voice that made me think she'd be surprised if it was.

"Afraid not," said Miss Eva. "Next."

This stringy Chapman boy handed over his dime and asked, "Miss Eva, can I ask a preliminary question? I seen it played that way one time." Miss Eva frowned in deep thought. "If I get the answer I'm after," the boy added, "I'll pay another dime to make my guess."

"Why I don't see anything wrong with that at all," Miss Eva said.

"Is it larger than a penny?" he asked.

"Nope," Miss Eva said. "Want to ask another question?"

"No'm," he said. "I thought it was a pocket comb."

Like everybody else, I was surprised at what happened next. Mr. Grover himself walked over and handed Miss Eva a dime.

"I guess a. . . ." He paused a minute like he was in deep thought. "I guess a. . . a . . . a clove."

"Why, that's right, Grover," Miss Eva said, looking real proud of him. "But how in the world did you ever guess it?"

Several of the others crowded around and seemed to have similar questions.

"Hold on," the stringy Chapman boy said. "I believe you seen Miss Eva bake that cake. I believe you seen her put a clove in that cake."

"Boy, you yourself was the one who give it away," Mr. Grover said in a very unfriendly way. "When you asked whether it was larger than a penny and Eva said no, I knew right off it had to be a clove."

Everybody looked confused. The Chapman boy looked like he wanted to say something, but neither he nor anybody else seemed agile enough to come up with a response. Mr. Grover took the cake over to the Kelvinator and slipped it in. He closed the door firmly.

"That man told a story," Elizabeth said on the way home that night, but Mama said, "We don't know that as an absolute fact, do we?"

For a while Daddy gave up sharecropping and worked at the sawmill, but we never had the sense that the job was permanent. We were happy for the time being though because we were able to move into a little better house, which we called the Marion Highway house. Mama and the girls would make out menus and grocery lists, and Daddy would bring home big sacks of good things to eat. In my mind, anything that came out of a can was preferable to anything that came out of the garden, and rice, macaroni, and dried fordhook lima beans, I thought, were premium items.

Every morning Mama would make a lunch for Daddy and put it in a syrup bucket with holes punched in the top. When it rained one day and he had to return early, he gave Julia and me his lunch bucket. We divided the four jelly biscuits we found in the bucket. They were sweating and warm, the grape jelly sharp and sweet tasting, and as I savored them, I suddenly felt a surge of love for Daddy.

Occasionally Daddy had to do night duty tending a slab fire at the sawmill site. Once he decided to take some of the children with him to spend the night in the woods. When I started getting ready to go, he told me I was too young. I threw a fit. "I'm almost six years old and I start to school this year. I'm big enough, and I *am* going," I screamed. Daddy and Mama finally relented.

In the late afternoon, we waved goodbye to Mama, Julia, and Kenneth, who had been born after we moved to the house on the Marion Highway, and we left for our walk to the sawmill. Elizabeth carried a grocery sack of food Mama had made, Marcille cradled a gallon jar of Kool-Aid in her arms, and Donald and I ran down the road in front of everybody. When we arrived, Daddy immediately started throwing more slabs on the fire, and Donald and I picked up some small pieces to throw on. "Watch out, Norman," Daddy said, "that slab's too big for you."

I turned away and went over where Elizabeth and Marcille were spreading a sheet on the ground and taking the food out of the sack—a pile of peanut butter and jelly biscuits, some chocolate muffins, and a brown bag of pop corn. There were also five jelly glasses for the Kool-

Aid. We all took our share and sat on the ground to eat.

The sky began to darken and the fire got brighter, lighting up the entire area and casting shadows on the nearby trees. Constant sparkles flew up into the sky. Somewhere a whippoorwill began to sing: "Chip-fell-out-of-the-white-oak."

"Chip-fell-out-of-the-white-oak," Donald yelled back.

"That's right," said Daddy, "don't ever let anybody tell you a whippoorwill says jack-married-the-widow. That's just what some folks think." The next time the whippoorwill called out, I heard it say "Jack-married-the-widow," but I didn't tell Daddy.

Everybody's face looked strange in the flickering light, and I got a little scared. I was glad when Marcille said, "Let's sing, everybody." We began singing loudly one of Daddy's favorite songs:

Had a little dog and his name was Fido,
He was nothing but a pup,
He could stand up on his hind legs,
If you held his front legs up.

Daddy didn't sing with us. He never sang with other people, but every now and then at night we would hear him singing "You Get a Line and I'll Get a Pole" and "Me and My Wife and a Bob-tailed Dog." He could not carry a tune in a bucket, but we liked to hear him.

"Daddy, would you say the books of the Old Testament for us?" Elizabeth asked, and he broke into his poem. I was so sleepy I could barely hear him, but I was still awake when he concluded:

Thus Malachi with garments rent,
Concludes the ancient testament.

I liked the poem, especially a part where it said that Ruth gleaned the corn with trembling hand. Although I didn't know really what Ruth was doing to that corn, I thought it sounded beautiful. It seemed to me that Daddy's poem was far superior to Mama's song about the New Testament: "Matthew, Mark, Luke, and John, Acts and the Epistle to the Romans." But I would not have told her that.

"Yeep, Yeep, Yeep, Yeep." High and keen, the unearthly voices sounded rapidly and frantically in the distance, threatening the safety I had been feeling. I ran and sat real close to Elizabeth. I wanted to ask what it was, but I was too scared to talk. Maybe I had just imagined the terrible sound.

"Yeep, Yeep, Yeep," they went again. My eyes were wide, and I began to shake. I knew this time they had to be real.

Daddy looked at me and said, "It's just a pack of coyotes, Norman. They're little old scrawny things. Don't be scared. They run in packs, and they'll attack a small deer, but they won't mess with humans."

He said it so convincingly that I stretched out on the ground under the stars. In the few minutes before I went to sleep I felt fortunate to be counted old enough to be out with Daddy and the others. I listened to them talk and sing, and I was happy.

The job at the sawmill ended, and once again we moved, this time to sharecrop on the Early Place. This house, which was constructed of cement blocks, sat back off the road, so we could no longer monitor the traffic on the Marion Highway. It was really just a shell of a house with no rooms laid off. All of the furniture was out in the open. It was sort of like camping out. But it had electricity, the first we had had. One naked light bulb hung from the ceiling.

We lived at the Early Place when I started to school. As the day approached, I could think of nothing else. "I hope I get put in Miss Jewell's class," I said.

"Put shit in one hand and hope in the other and see which one fills up first," Bill, who happened to be at home at the time, said in a real smart voice, but I was too busy hoping to worry with Bill. I had never seen Miss Jewell Rouderbush, but I knew hers was the better of the two first-grade classes at Powers School, where I would be going the following week.

"You know Miss Jewell only takes town kids," Bill said. "You're going to have to settle for Mrs. Thomas and a classroom of country kids like you."

I could live with that. I just wanted to go to school. I wanted to show off what I knew. Mama and the older kids were forever teaching me things. Mama corrected our grammar, and she prissed around the house quoting passages from Shakespeare and conjugating Latin verbs.

She was proud to point out that she had, as she put it, a classical education. Before I started school I could recite, "*Amo, amas, amant, amamus, amatis, amant.*"

I knew my letters and I could count to a hundred. I could color and sing. The first thing I intended to tell my teacher was that if she wanted any poems said or songs sung just to call on me. I'd put those other kids in the shade with what I knew.

I was worried, though, because I heard Daddy tell Mama several times that he didn't know how he was going to be able to send us to school that fall, that the money was just not there. That afternoon when he repeated his concern, Mama said in a cutting way, "Albert, just stop that talk right now. You've been saying that for years, and I'm sick of hearing it. Of course the children will go to school. I've prayed about it, and I know the Lord will provide." Mama's faith was absolute and infectious. At that time, I never questioned its correctness. Daddy wasn't so sure he agreed.

This time Mama was right. Later that afternoon when we were sitting around the front porch, a tan Pontiac pulled up in the yard. It was driven by Maideen Patton, a beautician in Greensboro who liked Mama a lot, a striking woman with dyed black hair piled on her head and lots of rouge. Wearing a white uniform and white lace-up shoes like a nurse, she looked like she had money in her purse, though Mama told us she had started off as a girl going door to door cutting hair for a nickel.

"Norman starts to school tomorrow, doesn't he, Mrs. McMillan?" she asked Mama as she walked toward the porch. "You mind if I take him down to Phineus Johnson's and get him some clothes."

"That would be nice, Maideen," Mama said, not at all embarrassed. She pulled me to her and straightened my shirt. "Go with Miss Maideen, Norman."

When Miss Maideen opened the door to the Pontiac for me, I climbed in, and even though I couldn't see over the dashboard I felt as big as a millionaire.

"You've gotten to be a big boy now," Maideen said. "I know you're gonna do real good in school, Norman. All of you McMillans are smart. You get that from your mama." She seemed to be driving fast, and I liked it. "Yes, sir, that Mrs. McMillan is one more smart woman. I heard her teach a lesson at church one time that could have been taught by a college professor."

I rejoiced when I heard people say good things about Mama. I thought Mama was perfect. She was in the middle of everything at school and church, and everybody seemed to admire her and respect her. About Daddy I wasn't so sure. He stayed at home all the time, and as far as I could see he didn't contribute anything to speak of to the community. On the whole, what I had seen of women made me think them far superior to men, and I thought that they were the people I wanted to be like.

In town Maideen took me into the department store, a narrow, dimly lit building. A frail woman leaning against a counter asked, "Who's that good looking boy you got there, Maideen?"

"This is Norman McMillan, Florine. You know who he is. Lucille and Albert McMillan's boy."

"Oh, yes," the woman said, looking very serious.

"We need two outfits and a pair of shoes," Maideen said, taking my hand and leading me to a counter with pants on it. "You want blue jeans?"

"Yes ma'am."

The sales lady took down a pair and held them up next to me, a sort of a bored look on her face. "These will do," she said. "You got some growing room in these."

Maideen held a shirt out towards me. "You like this, Norman?" It was a red plaid shirt.

"Yes, ma'am," I said.

"We'll get a green one just like it then," she said. "Come over and pick you out some socks." She pointed at a stack of colored socks and said, "You'll need that size."

I went over and selected a pair of red socks.

The saleslady sidled up to me and said, "I got a tip for you, son. It is the accepted thing that you choose your socks to match your trousers, not your shirts."

"Yes ma'am," I said, putting the red ones back and getting a blue pair. I wondered who had red pants. I'd never seen any.

"Get three pair," Maideen said, "and put on one pair to try on shoes with."

For the first time I thought about being barefooted, and I was embarrassed as I looked down at my dusty feet. The saleslady led me over to a row of chairs, and I sat down and pulled on a pair of the socks.

"What kind of shoes do you want?" the saleswoman asked as she measured my foot with the ruler.

I went perfectly blank. Nobody had asked me such a question before, and I couldn't think of what to say. Always before Mama had just got my shoes in town and had brought them home. "Any kind," I said, and the woman went to a row of boxes and came back with a pair of brown hightops. The heavy sweet smell of the leather delighted me as she took the shoes from the box and laced them on my feet. Then she mashed down and felt the toe with her thumb. "Plenty of growing room," she said. "And they look good too. Don't they Maideen?"

"Sure do," Maideen said, sitting down beside me. "Do they feel good?"

"Yes ma'am."

"Well, walk on them a little bit and make sure they're all right."

I walked around, and when I saw the gleaming shoes on my feet as I passed a mirror, I felt something close to ecstasy.

"You want to wear them?" the woman asked.

"Oh, yes ma'am."

The woman went over and made out the ticket at the cash register. Maideen opened her wallet. I could see lots of money in there. She took out some bills and handed them to the woman.

"The Lord's gonna bless you for this, Maideen," the saleswoman said, handing over the bags. "Hurry back," she called as we left.

On the street Miss Maideen asked me, "You want to go to the drugstore and get an ice cream soda or something?"

"Yes, ma'am," I said.

I had never been to a drugstore, and as we sat down on the stools at the marble counter I was amazed at how gleaming and beautiful the place was. It smelled sweet and clean. In front of me was a domed plate piled with thick doughnuts.

"I'll tell you what, Norman, let's get us a chocolate milk shake," Maideen said, placing her order with a teenaged boy behind the counter who was wearing a little white paper hat. I was not tall enough to see everything he was doing, but after a bit he put two big tin cups on a machine that made a loud whirring noise. Then he poured the contents into high glasses, put a straw in them, and handed them over with a tiny napkin.

What came through the straw was the best thing I'd ever tasted—cold, thick, and chocolaty. I had had chocolate milk a few times, but it was not in the running. I had had chocolate ice cream, but it was not so rich. If I could only freeze this moment, I thought, I'd be the happiest person in the world.

I hit bottom with a gurgling sound, and Maideen and I laughed. She paid the boy in the hat and we went to the car. As we drove home, I felt like I was a king or a prince. At home, I told everybody about the trip, and I expected that the others were jealous of my good fortune. I knew I would have been had it happened to them.

"See what I told you, Albert. The Lord *will* provide," Mama said happily as she spread my new clothes out on the bed.

"Let's see if he provides for the others," Daddy answered. He poured out some chalk-colored milk of magnesia into a tablespoon and took it. "My stomach is killing me," he said, slumping back down into his despair.

I guess I was my Mama's fair-haired boy. Even though she didn't talk about it much, it was clear to me that she always thought I could accomplish anything I wanted to, and she clearly assumed that I would excel at school. So I was quite confident having her by my side as we rode the school bus to Greensboro that day to register for first grade at Powers Elementary. As we went up the front steps, the brick school seemed gigantic to me. A woman standing in the hall checked a sheet of paper in her hand and told Mama I was in Mrs. Thomas's class, as Bill had predicted, and, though I felt sorry for a moment, I didn't dwell on my disappointment. That I got from Mama.

We went into the auditorium, and Mama folded down two seats for us. The whole room smelled of the sharp odor of the dye in all the new clothes, and I was excited to be wearing stiff new jeans like most everybody else. At the front sat two women who looked totally different, one fancy and one plain. I knew that the fancy one dressed in a black suit with a large red flower pinned to her lapel had to be Miss Jewell. She stood up with a giant smile and said, "Good morning, children! Good morning! Good Morning! I am Miss Jewell. I am principal of Powers School. Welcome, welcome, welcome! And you mothers too." Her face shone with rouge, and rings sparkled on her fingers.

"We are so very happy to have you here to start school at Powers Elementary. How many of you children are happy to be here? Raise your hands. Up high, now." I raised my hand high and I looked around. Only two or three others were following instructions.

"Let's try that again, children. Everyone who is happy to be here, raise your hand."

I raised my hand again and looked around. A few more raised theirs this time, but a little girl with corkscrew curls, who was sitting in her mother's lap, began to cry. Nearby a boy way bigger than me was making a face like a bulldog at Miss Jewell. I was shocked.

"Well, that's all right. You haven't had a chance yet to see how happy you are to be here," Miss Jewell said. "That's where Mrs. Thomas and I come in." She pointed over at the drab looking woman, who nodded her expressionless head. "We're going to make you precious things see how happy you are to be here. We're going to teach, teach, teach, and you are going to learn, learn, learn, and it's going to be fun, fun, fun," she said enthusiastically.

As I listened to Miss Jewell talking to us about Powers Elementary, I was impressed with everything about her. She was extremely beautiful, I thought, and she had a voice full of expression. And she never said anything that wasn't kind and nice. Mrs. Thomas, I noticed, did not smile. She was wrinkled and skinny, and her faded dress was a pale blue with little yellow flowers and a belt that was buckled tightly at her waist. But she was my teacher, and she would have to do.

"You who have been assigned to Mrs. Thomas can leave now," Miss Jewell said, and as Mama and I got up and went out with the other country children and their mothers I looked at the town kids and wondered what they would get to do once we were gone. I felt I properly belonged in there with them and Miss Jewell.

Once we were in our room, Mrs. Thomas told us to take seats at the tables and said to the mothers, "Now, ladies, you can be excused. Refreshments have been prepared for you in the lunchroom. When I finish, I'll bring the children to you and that will conclude our activities on this first day."

I felt, "This is it," as Mama got up to leave. Several children began crying, and one little girl would not let go of her mother's coattail.

"That's all right," Mrs. Thomas said to them in her flat voice. "Y'all can just sit in the hall until she gets more adjusted."

After Mrs. Thomas read our names off a sheet and we raised our hands so she could see us, she said, her eyes taking on a look of gravity, "Let me tell you about our room, children. This is my desk behind me. This is where I sit." She patted on it with her hand. "I can see *everything* from up here," she said very slowly, her eyes narrowing. "*Everything*."

She pointed at the tables we were sitting at. "You will do your work at these tables. Tomorrow each of you will be given a kit, with pencils, paper, crayons, and a few other things. And over here is the supply table where we keep our construction paper, paint, mucilage, and so forth."

She pointed to a bookcase. "These are our books, and before the year is over every one of you will be reading. How many of your mamas and daddies read to you at home, lift your hands?"

I lifted mine, and she asked me, maybe because I was so eager or maybe because I was at the table nearest her, "And what do your parents read to you?"

I went blank. I could think of nothing but a book Mama and Daddy and the older kids had been talking about. "*The Grapes of Wrath*," I blurted out.

"*The Grapes of Wrath*?" Mrs. Thomas said rather loudly. Her eyes lifted and she whispered almost as if to herself, "Think of that."

My face burned red because I knew she knew I was lying. But I didn't mean to lie. It just popped out.

Mrs. Thomas gestured to the door behind her. "That door goes into the cloak room," she said. "That's where you'll leave your coats when it gets cold. And I also keep Co' Colas back there, and every Friday if you have been good children all week you'll get one."

I wished I had a Coca Cola right then. I liked the peppery feeling in my mouth as the Coke foamed over my tongue. The only thing better I could think of was a chocolate shake, but I had no hope of having another of them any time soon.

At this point, Miss Jewell came to the door, a radiant smile still on her face. She asked Mrs. Thomas, "Ready?"

"Ready," Mrs. Thomas answered. "All you girls go with Miss Jewell," she said, and they got up and went out.

"Now, boys, follow me, one behind the other," she said. She started lining us up.

We went into the hall where Miss Jewell's boys were already lined up against the wall. All of us were marched together down the hallway to the boy's restroom, which smelled sweet, but not a good sweet like vanilla ice cream. I thought it stunk. The light in the room was very low, and everything looked spooky to me. A black man stood in a shadowy corner waiting on us. "This is Jerome," Mrs. Thomas said. "He is our janitor, and he will tell you all you need to know about the rest room. I'll wait outside."

Jerome didn't seem old, but he had a thin grayish beard. "Come over here this way," he said, pointing at a long trough along one wall. "This here," he said, "is what you call a urinal trough. You ain't likely got one of these at home, but this is what we make water or teetee in. Now, when you use it, always get up close to it, like this." He stood facing the urinal. "That way you won't wet on the floor. All you got to do is unbutton or unzip your pants and do your business. Everybody come up here and take a close look." I went with the others and looked down into the urinal. I didn't know what I was supposed to be looking for, but I noted that the sour, sweet smell got stronger the closer you got to the trough.

Then Jerome pointed at the two toilets, which were in stalls without doors. The floor around them was sweaty and slick. "You will not need to use these here very often, but when you do you just sit down and do your business. And make sure you flush when you get through. You ain't got to flush the urinal, now, but you got to flush the toilets. Everybody understand? Say 'Yes, Jerome.'"

"Yes, Jerome," I said along with all the others.

He then showed us where to wash our hands after every trip. "One other thing," he added. "You ain't never supposed to come in here without your teacher give you permission. Always ask her if you can be excused. Understand? Say, 'Yes, Jerome.'"

"Yes, Jerome."

"All right. Any questions?"

"Yes, Jerome," the big fat boy with the bulldog look, who was in Miss Jewell's class, said as he walked over to the urinal. He pointed at some shiny white chunks and asked, "What is that?"

Jerome thought a minute and said, "Well, you might say that's stuff to take the smell out of pee."

It worked, I thought to myself, but I'd almost rather smell pee.

Jerome ushered us back into the hall, and Mrs. Thomas took us down to the lunchroom, where we were given a little paper cup of red Kool-Aid and two Oreos. I took mine and went over to where Mama was sitting. "How did it go?" she whispered.

"Just fine, but we didn't get to do any work."

I caught a glimpse of Miss Jewell helping a little girl clean up some Kool-Aid she had spilled. Her bright colored face was still full of joy. I couldn't believe how beautiful Miss Jewell was.

My days at Powers Elementary School were on the whole quite happy. Mrs. Thomas was fine, though she must have wondered about me several times. One day she gave us chocolate milk to drink, and I drank not only mine but also the bottle that belonged to a boy named Rufus, who sat next to me. "You want it?" he had asked. "I don't drink cow milk." I took it, wondering what kind of milk he *did* drink. Shortly thereafter, as I sat at my desk copying letters in my book, I began to feel the pressure. I had to go to the restroom. I asked Mrs. Thomas if I could be excused.

"We'll all be going in about ten minutes, so let's just wait. Okay?" she said.

I should not have said okay. In no time I couldn't hold it any more, and the pee ran down my leg onto the floor. I was so ashamed. I looked down and saw the large yellow puddle moving slowly across the floor, gathering dust as it went.

"Mrs. Thomas, Mrs. Thomas," Rufus yelled, pointing at the floor. "Norman wet his pants."

Everybody in the room looked at me, and I turned red. Some of the children started laughing, even some of them who had had accidents themselves.

"Come with me, Norman. Everybody has an accident sometimes," Mrs. Thomas said, grabbing my hand and taking me in the hall. She began dabbing at my jeans with a handful of paper napkins. "We have to learn to be a big boy, don't we?" she asked, and I nodded. "And big boys don't wet their pants, do they?" I shook my head. She gave up on trying to dry me and said, "We're going to the play ground in a minute and you can lie in the sun and dry out."

"I'm sorry, Mrs. Thomas," I said to her, close to tears. When I got home and told Mama what happened, I did cry. Donald overheard me and said, "It's nothing to cry about, but you ought to have done like me. I used a wastepaper basket when the teacher wouldn't let me go."

In the first grade I pulled the worst of my stunts, although I didn't think I was doing anything particularly bad. Donald had taught me something to say to girls, and I decided to try it on Mary Maud Patton, who wore bows in her hair and nice lacy dresses. She was standing by the slide when I ran up to her and said, "You want to have some fun? Then pull down your britches and run." She looked confused for a minute, then broke out crying and ran to Mrs. Thomas, who stood nearby.

"Norman said something bad to me, Mrs. Thomas."

"What did he say?"

"I can't say it."

Mrs. Thomas got a stern look on her face and called me over. "Mary

Maud said you said something ugly to her, Norman. What did you say?'

I didn't want to say it again. I regretted saying it in the first place. "I can't say it," I said.

"You must say it. You said it to Mary Maud."

It hurt to say the words to the teacher, but I got them out. I might have been wrong, but I thought I saw a trace of enjoyment move over Mrs. Thomas's face. But she said, "Norman, I am surprised at you. Your Mama would be so disappointed."

That brought a chill over me. "Please don't tell, Mama," I pleaded.

"I won't if you'll promise me you'll never say it again."

"Oh, I promise, Mrs. Thomas. I swear before God I won't say it again."

"Don't swear either," she said, turning from me to another student who had come up.

I decided at that point that I wanted to be good. But I had this other side to me that I just couldn't seem to shake. And sometimes I couldn't tell what was good from what was bad. That was what worried me.

I had one triumphant moment with Mrs. Thomas that could have gotten me in big trouble. Almost as soon as I learned to talk good, my older brothers and sisters had taught me to say, "Have you the audacity to doubt my veracity or even to insinuate that I would prevaricate?" I didn't really understand the words, but I knew full well I was supposed to use them when somebody accused me of not telling the truth. Elizabeth had told me that they might come in handy at school.

One day just before lunch while we were gluing pictures on construction paper, Mrs. Thomas announced, "It's time for dinner, children. Now, everybody, put your mucilage and extra paper back on the supply table."

I put mine up, but when we returned from lunch Mrs. Thomas spotted a bottle of mucilage on our table, and she immediately said, "Norman, did you leave out that mucilage?"

"No, ma'am," I answered, absolutely sure that I had put mine up.

"Yes, you did too," she said. "You were the last one using it. I saw you."

Almost automatically I said in a loud voice, "Have you the audacity to doubt my veracity or even to insinuate that I would prevaricate?"

Mrs. Thomas's mouth fell open and she wheeled and walked out of the room for a while. I felt like I probably shouldn't have said it to her, but it felt real good at the same time. Unfortunately, I never was able to use the phrase at school again.

The most thrilling thing about school was that Miss Jewell knew who I was. As my class was filing out to have play period one day, I saw her standing in the hall. I was astonished when she crooked her finger at me. "What have I done?" was my first thought.

I was relieved when she said in her nice voice, "Come in here with me, Norman. I've got something nice for you." Her first graders must have been on the playground too because her room was empty and dark. We went up to her desk, and she reached in a drawer and pulled out a large shiny apple and a sharp paring knife. In one deft movement she cut the apple in two and gave me half. She returned the other half and the knife quickly to the drawer.

"Thank you, Miss Jewell," I said, stunned that this woman had singled me out. She could have given that apple to anyone, but she had chosen me.

"You are welcome, Norman," she answered. "Mrs. Thomas brags on how smart you are, and you can count this as my little prize for you. You can go on out to the playground now."

I sat on the swing and ate the apple slowly, moving back and forth. I had never tasted a sweeter apple in my life. I ate it right down to the thinnest core. All the while I was thinking about the other half. For days afterwards, its image would pop into my head and I would wonder what had happened to it. Did Miss Jewell herself eat it or give it away? Did it turn brown?

I was becoming obsessed with Miss Jewell. At home I would go to the window ledge and pretend to play the piano the way she did. When I sang, I would try to copy her vibrato, and I tried to match her enthusiasm in my daily life. I longed for her to call an assembly at school, and any time I passed her room I would look in at her adoringly.

In time, I made lots of friends at Powers School. Even with my ill-fitting clothes and poorly cut hair, even as the recipient of free school lunches, I constantly exuded a self-confidence worthy of my noted ancestors, the Averys. It didn't occur to me at the time that much of what I was told about my Avery ancestors was pure myth. All I knew was that I was not common. I told my classmates that my great-grandfather had invented the horse drawn gin and was a millionaire, and they looked impressed. I told them I was descended from Robert E. Lee, and like all southern children they knew that name and were appropriately in awe. I told them I could play canasta, which I could, and bridge, which I couldn't. I told them the jokes I heard from my grandmother and brothers and sisters, even if I didn't understand them perfectly. I wasn't any good at team games, but no one seemed to care. I discovered happily that I was popular, and even the town kids wanted to hang around me.

After the first grade I was put in the class with the town kids, and I found that it was with them that I really belonged. They were generally smarter and seemed better liked by the teachers. Many of them got placed with me in the superior reading group, the bluebirds. As we would sit in our circle and read, I would occasionally glance over at the blackbirds, huddled in the corner over their remedial readers, their fingers tracing the words on the page, and I would feel about equal parts of pity and pride.

It was mainly the town kids who had birthday parties at school, and I lived for those days. The mothers would arrive in the afternoon with a case of Coca Colas and brown paper grocery sacks filled with little cups of vanilla ice cream and wooden spoons, cupcakes with bright-colored icing, and little cellophane bags of peanuts. I watched and noticed that the boys always poured their peanuts into their bottles of coke, and, though I thought neither one tasted as good that way, I faithfully did the same thing.

One day when I was in the second grade Miss Jewell called the entire school into the auditorium, which meant something important was going to happen. Sitting in the front was a large woman in a nurses's uniform. Two big paper bags sat on the floor beside her. Miss Jewell got up and said, smiling all the while, "This is Mrs. Crawford, boys and girls. Mrs. Crawford is the County nurse. There is a little problem Mrs. Crawford wants to talk to you children about. So let's clap a welcome for her." We did so immediately because we were used to clapping welcomes for every visitor that came.

The woman had a tiny cap on the top of her head, and her hair was pulled up and pinned. “Boys and girls,” she said seriously, “we have a bad health problem in this county, and we find it a lot in little boys and girls like you. So I'm going to ask you to do something for me.” She reached in one of the bags and pulled out a little can about the size of Daddy's snuff tin and held it up. “What I want you to do is to take this little can home with you, and the first time you have to do number two—does everybody know what number two is?”

“Yes, ma'am,” everybody answered in unison.

“When you have to do number two, I want you to do it in this can.”

The can looked awfully small to me.

“Then get your Mamas to print your name on the can or if you want to you can do it yourself and bring it back to your teacher. Would you do that for me, now? Any questions?”

There was a lot I didn't understand, but I was not going to ask any questions. Neither was anyone else.

At home, I asked Mama why they would be interested in my doodoo. She had already read a little note that came with the can, and she said that it was a hookworm test. We could expect results in two weeks. “Nothing to it,” she said.

There was something to getting the turd in that little can, but I did it. “Nasty,” I thought as I placed the metal lid on the can. I wondered what it would smell like when over a hundred of those cans were returned to school. “Pew,” I said aloud.

Then, as I printed my name on the can, I began to fear that I had hookworms. What would the worms do to me? I wondered. Would they eat up my insides? Would I have to quit school? During the next two weeks, the matter was not off my mind more than a few minutes, and the day I received a clean bill of health I felt as if an iron blanket of worry had been snatched from me and I could walk upright again.

When I was in the second grade, we moved again. This was the longest move we had made, about twelve miles, to a community called Bucksnort on the Tuscaloosa side of Greensboro, but I still went to

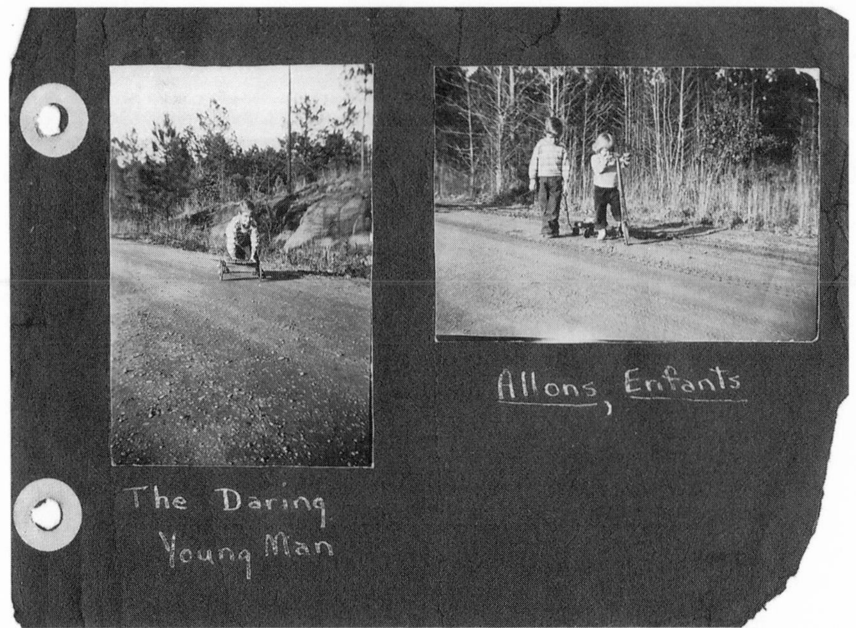

Pictures from Evelyn's scrapbook, made at Bucksnort in 1950. I am in the picture on the left, Julia and I in the one on the right.

school at Powers Elementary. The new house at Bucksnort was called the Lyons Place, a falling-down house with four small rooms. We began sharecropping with a man named Mr. Bryan Rose, who lived a short distance down the road with his wife and two daughters named Patricia and Sharon in a nice white house with a blue Chevrolet parked in the driveway.

In the front yard at the Lyons Place there was a well with a shed over it which had a windlass to draw the water with. When Evelyn, who taught school in East Alabama now, came home, she noted correctly that the well was in much better condition than the house. She took her new Brownie camera out in the yard and snapped a picture of it. Later the picture was put in her scrapbook with the caption, "Greensboro Water Company."

In Bucksnort, Donald, Julia, Kenneth, and I created a playground called Death Valley, painting the name on a piece of tin and placing it on a cattle gate, and we walked the half mile to Big Creek pretty often to fish. We seldom would have any bait, but we discovered that a crawfish would bite a naked hook, and when we caught one we would crack it open and remove the meager meat inside to bait our hooks with. We sometimes caught little bream, but even if we caught keepers it would do no good to take them home. Mama wouldn't cook them because she had a great fear of one of us getting a bone caught in our throat.

Once Donald and I came upon a giant turtle when we were fishing. Donald went over and broke a branch off a gum tree and wiggled it in front of the turtle's head. He snapped at it and clamped his jaws over the branch. We knew we could take him home safely because there wasn't a cloud in the sky. Daddy had told us a number of times that a turtle wouldn't turn loose anything until sundown unless it thundered. At home, Daddy killed the turtle with an ax, and Mama fried him, like chicken, in a skillet. But the turtle, unlike chicken, jumped around in the skillet for a while.

"The turtle is said to have seven kinds of meat in him," Mama said at the supper table.

"What are they?" we wanted to know.

"I'm not sure. Chicken, beef, and pork, I guess, but I don't know the others."

"Cat and dog," Donald said.

"Oh, Donald, that's sickening," Marcille said.

I looked down at my piece. It looked like chicken to me.

My little brother Kenneth was growing fast. He was Daddy's favorite, and he could get away with anything, I thought. He even took to cussing like Daddy did. One morning before anybody in the house had gotten up, Kenneth awoke and somehow got it in his head that Donald and I had gone fishing and had left him behind. He ran out the front door yelling, "Wait for me, dod damnit, wait for me." Even Mama couldn't keep from laughing a little bit.

Although Mama often said proudly that her children were not jealous of each other, I envied Kenneth the attention he got from Daddy, who called Kenneth Bud and bragged on him all the time. Daddy was also crazy about Julia, whom he called Doozy Gal, and he would tell her she was pretty and would hold her in his lap. It grated on me that I never got an affectionate nickname and that he never held me in his lap. I did my best to ignore him, but the truth was that I craved his attention, and the few times I got it stand out prominently in my memory.

The main time Daddy seemed to pay any attention to me was when I was sick. His nurturing instincts in many ways far outshone Mama's. She was far more interested in delighting in the victories of the strong than in ministering to the needs of the infirm. While we were living at Bucksnort, I got a bad boil on my shin, and it swelled up and turned purple and ached. It got so bad I started crying with it one night.

"Here, let me see that," Daddy said, bringing over the kerosene lamp to the bed where I was sitting. He turned up the wick a little and peered closely at the boil over the top of his glasses. "That is one more bad carbuncle," he said, walking over to the dresser and taking a big sewing needle out of the drawer. He took off the lamp globe and put the needle in the lamp flame to sterilize it. I whimpered in fear.

He came over and began gently to lance the boil.

"Does it hurt?" he asked. "I'm trying to be as easy as I can." Before I could answer, the bloody core shot out of the boil.

"There," he said. "You won't have any more trouble with that." He got some brown salve and put it on the open boil, and he took an old sheet and cut a piece to wrap it in. "Give it two days, and it'll be healed," he said with authority.

No day in my early childhood stands out more in my memory than one involving Daddy that happened while we were sharecropping at Bucksnort. It was 1950, a warm September afternoon. I sat on the front steps looking at a book on American birds I had brought home from school, Julia kneeling behind me and looking over my shoulder at the brightly-colored pictures. I lifted my eyes to gaze at the front yard where two gray mules stood in their traces, heads lowered to the ground to get any sprigs of grass they could. They were harnessed to a wagon with tall slatted sides, mounded high with cotton.

Daddy walked out of the house and motioned for me to follow him. I knew exactly what that meant because he always carried one child with him when he took in the first load of cotton to be ginned every year. I quickly handed Julia the book and raced to the wagon, my heart pounding. Daddy lifted me up on top of the cotton, and, saying nothing, mounted the driver's seat and took the reins, clicking the mules into action.

I lay on my back, half buried in the cotton, and I listened to the iron wheels scraping along the gravel road. Smelling the clean cotton and looking up at the blue sky, I felt a mantle of contentment beginning to lower over me.

When we got to the gin, we took our place in a line of loaded cotton wagons and trucks so long that by the time our turn came the sun was setting. We pulled up into the bay under a long tube hanging down from the rafters, and Daddy climbed up into the wagon and started sucking cotton up through the tube. Daddy passed the tube to me, and, operating it for a little while, I felt more grown up than I ever had before.

When Daddy finished sucking the cotton up, he took the wagon and parked it under some trees. Then he took me inside the gin and showed me the whole ginning process from beginning to end, explaining each step. "This is the deseeder," he said, and the sound of the seed flying through the pneumatic tubes coupled with the roar of the machinery was deafening, but I didn't mind. I loved the piercing smell of the place and the excitement of the workers moving about hurriedly to do their jobs. I decided that I wanted to work in a cotton gin when I grew up. "Gosh, this is interesting," I said to Daddy.

"I wouldn't want to be cooped up in a hot place like this myself," Daddy said, as we walked to the store next door. When we got there he said, "Get yourself a coke and piece of candy," and I walked to the drink box and, identifying the cap of an R. C. Cola, plunged my hand down into the icy water and pulled out the drink and opened it. Then I went to the candy case and told the woman in a bib apron that I wanted a Baby Ruth.

Daddy came over and stood by me. He was drinking an Orange Crush. "This is my boy Norman," he said to the woman, who had a faraway look in her eyes, and she didn't say anything, only smiled a weary little smile in acknowledgment.

We took our drinks outside and joined some other farmers in overalls who were smoking and, from what I could figure out, telling jokes. One of them with a large hairy wart on his chin asked, "Did y'all here the one about Big Jim Folsom and the country girl?"

Daddy cocked his head in my direction. "There's a boy here," he said to the man.

"Oh," the man said and stopped telling his joke. I was sorry because I knew that Big Jim Folsom had been governor and I knew a song about him Evelyn had taught us:

She was pore but she was honest,
Victim of a rich man's whim,
When she met that Christian gentleman
Big Jim Folsom,
And she had a child by him.

We finished our drinks, and I went to the office with Daddy to get the money for the cotton. A man in khakis went to the safe and got out a stack of bills, which he counted out on the counter. Daddy recounted them and put them carefully in his billfold, and I thought he seemed proud when he walked out. I know I was. A father who was sober earning money and spending time with his son—that was what I would have given anything to have all the time. As I sat on the seat beside Daddy, silent as we rode home in the moonlight, I choked up because I knew the evening was ending. I didn't thank him, but I thought he sensed my gratitude.

That day was to haunt me for many years as a reminder of what life might have been. When I would see Daddy bent-over drunk or hear him cursing in anger or being so hopeless as he looked at the world's prospects, I would think of that day. But only for a moment.

As the fifties arrived at Bucksnort, things began to change quickly for our family. Evelyn had been away teaching high school since the late forties, and Sarah had fallen in love with Howard, a man she met at the University of Alabama, and had married him, moving to the Wiregrass in the southern part of the state. Now Bill was leaving, and it looked as if Elizabeth would be going soon too.

Bill had spent so little time at home in recent years that when he joined the air corps after graduation I realized that I really didn't know him very well at all. When he had been at home, I found myself somewhat wary of him. For one thing, he wouldn't join the church, no matter how much Mama pled with him, and I knew that if he died he would go as straight to hell as a martin to its gourd.

I also found out that Bill had taken a pistol that belonged to an old cousin in Newbern. He said that he was carrying it around with him for protection, but he never said protection from what or whom. One day when he was at Aunt Elizabeth's house in Greensboro he dropped the pistol on the floor and it discharged, shooting him in his foot. After the wound was treated, he was brought home to Bucksnort, feeling quite humiliated, having had to confess to having taken the gun and having to come back to the house he had vowed to be free of.

He was there for over a month, mostly lying on the bed with his leg propped up and sighing repeatedly. I would come to the door and peer in at him and listen to him sigh. His skin was oily and translucent, very light, not tanned like mine. You could see little red blood vessels through his skin. I didn't want to get too close to him. I knew that normal people didn't shoot themselves in the foot with a stolen pistol, and to rebel as he had done seemed amazing and dangerous to me.

When Bill took off to Texas six weeks later for basic training, there were only six kids left at home. Marcille and Elizabeth spent all of their time trying to beautify themselves to attract boys. They gave each other permanents, and they spent hours brushing their hair and putting on their makeup.

Elizabeth had one special problem with her appearance, and she worried about it a lot. She was very thin and almost altogether unendowed with the first measurement. Afraid that no boy would look at her

Bill in his Air Force uniform

Elizabeth and Marcille

twice, she begged Mama to get her a pair of falsies. But Mama thought she was too young to even think of such a thing.

When Sarah and Howard invited Elizabeth and Marcille to go to Panama City with them, Elizabeth couldn't stand the thought of walking flat-chested on the beach so, without letting Mama know, she fashioned her some home-made falsies out of a pair of shoulder pads she removed from an old dress. She inserted them into the bra of her swimsuit and went to the mirror to check them out. Turning sideways, she said to Marcille, "I may not look like Dagmar, but at least I don't look like Frank Sinatra."

After swimming one day at the public beach in Panama City, Elizabeth and Marcille went to the bath house to shower and change, and as Elizabeth stood at the lavatory she reached up to her breasts, took hold of the shoulder pads through her suit, and wrung them out vigorously. An old lady standing at the next lavatory turned pale when she witnessed the exercise. Her mouth flew open, and she pointed at Elizabeth. Only then did Elizabeth realize what she had done, and she fled the room without even changing.

Elizabeth's new titties might have worked or maybe it was just coincidence, but some boys started coming to Bucksnort to take her out. One of her suitors was a raw boned, red-headed country boy named Raymond Rasher, who worked at the Woco Pep filling station in Greensboro. He drove a huge old Studebaker President, and I liked the car so much that I begged Elizabeth to marry him, even though I knew Mama thought he was common.

Raymond kept the car's black paint and the chrome hood ornament polished to a high shine, and he had installed imitation leopard skin seat covers. The horn went uga uga, and he used it often. When he took us younger kids for rides, we sat on tiny folding seats in the back. Elizabeth sat pressed up against Raymond far up in the front seat, while he steered with one hand and put the other arm around her.

Unfortunately, the romance between the Elizabeth and the guy didn't last for long. Sarah said the way she figured it the boy was not good enough for Elizabeth and the car was too good.

One day when she was a senior in high school, Elizabeth sat down by me on our bus ride back to Bucksnort. I was in the third grade, and Miss Dailey, my teacher, had said that day that the school had been given some surplus pears and that as we left each of us was to take one. I reached in and took mine. It was wrapped in slick red paper, and I could smell it as I went to the bus.

I sat down by Elizabeth and unwrapped the pear. It was mellow and sweet and bursting with juice, and I ate it very slowly, looking out the window.

Elizabeth touched me on the arm and asked, "May I have a bite, please?"

"No, I want it all myself," I said, and I continued to eat, not even looking at her.

When we got off the bus I heard Marcille tell Elizabeth that she looked pale, and I heard Elizabeth answer, "I'm sort of trembly. I didn't have money to buy lunch today." A gush of pain circled through my

Aunt Elizabeth Otts

heart like a router. It had never dawned on me before that she would not have been automatically able to eat lunch in the cafeteria, as I did.

I would not even look at Elizabeth. As much as Adam and Eve's apple, that pear was my clearest introduction into the world of guilt and sorrow. I would lie on my bed at night agonizing over what I had done. The Lord's prayer, which we often said at school, begged God to forgive us our trespasses, but before this I couldn't think of any I had. Sin I had always felt immune to. Now in some vague way I knew what a trespass was and I knew what a sin was. And I also knew that I would have to live with the knowledge that there was no way in the world to make amends. I had eaten the pear. I was no longer an innocent.

There was little to break the monotony of those days in Hale County. But every once in a while we would get to go into town and visit at my Aunt Elizabeth's house. While Daddy had squandered his inheritance, she had invested hers well, I was told, and she lived in a fine house on Tuscaloosa Street. A slim, high-cheeked woman who smoked cigarettes quite elegantly, she had married into a prominent Greensboro family. She was quite aware of Daddy's failures, but she remained close to him and his children despite them.

Aunt Elizabeth had the remarkable ability to let people, even children, know how much she valued them. When she talked to me, I felt as if I were the only person in the world. She told me several times that her grandfather David Avery was a leading citizen of his day and that he valued the life of the mind, that he wanted the best for his family, and that we had all been blessed by his example. She would pull out manila envelopes of family documents and show me receipts for the purchase of slaves, bills of lading from England for steel he ordered, essays written by my grandmother and my great-aunts and uncles, old report cards of the Averys. She told me that when I got big enough she would give some of the documents to me.

Aunt Elizabeth said that neither she nor Daddy looked like the Averys, but that was all right because the McMillans were much better looking people. And she also spoke reverently of PaPa's character. I adored her and could have listened to her forever, I thought.

Aunt Elizabeth's house could not have been more different from the ones we lived in. I thought it was a mansion. There were twelve high-ceilinged rooms and four bathrooms, and the house was filled with heavy antique furniture, all stained a deep mahogany. In the summers the house was cool, and in the winters it was warm. Aunt Elizabeth kept ivy in vases on the mantels year round, and on the walls she had good oil paintings. There were also many cases full of books. When it was warm, she served us lunches on a glassed porch filled with Boston ferns and heavy wicker furniture.

Outside there were pear trees, pecan trees, and all kinds of blooming shrubs. The house sat up high on a hill, and it had concrete steps leading down to Tuscaloosa Street. I would sit out there watching the cars and pedestrians passing by, pretending to live there.

Other than these occasional trips into town, we seldom traveled anywhere. I didn't go out of the county until I was eight or nine. Luckily, fun occasionally came to us, most often when Sarah and Howard came for week-end visits from South Alabama. By now Sarah had a good job as a bookkeeper for the Rural Electrical Association in Hartford, and Howard was doing well as a manager at the Philips-Van Heusen plant. They had no children to spend their money on, so they spent a lot of it on us. Howard, who was ten years older than Sarah, had been orphaned as a boy, and he seemed to relish being a part of such a large family as ours.

Invariably Sarah and Howard's visits included an outing, usually a picnic to a nearby place we called the Submarginal, a large lake built on land unfit for agricultural purposes, a creation of the federal government during the depression. There was a spillway there in which we waded and a fire tower we would climb. And we would swim in the lake itself, which was full of rather brackish water and had a soft muddy bottom.

We would all cram into Sarah and Howard's Chevrolet for the short trip. Julia, Kenneth, and I stood in the floor behind the front seat, breathing down the necks of Sarah, Howard, and Mama in the front seat. The older kids were crammed into the back seat behind us. We never thought of this arrangement as being unusual and certainly not dangerous, nor did we find it strange that Daddy never went on these outings.

Sarah and Howard also brought huge sacks of groceries when they came, and during their visits we got a break from our customary home-grown diet. We would gather around as she would unpack the grocery sacks, and our mouths would water as we saw the bananas and cans of pineapple, the hot dogs, the potato chips, the purple grapes, and the Oreo cookies coming out of the bag. When we went to the store about all we got was twenty-four-pound sacks of flour and twenty-pound buckets of lard, large bags of sugar, sacks of coffee, jars of Golden Eagle syrup, and cartons of margarine, which Mama worked the coloring into. Almost everything else came from our garden and fields.

When Sarah came she would always give the house a good cleaning. If Mama had ever been a good housekeeper, by the time I came along she had lost any interest. Although she never said it, she must have felt defeated from the beginning. If she cleaned the place, it got cluttered again immediately.

In the kitchen every square inch was always covered with something—unwashed dishes, the hulls of peas and beans, rotting tomatoes, open jars of syrup. Slimy dishrags and drying cloths made from flour sacks gave off a sour smell. Elsewhere in the house beds went unmade for days, and papers, magazines, and books were stacked everywhere. Clothes lay in random heaps throughout the house.

All of the children were so embarrassed about the condition of the house that we didn't want to bring our friends home, and we seldom did. If Aunt Elizabeth or somebody else drove up, we would scurry around to take care of the worst of the clutter, but Mama seemed not to notice. She spent a great deal of time lying on the bed studying her church lessons or reading books. In the midst of the greatest turmoil in the house, she could call upon some quiet center and relax thoroughly. That capacity might have saved her sanity.

Julia, the youngest girl in the family, started to Powers school when I was in the third grade. She was very pretty, with bright blond hair cut in bangs, and she had early become my soul mate. Donald and I were not close, even though we played together some. He kept his own counsel and, for the most part, thought his four-year seniority put him in another category. Julia, though, loved me and was always anxious for me to tell her what was going on in school. When they took my second grade class down town to see *Stars in My Crown*, my first movie, I came home and recounted everything that happened in it to Julia. When there was a puppet show at school she heard all about it. She knew the names of all of my classmates.

When Julia started the first grade, I felt well-established at Powers School. Being an older brother inflated my sense of importance even further. One day, because Julia had been sick on the day shots were given at school, Miss Jewell called me out of my class to come and walk Julia the couple of blocks down to the county health building, where she would get a makeup shot.

Julia

My third grade class. I am third from the left on the first row, the only one not crossing his feet at the ankles.

When we arrived, we were sent into a room with the nurse, whom I immediately recognized as the hookworm lady. She looked at a piece of paper on the table and said, "So it's Julia who gets the shot, is it?"

"Yes ma'am," I said, happy at the answer. "She was sick the day they gave them at school."

"All righty, Julia, come over here," the woman said cheerily. Julia's eyes began to cloud as the nurse lifted a syringe with a long needle, making a mist go skeet skeet out the end to check it.

The nurse patted Julia on the shoulder and said, "Now, would you please pull down your panties for me, honey?" Julia froze, and when she began crying I for some unaccountable reason started laughing. I knew I shouldn't, but I couldn't stop. I could see the hookworm lady getting red in the face, and my heart sank when she shook the needle at me and said, "Well, if you think it's so durn funny, I'll give you one too. And with an extra long needle to boot."

That wiped the smile off my face. I hated needles, and for years I feared more than anything what was going to happen to me in the ninth grade. My older brothers and sisters had told me about it. All students were required to line up and present their arms to a nurse, who stuck a big needle in the bend of the arm and drew out a large vial of blood. I understood they were checking for syphilis, a disease some young people inherited. Some students passed out, they said. "You ought to have seen Mattie Louise Crow," Bill said. "The more blood they pulled the paler she got until she just hit the floor. It ripped her arm real good."

Once I woke up screaming, "No, no," after I dreamed that Mattie Louise Crow was getting her blood pulled, but before my eyes her face molted into my very own, and I felt myself fainting away.

The smell of the alcohol the nurse had rubbed on Julia pulled me from my thoughts, and I found that she was not crying anymore. Intuitively, Julia seemed to know that my laughter in the clinic that day was caused more by nervousness than meanness, and she did not hold it against me afterwards, although I knew she had every right to do so.

Like me, Julia became a great fan of Miss Jewell. When Easter came my third grade year, Miss Jewell decided to put on a program in the auditorium. On Good Friday when we were all assembled, she stood up real straight and, wearing a black dress with red beads and red ear bobs, read to us out of the Bible about Jesus dying on the cross. Then she said, "Boys and girls, we don't like to think about people dying, do we, but the good thing about Jesus was that he didn't really die. Well, I guess you could say he died for three days, but then he became alive again. Where does he live, boys and girls? Do you know?"

"Heaven," several eager voices yelled out in unison, but Miss Jewell tapped her bosom and said, "He lives right in here." Sam Stubbs, who was sitting next to me, looked down at his chest and frowned.

"And we are glad he lives in our hearts, aren't we, because if he didn't we'd go to the bad place. And we don't want to go to the bad place, do we?" She paused, her rouge gleaming on her face, and when we didn't answer asked emphatically, "Do we?"

"No ma'am," we roared.

"So you are lucky children that Jesus died, and you are lucky children that he rose again. I want to sing you a little song about that right now."

As she walked to the piano my heart started thumping because I knew we were in store for something wonderful. I thought she played the piano perfectly, and she could sing better than anybody I had heard on the radio. She began softly singing a song I recognized from church: "Low in the grave he lay, Jesus the Savior. He tore the bars away, Jesus the Lord." I mouthed the words along with her.

Then she struck the keys hard and picked up the tempo, singing triumphantly:

Up from the grave he arose
With a mighty triumph o'er his foes.
He arose a victor from the dark domain
And he lives forever with his saints to reign.
He arose, he arose,
Hallelujah, Christ arose.

The beauty of the song hit me so hard I thought I would faint. The way Miss Jewell thrust her head back and forth, the way she leaned over the keys, the way she would shape her mouth to the words—I thought that her presentation of the song was the most beautiful thing I had ever heard and seen. I was overcome with love for Miss Jewell. I wanted, in fact, to *be* Miss Jewell. I wanted to play the piano. I wanted to sing "He Arose" like that. I wanted a little black dress.

I went home that day, driven. I knew that I would do it, even though I didn't want to. I went to Mama's dresser and got her lipstick and smeared it on my lips. I put rouge on my cheeks. I found an old black dress hanging on the door of Mama and Daddy's room and stepped into it. I screwed some pearl earrings onto my ears, and I slipped into Mama's high heel shoes. I looked at myself in the mirror, and a thrill shot through my body.

"What in the world are you doing, Norman?" Mama asked from the doorway.

"I'm dressing up like Miss Jewell," I said sheepishly.

"Oh," Mama said, not particularly bothered. She seemed to think it was just a stage I was going through. It would never have dawned on her that I was showing any marks of perversity.

Donald walked in as I stood there in full costume. His face registered shock and disdain. "Now that is sickening," he said. "Mama, make him take that stuff off."

Mama didn't have to make me take the things off. As I put the clothes back, I heard Donald say, "If you ask me, he was cut out right but sewn up wrong."

I was ashamed of what I had done, and I went to get soap and water to remove the makeup. I told myself that I would never do it again, but for the next several months the desire would become so overwhelming that I couldn't resist, and I would become Miss Jewell all over again. Never in my life had desire and shame fought such an evenly pitched battle, and I would be filled with self loathing at the same time I experienced a great secret thrill.

At Bucksnort we attended a Baptist church for the first time. I couldn't tell much difference between Rhodes Chapel Baptist and the Methodist churches we had been going to except that the Baptists sang faster and when they baptized they dunked people rather than sprinkling water over their heads. Mama wasn't much worried about minor doctrinal differences, and she shifted to the Baptists without blinking an eye.

On Homecoming Day, Rhodes Chapel Baptist brought in gospel quartets to sing, and the place really rocked. The quartets were accompanied by pianists who played in a sort of boogie woogie fashion, and I thought all the performers with their greased-back hair looked like criminals. After a morning of singing and praying and preaching, we would go outside to the makeshift tables made out of lumber and saw horses and stuff ourselves with cold fried chicken, potato salad and deviled eggs dusted with paprika, field peas, home-made rolls, and apple pies with golden crusts and tall caramel cakes. Sometimes there were freezers of sweet vanilla ice cream made with Pet milk.

Every Sunday night we had what was called BYPU, which stood for Baptist Young People's Union. My teacher gave prizes for memorizing Bible verses, and I worked hard to win. I got a little kaleidoscope made from paste board for learning to recite Psalm 100.

It was about this time that the Baptists started a competition called the sword drill, designed to make one familiar with the Bible and able to use it with alacrity. I was too young to compete, but I was keenly interested. The competitors stood in a line with Bibles at their sides, and the person in charge—the drill sergeant—would stand before them. When he called the soldiers forward to present arms, the participants would lift their Bibles.

Then the sergeant would call out a Bible verse and say, "Ready, aim, charge," after which the competitors would frantically seek out the passage, the first to find it stepping forward and reading the verse aloud. Prizes were given in this contest, and I couldn't wait to compete.

In Rhodes Chapel Church there was a rotund and acned teenager named Floyd Watkins, a socially mal-adjusted boy who decided that the sword drill was his ticket to fame and popularity. He practiced constantly, representing our church in the Baptist Association contest in Greensboro, which pitted him against all of the other church winners from our area. His reputation went before him, and everyone assumed he would take home the honors for Rhodes Chapel.

But on the day of the contest just before the drill was to begin, someone went into the room Floyd was practicing in and found him dusting the pages of his Bible with talcum powder. It was judged that doing so gave him an unfair advantage over the others, and he was disqualified. He came home with his head hung low. The most he could get out was, "Didn't nobody tell me any different. And it wasn't in the rules either." The ruling went unchallenged, and sword drill became much less the thing at Bucksnort after that.

Widely known around Bucksnort was a biting dog named Grit. He belonged to the Pinkins, who also sharecropped with Brian Rose—a family we didn't know very well because they were distant and reclusive. Mama said their backwardness was beyond words. It did not seem to bother them in the least that their dog was constantly biting people, and, because the bites were minor, no one pressed the Pinkins to do anything about him.

I didn't like Grit's looks one bit. He wasn't a big dog, but he was tightly packed, his brown, red, and black fur bristly, suggesting that there had been some German Shepherd somewhere in his lineage. He was a lazy dog, and even when he wanted to bite someone he never ran any faster than he had to.

One day when I was going with Daddy to get the mule, which was kept in a lot behind the Pinkins' house, I noticed that Grit was nowhere in sight, but I didn't worry much since Daddy was with me. As we rounded the corner of the house, however, Grit suddenly appeared, his dull eyes locked with mine. I knew without a doubt that he would bite me. Before Daddy realized that anything was happening, Grit tore into my leg, just at the top, right next to my incipient manhood. Daddy rushed at him and screamed, "Get out of here you son-of-a-bitch," and Grit backed up under the house slightly and watched us coldly, neither growling nor barking.

Daddy looked at my wound. It was ragged and bloody, and it hurt so bad I was crying in pain. He picked me up and took me to the Roses' house, and Mrs. Rose drove us to the doctor in Greensboro, who frowned when he looked at the wound. He said, "This is a bad one. It's ripped so bad that it won't even hold stitches. I'm gonna have to use surgical tape." He cleaned the wound and applied ointment, and I screamed in pain. "This is going to hurt a little," he said, and I braced myself as he squeezed the wound together so he could close it with the tape. Then he turned to Daddy.

"Albert, you got to cut that dog's head off and send it to the lab in Birmingham. It's the law. We can't take any chances with hydrophobia."

I had known what hydrophobia was since we lived at the Walker Place, and I regarded the prospect with horror. I had heard about a man that started foaming at the mouth and barking when he went mad with it, and in my gut I began to feel a gnawing terror. What if I went mad? When I got home I told my brothers and sisters to stay out of my way and to run if I started chasing them because I wouldn't be able to help myself.

Daddy sent the dog's head to Birmingham, and fourteen days passed before we got a report. These were among the worst days in my life. When I slept I dreamed that I turned into a biting dog, and when I awakened I more or less sat waiting for the death sentence. At times, though, I thought I would have rather died than to take the series of shots for hydrophobia which Donald happily described repeatedly in graphic detail. When the "Not rabid" verdict arrived from Birmingham, no criminal pardoned from death in the electric chair by the governor could have felt better than I did.

I was happy to learn a little later that the Pinkins had decided to quit sharecropping with the Roses, mainly because that allowed us to leave the falling-down Lyons House and take over the house the Pinkins had had. Mr. Bryan knew how cramped we had been in the Lyons place so he told Daddy he would make things better in the new house by adding on a new kitchen, which would allow us to use the old one for a bedroom. The new kitchen smelled richly of new pine lumber and we were proud of it, as we were of the state-of-the-art metal toilet he put in out back.

Other than the Roses, whose house now faced ours across the road, the Highsaws were now our next nearest neighbors at Bucksnort. Their names were Huck, Birdie, Mamie, and Miss Octavie, and they lived in a small unpainted cement block house with a tin roof. I never went inside the house, but I spent a lot of time on the front porch in their split-oak swing, which I coveted very much.

Huck was the one who fascinated me the most. A bachelor in his thirties, he would disappear to Florida for extended periods, working construction. When he returned he would be wearing boldly-colored printed shirts with palm trees or parrots on them, and he would be filled with magical stories about this mythical place he had been to. When I listened to him, I thought that I would rather be in Florida than any place in the world.

Huck was bad to drink, and when he and Daddy were in their cups they would spend a great deal of time talking. I'd get as close to them as I could without attracting their notice and listen.

"Florida," Huck once told Daddy, "is just like heaven. A beer joint on every corner." Then he lowered his voice and said, "And there are houses full of women down there that'll do it for just a dollar." I noticed that Daddy looked sort of embarrassed, and I wondered what it was the women would do. A dollar sounded like a lot of money to me.

"Hey, Mr. McMillan," he said another time, "did I tell you about going in this snack bar down in Ocala? They had this big sign out front that said 'All the orange juice you can drink for a dime.' That looked like a good deal to me so I went in and ordered me a glass. I drained it off real fast and asked for another."

"'That'll be another ten cents,' the waitress said.

"'But the sign says all you can drink for a dime,' I said.

"Then she looked at me straight in the face and said, 'That's right. That *is* all you can drink for a dime.'"

And Huck threw back his wide red head and laughed the happiest laugh I had ever heard.

Huck's sister Birdie was a slight, compact person with a tiny sunburned head that looked as hard as a little cooking apple. I was frightened of her because she wasn't right, and it seemed to me that there was something unspeakably sorrowful dammed up behind her troubled eyes and her thin snuff-stained mouth.

Birdie hardly ever said anything, but she was a hard worker. Donald said she could pick a bale of cotton a day, and I believed him. And she was a fast and accurate cotton chopper. I never knew Birdie's age, but I would guess she was a little older than Huck, probably in her forties.

Birdie and Huck had a niece named Mamie who didn't live there all the time, but she came there for long periods. She was in high school, somewhere around Marcille's age, and she was not bad looking. Lots of people said she was fast, though, because she wore heavy makeup and lots of costume jewelry.

Mamie had a good battery radio off of which she learned the latest songs. She kept it on the front porch, and she would swing back and forth as she sang:

Tra-la-la-tweedledy-dee-dee
It gives me a thrill
To wake up in the morning
On Mockingbird Hill.

At school, we were told, Mamie had behavior problems. One day she came home with her hand and arm in a bloody bandage after having gotten mad and driven her fist right through a plate glass back door at the school.

Mamie was always telling Elizabeth and Marcille about the moral lapses of the Rose girls, and she told the Rose girls about the lapses of my sisters too. If I heard Mamie say anything behind any one of their backs, I'd go straight to them and tell them what she said.

I made a grave mistake one day, however, when all of us, including Mamie, were in the Roses' garden picking peas. I went over to Sharon Rose and said, "Hey, Sharon, you know what Mamie said about you? She said you would let boys put their hands on you anywhere they wanted to. I heard her say it on the bus."

As soon as I got it out of my mouth, Mamie ran at me with homicide in her eyes, screaming, "Shut your mouth, you nosy little bastard." I took off, but I felt her galvanized bucket of purple hull peas clip me on the ear as I fled. When I got away and looked back, I could tell that Mamie was lying up and down, telling them that I had made it all up. A few nights later in a fitful sleep I dreamed that Mamie crammed me down into a large galvanized bucket and threw me with main force through a plate glass window.

I assume that Miss Octavie, the matriarch of the family, was a widow. No mention was ever made of a Mr. Highsaw. She had bruised looking splotches on her arms, and on her legs she wore heavy mauve-colored stockings.

Despite being stuck with Huck, Birdie, and Mamie, Miss Octavie walked around in a state of good-natured serenity most of the time, dipping snuff and humming hymns. We were therefore quite surprised one night to be awakened by a loud clanging sound coming from down toward her house, which we interpreted as a clear call for help. Mr. Rose heard it too, and he and Daddy got there about the same time. Donald and I were not far behind them.

Miss Octavie stood on the font porch wearing a white nightgown and some kind of nightcap. She had a hammer in one hand and a plow sweep in the other.

"What in the world's the matter, Miss Octavie?" Mr. Rose asked.

"Somebody's been throwing rocks on the top of my house," she said.

"Throwing rocks on top of you house?"

"That's what it sounded like to me," she answered.

Daddy and Mr. Bryan looked around. The moon was full that night so it was easy to see. Suddenly Daddy said to Miss Octavie, "Where's your ladder?"

She pointed to the wooden ladder leaning against her barn, and he got it and carefully went up to the roof without a word. He reached over slowly and drew back a squirming animal. He backed down the ladder carrying a very large brindled cat—Miss Octavie's own cat—who had for some reason decided to climb up on the galvanized tin roof and try to walk around. "This is who has been throwing rocks on your house," he said to Miss Octavie.

Miss Octavie stared at the cat with about equal parts of disgust and malevolence, but her countenance changed to pure embarrassment as she looked back at us. "Well, if that don't beat it all," was all she could get out before retreating into her house.

Later Elizabeth and Marcille composed a mock epic poem on the incident, the beginning of which went

In the night dark and deep
Miss Octavie beat the sweep.
And then she began to weep,
"Oh, my friends, I'm losing sleep
For something on my house doth creep.

The poem went on for many lines, with every line rhyming, and we all learned to recite it.

Our days at Bucksnort were fast coming to a close. Daddy had determined that Mr. Bryan Rose was a snake in the grass just as he had with all the others we had sharecropped with, and Elizabeth was hoping to study art at the University of Alabama in Tuscaloosa in the fall. Marcille would also want to be going to college before long. "There's no way they can go unless we move near the University," Daddy said, and we were excited at the prospect. "We're going to move to town," Julia and I sang over and over. That's where all of us thought we belonged anyway.

As it turned out, Daddy by some miracle acquired a twenty-six-acre farm twenty miles south of Tuscaloosa in a little community called Ralph, but here things would be quite different. In the first place, we would be moving out of Hale County for the first time, which to us meant that things were bound to get better. And, second, we would not sharecrop but would own the place.

"There's a lots of money in truck farming," Daddy said, and we believed him because we wanted to. It sounded much better to be truck farmers than sharecroppers.

When the truck taking us to our new home pulled away, Miss Octavie and Mrs. Rose stood in the road to tell us goodbye. Tears streamed down Miss Octavie's face as she hugged Mama and said, "I hate to see y'all go, Mrs. McMillan. Y'all were civilized." As we rode off down the road, I didn't feel particularly civilized as I lay on a mattress atop our worldly goods, but my heart pounded as I listened to the whine of the wheels on the blacktop and thought of an entirely new life.

PART 4

Ralph

It was a cool November day in 1951 when the truck took us to our new house at Ralph, and, although the trip from Bucksnort to Ralph was just a little over fifty miles, it was the fartherest I had ever traveled. When we finally pulled up the long driveway to the house, I could hardly believe what stood before me. The house looked like a mansion. Maybe not as good a mansion as Aunt Elizabeth's, but a mansion anyway. Up until then I had never lived in a painted house, but this one was gleaming white, and it had deep green shutters on the windows and a stamped tin roof which was silver-colored. There was a screened-in front porch with balusters in the shape of the fleur de lis, and over the double front doors was a transom. This was no sharecropper's house, I thought to myself, and I wondered how it could be ours.

Daddy was the only one who had seen the house before we arrived, and he hadn't told us much about it because, he said, he wanted to surprise us. "How in the world were you able to get a place like *this*?" Donald asked Daddy, who was unlocking the front door with a skeleton key.

The house at Ralph

"Robbed a bank," he answered with a smile. You could tell he was proud.

"Is it really ours? Do we really own it?" Marcille asked.

"Yep, it's ours—lock, stock, and barrel."

I looked over at Mama, who had her back to us and seemed to be looking out at the fields around the place. I went over where she was, and I could see she was crying.

"What's wrong, Mama?" I asked.

"Nothing's wrong. I'm just overcome with joy I guess," she answered, dabbing at her eyes. I knew that she had grown up in a nice house in town, and the places she and Daddy had had in Greensboro during the first few years of their marriage had been very good. Now, I thought, she was at least facing the payoff for the intervening years of existing in inadequate hovels. Her indomitable optimism was being validated.

We all went in, and I couldn't help but notice that the entrance hall was bigger than some of the rooms in our previous houses. I looked up at the fourteen-foot ceilings, just like at Aunt Elizabeth's, and I noted that the windows were twice as high as the ones in our other houses. The walls in some rooms were covered with flowered wallpaper while others were neatly painted. The doors, which were all painted white, had bulls-eye decorations on their facings. Everybody was talking at the same time, yelling out, "Look at this" and "Wow" and "Gollee."

I was amazed when I saw that every room had electric lights, a far cry from the one naked bulb at the Early Place. Some of the rooms even had chandeliers, which were golden from the dust that had settled on them during the two years the house had been unoccupied. We pulled the chains on all the lights to make sure that they worked.

The biggest surprise to me, though, was the running water, the first we had ever had. There was no bathroom—that would just be too much, I thought—but there was a spigot at the sink in the kitchen and a faucet in the back yard. I turned on the backyard tap, and rusty looking water came out. "Let it run a while," Daddy said, and when it finally ran clear I leaned over for a swig. I was surprised at the sharp, bitter taste, and I knew I had some adjusting to do.

We ran through all the rooms. "Let's see," Elizabeth said, "a living room, a kitchen, a dining room, four bedrooms, an entrance hall, a pantry, and three porches. Not bad. Not bad."

Daddy said the house had once been two apartments, and the room Donald and I were given as our bedroom had been a kitchen at one time. You could see where the cook stove had been, and there was a corner cupboard Donald immediately claimed as his.

I was exploring the side porch, which was next to our bedroom, when Donald ran out and said, "Follow me. I got something to show you you aren't gonna believe." He led me up a narrow dim staircase to a large attic, which smelled richly of wood and dust. There was one small window, through which spilled a bank of light filled with the motes of dust we had kicked up. As my eyes adjusted, I could see that the place was full of all kind of loot, stuff which I later learned had been left there by the previous occupant of the house, a medical doctor named Simpson.

I picked up a little black leather case covered in dust, and when I opened it I found rows of tiny wire-rimmed glasses resting on a rich blue velvet lining. "Hey, Donald, look at these," I said, selecting a pair and putting them on. "These glasses sort of make things go fuzzy," I said.

"You'll get used to them," he said, rummaging in a corner. "You always have to adjust to glasses." He was examining something he had pulled out of the corner. "I can't believe this," he said. "It's a single-shot .22 rifle. These people must have been rich to leave something like this."

"Yeah, and you look at these," I said, holding up a stack of x-rays I found. I took one over and held it up to the window, and I could barely make out what looked like somebody's ribs. We also found a box filled with medical books and another with small brown bottles of medicine. In a metal trunk there were some old dresses and two pair of high-buttoned black shoes, which were shiny and cracked. There was a spinning wheel in the corner. It creaked and squeaked when I gave it a spin. I also found a huge wooden plane with a rusty blade.

"Hey, look, Norman, here's a bunch of old letters," Donald said, peering down into another trunk. He pulled one out, walked over to the window, and began to read silently. "Wow," he said. "This is good. Just listen to this: 'My dearest Margaret, I cannot wait until I can feel your billowing breasts heaving against me once more. Lying on my lonely bed as I write this, I think of your bare white skin and your alabaster bosom. . . .'"

"That *is* good," I interrupted, "but I want to read one myself." I pulled out a yellowed letter and took it downstairs where the light was better. I sat on the floor of the dining room trying to figure out the old-fashioned handwriting. With difficulty I mouthed the words to the first sentence, "My dearest Margaret, as I lie in my bed my very manhood cries out to you." Before I could read further, Mama walked over and asked what I was reading.

"Just a letter Donald and I found upstairs."

"Let me see that."

I surrendered the letter reluctantly. As she read, her brow began to contract, which meant she didn't like something. "This is not appropriate reading material for boys," she said, wadding up the letter. "I'm ashamed of you. Don't you ever read a letter like this again, and take those silly glasses off before you put your eyes out."

"Yes ma'am," I answered, removing the wire ear pieces as I wondered what was wrong with the letter.

I called Julia and Kenneth to come with me, and we began to explore the back yard. We went into the smokehouse first. Around the walls were shelves filled with jars of canned vegetables and fruits, but when I knocked the dust off of one jar and shook it up, I couldn't even tell what it contained. A milky slime swirled round and round. "That's nasty," Julia said, and I agreed.

In the back yard underneath a big pecan tree we found a few small oily pecans in the brown grass. Most of them had wormholes, but we found a few good ones and put them in our pockets. There were lots of black walnuts still on the ground, but we had no idea what they were. We picked up some of them and flung them at the side of the barn. Then Julia and I spotted a towering October pear tree, on which a few last golden pears still hung. We climbed the tree, picked one apiece, and sat in the crook of the tree eating them, staring out over our new-found domain.

How we acquired this domain was a mystery to us children. Such matters were grown-up business in our household. Before we moved from Bucksnort, I did overhear Daddy say to Mama that the house and its twenty-six acres of farmland had cost $3,000, an amount of incomprehensible magnitude to me. Donald said he thought Aunt Elizabeth paid for it, and Marcille suspected that Evelyn did. Maybe it was a combination. We really didn't know.

It all seemed like a fantasy. The thing that was the hardest to take in was that there was a tenant house down the hill behind our house that went with the place, and I thought it looked very much like the houses we had been living in. It even had its own spigot in the yard.

When Donald and I got into bed exhausted that night, I hardly noticed the chill in the room. Staring into the darkness, I silently prayed, "Dear God, thank you for all of this. Amen." It didn't matter in the least at that moment that we would still cook on a wood stove, that we had no frigidaire or any other appliance to hook up to the electricity, that we lacked indoor plumbing, that the house was inadequately heated—I thought we had it made, and I was grateful.

Mama had taught us to be good stoics. "Whatever bad you are going through now is only temporary, so buck up and bear it," she would say. On this glorious night I thought Mama was right. The payoff for all my previous deprivation had come.

We awakened on our first morning at Ralph with the sun. Mama had heated water, and as she brought the wash pan to the hearth in the living room, she said, "Wash yourselves carefully, now. You want to look good on your first day of school. First impressions are the most important ones." After Marcille, Donald, Julia, and I had finished our sponge baths and had dressed in our best school clothes, she called us to the dining table, on which sat a huge pan of golden biscuits, a saucer of margarine, and a quart jar of Golden Eagle Sopping Syrup. After I made finger holes in four biscuits and poured syrup into them, I ate them all, even though I felt a little nauseated in my excitement. I knew a lot was riding on what happened in the next few hours.

Mama thought Julia, who was in the second grade, was old enough to enter school without her, especially since I would be there. She handed me a brown manila envelope containing our Greensboro school records, and we went down to the road to wait on the school bus. Donald and Marcille, who would ride the bus to Tuscaloosa County High School in Northport, waited with us.

When we saw the yellow bus with number fourteen on it come over the hill, Donald went out stiffly and flagged it. The little man driving the bus looked surprised as we piled on, but Marcille stood in the front and explained everything to him as he pulled off. The other children stared at us as if we had come from some other planet, and I was relieved to find an empty seat for Julia and me.

On the seat opposite us, a big boy with pimples on his face eyed us closely, and I could tell he was working up to a question. Finally he asked me gruffly, "What grade you in?"

"The fourth."

"Really? You look awfully scrawny for a fourth grader," he said. He paused a minute, then said proudly, "I'm in the sixth. I'll go to County High next year."

I was impressed. "My name's Norman," I told him, "and this is my sister Julia. She's in the second grade."

"She goes to Miss Snow's room. You're in Miss Maurine's room with

Ralph School

me," he informed us. When we arrived at school and walked up on the porch, he directed Julia through one door, and the two of us entered another.

I was confused. He said he was in the sixth grade. Then how could I, a fourth grader, be in his room? Inside, he explained to me that there were only two rooms for all six grades, the first three grades taught by Miss Snow Drop Thompson, and the fourth, fifth, and sixth by Miss Maurine Rodgers.

"I'm gonna tell you something important about Miss Maurine," he said confidentially. "She don't take no crapola." Then he added, "Her husband runs the store next to the school here. He's a dope fiend."

"A dope fiend?" I asked.

"You mean you ain't ever heard of a dope fiend? It's those people who take happy stuff and it makes them act crazy. Mr. Luke don't take it all the time, though. But I'd say about every two months they have to send him to Meridian."

"To Meridian?"

"To the hospital."

I was getting information so fast I couldn't take it all in so I slowed things down by asking, "What's your name?"

"Oh, I forgot. Johnny Ray Stoneman. I'm from up at Shiloh. You're from Bethel. Some of the other students are from Wesley Chapel." I was to learn that the three spheres represented at Ralph School were determined by the three white churches in Ralph, two Baptist and one Methodist. "Hey, look," he said, "I can't talk no more. I got work to do. Chores. If we don't get our chores done before Miss Maurine gets here she gets on our asses."

"Can I help you?" I asked, thinking it might be good to get in with Johnny Ray because he seemed to know all the ropes.

"Well, you could go get some more coal for the fire," he said.

"Do you have a wheel barrow?" I asked. Jerome, at Powers School, always used a wheel barrow to carry the coal to the furnace so I assumed that was the way it was always done.

"A what?" Johnny Ray asked.

"A wheel barrow to carry the coal in."

"Oh, new boy, you mean wheel BAR. No we ain't got no wheel bar. You get coal in a scuttle." He looked irritated by my ignorance as he walked over to the potbellied stove and picked up the bucket and shovel next to it. "This here is a scuttle. Take it and go out that back door there and you'll see the pile of coal on the edge of the playground."

As I went for the coal, I realized I was in a different world. This school, compared to the one I had attended in Greensboro, was really backwards. Beyond some swings and a spinning jenny I could see a pair of outside toilets, painted a dull green, and I spotted an artesian well from which two girls were drinking water.

I shoveled the shiny coal into the scuttle, and when I took it back inside I heard someone yelling, "Here comes Miss Maurine." Everybody rushed to the front porch to meet her, and I followed them. Coming across the school yard was a short lady with brownish gray hair, not fat but solid, walking with a shuffling waddle. She wore a matching pink sweater and skirt and navy blue wedge-heeled pumps. A pair of reading glasses dangled on a chain around her neck. Two girls ran out and took her hands, and both started talking at once about the county fair they had just been to. She seemed to be trying to listen to both of them at the same time.

"Miss Maurine," Johnny Ray interrupted, "we got a new boy."

"Oh, where?" she asks as she scans the faces for me.

I raised my hand.

"We're pleased to have you. What's your name?"

"Norman McMillan." My name always sounded funny to me when I spoke it aloud, not like it sounded when others said it.

"A good name. A very good name," she said, like she was impressed. "Fourth grade?" she asked.

"Yes, ma'am."

"Let's go in," she said, putting her hand on my shoulder. "We'll find you a place at the fourth grade table."

I handed her the manila envelope as we went in the room, and after she showed me my seat, she went to her desk and looked over the papers in the envelope. I watched her closely. She nodded a few times, but once or twice she sort of frowned, I thought. When she finished she said to the class, "For you who didn't hear it, Norman McMillan is your new classmate. He comes from Greensboro, Alabama, where he was a very good student. He has a sister Julia in the second grade. Now while I carry these papers over to Miss Snow, get the flags ready for the devotional period. Let's see. Bessie Jean is in charge today, I believe."

When she returned, Bessie Jean, a tall sixth grader with decayed teeth and oily hair, stood up and said, "We'll now salute the American flag." We all turned to face the drooping flag, placed our hands over our hearts, and recited the pledge. This I was used to doing in Greensboro. Then Bessie Jean reached over and picked up a red Bible, raised it up over her head, and said, "I'll read the words of Jesus written in red, which reminds us all of the blood he shed." That rhymes, I thought, but I didn't pay any more attention to her because I was thinking about Powers School in Greensboro. I thought of Miss Jewell reading the Bible and singing and playing the piano, and for a moment I longed painfully to be back in my old school.

Bessie Jean's reading went on and on, but finally she stopped and said, "Let us now pray." She paused dramatically before beginning:

"Dear Heavenly Father, thank you for this beautiful day, and thank you for our teacher Miss Maurine. Bless the missionaries on the foreign fields. Shield and protect us from the godless communists who move among us secretly. And bless President Harry S. Truman and Governor Strom Thurmond and all of our other representatives as they lead our country. Be with us throughout this day, Heavenly Father. In Jesus' name we pray, amen."

I was quite impressed with Bessie Jean's prayer. I knew that I could never come up with anything that good. It wasn't long, however, before I found out that Bessie Jeans's prayer was pretty much the same one everybody used, and it was repeated with only slight variation at church as well as at school.

For three years in the same room at Ralph School, I was under the strict tutelage of Miss Maurine Rodgers. A teacher of the highest standards, Miss Maurine was obsessed with sending on to Tuscaloosa County High School a group of students who would reflect well upon her and her community. No one before or since ever pushed me harder than she did.

Miss Maurine took no shit off anyone. All students were expected to live up to their greatest potential or she would know the reason why. She had a long cedar paddle under her desk, and we all knew she was fully willing to use it. Although she seldom ever pulled it out, it served as a mighty deterrent to classroom misbehavior.

Miss Maurine taught so hard she would get a sick headache by the middle of the morning almost every day, and she would have to send a student to the store to get her a BC headache powder and a Coca-Cola. She would pour about half the Coke into a cup and hand the remaining part to the student who had gone to get it. Then she would tap the BC powder onto her tongue, make a strange face, and wash it down with the Coke. Sometimes it made her better; sometimes not.

I made a terrible mistake there at Ralph School when I was in the fourth grade by listening to all the fifth and sixth grade lessons. By the time I got to them, they were old hat, and I was bored much of the time. Often I would just sit idly and wait for play period or lunch.

To keep us busy, Miss Maurine would give us page after page of mimeographed math problems, science questions, and language exercises. She would even duplicate puzzles and riddles on the copying machine, and when she would pass them out we would smell of the copies before we even looked at the purple print, agreeing that they smelled like embalming fluid, a liquid none of us could claim to have smelled. Sometimes she would write puzzles on the board and ask us to solve them. Once she wrote:

YYUR
YYUB
ICUR
YY4me.

We were to discover that it meant, "Too wise you are, too wise you be. I see you are too wise for me."

But even with all the extra things to do and the bookmobile books that we could read, I seldom had enough to keep me busy. On my report cards she would always write, "Does not use his leisure time wisely," and when she found me in a brown study I was made to copy long passages out of a textbook. Once, when she was especially aggravated by my sitting and doing nothing, she made me write "I am not living up to my potential" five hundred times. At church, she would tell Mama that she couldn't find enough to keep me busy.

Miss Maurine had a mean streak. She was particularly hard on Abner Jenkins, our closest neighbor and someone I played with pretty often. When we moved to Ralph, Abner's father Alton was serving time in prison for shooting a revenuer who was trying to break up his whiskey still, but he was given parole shortly after we moved there. At that time, the state of Alabama required four weeks of church attendance when they let somebody out of prison, and I first saw Alton when he brought Abner and his other children to Bethel Baptist Church and sat on the back pew, a slight snarl on his lip. After the four weeks he never came back.

Abner, the oldest boy in the Jenkins family, had a great problem with spelling. Once in a required spelling bee he was asked to spell church, and he rared back and said quite deliberately, "H-s-r." He was eliminated in the first round. If he failed a spelling test, Miss Maurine would get right up in his face and say, "Abner, if you don't apply yourself more than you have been, you're going to wind up in exactly the same place your father did." Abner would turn red in the face, and I would feel sorry for him because I knew he was doing his best.

After thinking about it long and hard, I decided that Miss Maurine did not intend to be cruel. She just didn't want Abner to be satisfied unless it was the best he could do. But that didn't make it any easier on Abner. Once he said to me, " I'd kill the old bitch if I thought I could get away with it," and I understood why.

Miss Maurine wanted to give her students as many opportunities as possible. Once she formed us into a rhythm band, and I played the triangle. Another time she purchased tonettes for us, but none of us could learn to play them. She would get educational movies from the County School Board to show to us, but she was not very adept at running the projector. Once she showed us an entire film backwards because she couldn't figure out how to stop it. It was the most interesting educational film we had ever had, and we hooted as we saw cotton pickers putting cotton back into its boles, a man uneat an apple, and a diver flip backwards out of the water onto a diving board—all in one movie.

When Miss Maurine found out that Elizabeth was studying art at the University, she hired her to come once a week and give us an art lesson. Art supplies at Ralph School were limited, but there was a good supply of tempera paints, large brushes, and pads of coarse-grained art paper. In addition there was a big roll of sleek white paper which we would unwind and tack around the walls so that we could do communal murals depicting holidays.

I was quite proud to have my sister teaching us, and I would try to sit next to her when she rode the school bus down to give us our lessons. We arrived at school about thirty minutes before class actually started, and during that time we did our assigned chores. One day when my job was to sweep the room, I wheedled Elizabeth into sweeping for me. When Miss Maurine came in, she began to check as she always did to make sure that our work was satisfactory. Going into the supply room and coming out with the broom, she began kicking up dust between the boards in the floor. "Who half-did this?" she asked in disgust. "Can't you see this dirt?"

"Elizabeth did it," I told her gleefully.

Miss Maurine did not seem in the least embarrassed as she handed me the broom to resweep the floor, and I felt a little disappointed about that. For once I wanted to see her hem and haw. I looked over at Elizabeth, and I thought at the time she looked a little bit gotten away with, but she was laughing about it at home that night.

There were only six of us students in my class. My best friend among them was a blond-headed boy named Randy Harris, and I also especially liked a plump freckled-faced girl named Betty Boyd Bunn, who would be asked after we finished lunch to go to the piano to accompany us students as we sang. I loved to sing the boy-girl call and answer song that began

Reuben, Reuben, I've been thinking,
What a grand world this would be,
If the men were all transported
Far beyond the Northern Sea.

Almost every week we sang "My Grandfather's Clock," and we often sang "Three Blind Mice" and "Frere Jacques" in rounds. Occasionally Miss Maurine would ask somebody to sing a solo.

I brought a song from Greensboro with me that seemed to be a hit with everybody. Beginning with "The circus is a jolly place for anyone to be," it went on and enumerated what all you could see there. "I've got a request for the circus song, Norman," Miss Maurine said one day.

As I went proudly to the front, I thought I heard some snickering behind me, but I decided to ignore it. I sang the song in my best voice. Everybody clapped, but when I went back to my seat, my glory faded quickly. Johnny Ray, who was at the next table, leaned over and whispered, "Check the ass end of your pants, Bud."

I eased my hand back there and I could feel my hot skin through an open hole in my jeans. I remembered in a flash that when I had not been able to find any underwear that morning I had pulled on the jeans without any. I obviously had missed seeing the hole. I could feel the red crawling over my face, and I could hear Johnny Ray and a couple of others laughing. If I could have, I would have stayed in the chair forever, even as everyone was leaving the cafeteria. "You might as well come on, Norman. Everybody's seen your ass already anyway," Johnny Ray said loud enough for a few of the sixth graders, but not Miss Maurine, to hear him.

If we were good Miss Maurine would read aloud a chapter out of a book after lunch. But sometimes she would say, "Y'all are acting so bad, I'm not ever going to read another word to you," and you knew there was no reason to try to change her mind for that day. But invariably on the following day she did read, in part, I think, because she really enjoyed it. She would read to us about Miss Bluegum Tempy Peruney Perline in a thick book called *Miss Minerva and William Green Hill*, and each year she read us my favorite book of all, *Little Britches*.

On my own I began to read from a set of orange biographies for young readers we had in the room. I finished the entire set, devouring titles like *Andrew Jackson: The Fighting President, Davy Crockett: Frontier Hero,* and *Daniel Boone: The Opening of the Wilderness.* I also got a sense of being a part of a larger world from reading the *Weekly Reader*. I learned the names of kings and princes, presidents, and prime ministers. I learned about new inventions. I felt like I was up on things.

At home we always had magazines, but most of them were not current. The only publications I remember coming regularly into our home were *The Progressive Farmer, Home Life* (which came from the Broadman Baptist Press in Nashville), the *Alabama Baptist*, and a little newsletter called *Now*, which was circulated by an evangelical businessman named R. G. Le Tourneau. It always included pictures of the giant earth-moving equipment he manufactured. None of these publications did a thing for me.

We also took the *Tuscaloosa News*, which I read daily, all except the funny papers, which never interested me in the least. We made a game of guessing grocery prices, using the ads in the paper. "How much are red grapes a pound?" one of us would shout out. "A pint of Kraft mayonnaise?" "A pound of sirloin steak?" The caller recorded answers and matched them against the advertised prices. The winner got to call the next game.

Most of our magazines came from Aunt Elizabeth. She would save them for us, and when she visited she would bring boxes crammed with copies of the *Saturday Evening Post, Life, National Geographic, and Reader's Digest*—all of which I loved and read from cover to cover. For almost every young boy in those days, the *National Geographic* supplied the most daring pictures of women we saw anywhere, and we would check out every issue for barebreasted Polynesian or African women.

The *Reader's Digest* had interesting articles that could be read quickly, and I became addicted to trying "It Pays to Increase Your Word Power" while I was in grade school. Even when I couldn't get many of them at all, I loved to look at words like *vicissitude*, *vouch*, and *voluptuous*. I also regularly read "Life in these United States," but its blandness was always a bit disappointing to me.

My two favorite books when I was small were brought home by Elizabeth when she was a student at the University. The first was a book of paintings by Vincent Van Gogh. I would particularly stare at Van Gogh's self portrait and wonder how anybody could cut off his own ear. The other book, a collection of cartoons by Charles Addams, was called *Monster Rally*, and, without knowing it, I was learning a wonderful lesson about irony as I looked at it. My favorite one depicted Mona Lisa sitting in a crowded theater with her enigmatic smile while everybody else is laughing uproariously.

Much of what I learned in my elementary years came from the older brothers and sisters. Evelyn taught us to sing the opening lines to *The Canterbury Tales* in Middle English to the tune of "Dark Town Strutter's Ball," and she taught us the Titanic song, "It Was Sad When That Great Ship Went Down," singing the line, "Hit the bottom, Lordy" in an exaggerated bass voice. We could mimic her perfectly.

Sarah taught us a hillbilly version of the popular song "Temptation," and before Kenneth had started to school he was already singing "Ninety-nine Bottles of Beer on the Wall." Once when some cousins from Tuscaloosa came down to Ralph, the mother proudly said that her little son, who was Kenneth's age, could sing "Jesus Loves Me." "Sing it for them, Stevie," she said, and after he finished I responded by saying, "That's nothing. Kenneth can sing 'Ninety-nine Bottles of Beer on the

Wall.'" Mama didn't think that was funny and gave me a talking to after they left.

Sarah and Evelyn thought Edgar Allan Poe's "The Raven" was the worst poem ever written, and they instructed us to recite it in high sardonic voices. We had little idea of what "surcease of sorrow" meant, but we yipped the poem out in glee.

Evelyn especially liked to read aloud to us. She introduced us to Sister and Stella Rondo in Eudora Welty's "Why I Live at the P. O," and we would beg her to read it again and again. She also read us James Thurber's "Sitting in the Catbird Seat" and Faulkner's "A Rose for Emily."

Mama recited a good bit of poetry to us, things like "Little Orphan Annie," but more often she sang sorrowful songs about drunken husbands, long-suffering wives, and afflicted children, and these she sang in a trembling voice as if she were telling her own story. She seemed unsatisfied if she couldn't elicit a few tears from our eyes, and she seldom failed when she would sing:

Mother, when I get to heaven,
Will the angels let me play?
Just because I am a cripple,
Will they say I'm in the way?
Other children here don't want me,
I'm a bother they all say.
Mother, when I get to heaven,
Will the angels let me play?

Mama also sang a song called "Stay in Your Own Backyard," in which a little black child—a kinky-headed pickaninny as he was called in the song—complains to his mother that he has been mistreated by some white children. We never questioned the advice his Mammy gave him—to stay in his own back yard—but we felt terribly sorry for the little pickaninny.

But there was happier singing around the house too, singly and together. Sometimes Elizabeth and Marcille would harmonize on songs

Daddy

like "I Love You Truly," and they would shoo the rest of us away if we tried to join them because they said we drowned out Elizabeth's alto. Usually we sang hymns, folk songs, and hillbilly music, and after we got a radio we added rhythm and blues to our repertoire.

That first spring in Ralph, Daddy was eager to plant our first truck crops, even though he didn't own a truck. He went to Tuscaloosa and bought seeds and sets and slips to plant acres of purple hull and crowder peas, Kentucky Wonder pole beans, bush beans, butter beans —white and speckled, potatoes—Irish and sweet, Marglobe tomatoes, green peppers, hot peppers, cabbage, eggplant, okra, yellow crook-necked squash, cucumbers, sweet corn and field corn, cantaloupes, and Snider watermelons. He got bags of 8-8-8 fertilizer and sodium nitrate. And he acquired a mule, whom we named Mary.

"Everybody's got to pitch in, all of you," Daddy said at the supper table the night before he started putting in the crop. "If we all do our part, we can make some good money. We'll set up a fruit stand and sell our stuff out in front of the house, and I've already made some arrangements with Roy Claiborne to haul stuff to Tuscaloosa, Eutaw, and Boligee. We just all have to do our part."

I did not want to do my part. I hated farming, and I had to be made to do anything. I'd perk up slightly when Daddy announced that he'd pay us two bits for each bushel of peas we picked, four bits for a peck of beans, and this and that for other vegetables, but even that was not enough motivation.

Daddy stayed mad with me much of the time. "You are the laziest white boy I've ever seen," he'd say. "Put that goddamn book down and get your work done." I'd obey, but in an unenthusiastic and surly way.

Marcille hated the field work as much as I did, but she was expected to do some work too. She thought hoeing was the most humiliating of all the jobs, and when she heard a car coming along the road when she was hoeing, she would throw down her hoe and pretend to be looking up at the sky. "You better stop that or people are going to think you are a scarecrow," Donald would say.

One blistering hot afternoon Daddy told Kenneth and me that we had to pick four long rows of tomatoes. As we walked into the field, the hot dirt scorched my bare feet, inspiring in me an idea of how to get out of this job. "Hey, Kenneth," I said, "if you'll eat a whole pod of that hot red pepper there—just one—and if you'll do it without drinking any water—I'll pick all of the tomatoes myself."

"Shoot, I can do that," Kenneth answered.

"But wait just a minute," I said. "That's not all the bet. If you can't eat the whole pod of pepper, then you'll have to pick all the tomatoes by yourself."

"It's a bet," he said, going over confidently and picking a shiny pod of the pepper. He took a little bite. "That's nothing," he said, chewing tentatively. But after one more bite he began to wheeze a little. Then he spit on the ground. That apparently did little good, so he rushed over to the backyard faucet and flooded his mouth with water. That didn't seem to help either, and he threw up a little reddish liquid on the ground. He finally had to sit down on the back steps and hold his head down.

"What you sitting down for?" I asked. "A bet's a bet. Are you going to finish that pepper? If not, you better get to picking those tomatoes."

That was too much for Kenneth. He began crying, and instead of going to pick the tomatoes he ran out to where Daddy was. "Daddy. Daddy. Norman made me eat a hot pepper and I'm sick."

"What do you mean made you eat a hot pepper?"

"He said if I'd eat a whole hot pepper he'd pick all the tomatoes, and I tried to, but I got sick, and now he's trying to make me pick the tomatoes."

"Get your ass over here," Daddy yelled at me as he went over to the hedge and cut a fat switch. "Don't you ever treat your brother like that again," he screamed, taking my hand and switching my bare legs. I ran round and round, so he wasn't making very good contact, but it stung pretty bad anyway. "If you ever pull something like this again, I'll beat you within an inch of your life."

Then he told Kenneth to go inside and lie down, and Kenneth couldn't help grinning at me when he heard that. I felt mad enough to kill him, and, as I was thinking about how I'd get his skinny ass good, Daddy turned to me and said, "And you can pick all the goddamn tomatoes by yourself, Norman. We'll see how you like that."

I didn't like it very much. Feeling grossly mistreated, I picked up the bucket and stomped down the tomato row. I threw some of the tomatoes in the bucket so hard that they split open.

The only good thing I could see about truck farming was getting to meet the people who turned up at our stand to buy vegetables. Business was pretty slow because we were not on a major highway and it seemed like most country people grew their own vegetables. But we did have our regulars who came every day or so to buy.

A woman with a tiny baby and a little girl who lived up on the highway was our best customer. She was from up north, and she had money because her husband, as she put it, was "in management" at the B. F. Goodrich Tire Plant in Tuscaloosa. One day she drove up in a brand new two-toned Pontiac, and after she selected her vegetables and got ready to go she found that the car wouldn't start.

We went and got Daddy, who had no idea what was wrong. "We'll just have to push it off," he said. "Come on, children." We all lined up at the back bumper and started pushing. Since the driveway went down hill, we got up some pretty good speed, but it still wouldn't start.

"I'll never have another Pontiac ever again as long as I live," the woman said in a spoiled-sounding voice.

"Let's try once more," Daddy said. "And put some shoulder into it this time, Donald."

No luck. We tried three times, and we were about to give out. The woman got out of the car, the baby in her arm and the little girl holding onto her skirt. She looked like she thought she was trapped in that exact place on the side of the road forever. I guess we all sort of looked that way when Mr. George Taylor drove up in his pickup. "Y'all got a problem?" he asked.

"This sorry car won't start," the woman said.

Mr. George got out of his truck and went to the car and got in. In no time we heard the car start. He then turned back and said in a voice tinged with scorn, "That car was in drive. I thought everybody knew that an automatic transmission had to be in park or neutral to start."

I knew six sweating people who didn't.

"Thank you, sir," the woman said sheepishly, getting back in the Pontiac. I thought she drove off faster than necessary.

"Much obliged," Daddy said to Mr. George, who was getting back in his truck.

"Think nothing of it," he answered, cranking up the pickup. As he drove away, I could see him shaking his head, and I figured he was going down to Luke Rodgers' store to report on our stupidity to whoever was down there. "They may have book learning, but they don't have any common sense" was what people said about us. Abner Jenkins had reported to me that he had heard people say that on more than one occasion.

For two years we truck farmed without any transportation, but one day in 1953 Bill drove in from Texas driving a 1939 Ford coupe. "That's the worse looking car I ever saw," I thought. It had only one back fender and a side window that was cracked, it lacked a muffler, and heavy exhaust smoke rose up through the floor into the car. It had broken down on Bill three times on the way home, and he said he had had it with the piece of junk. If Daddy wanted it, he could have it free of charge.

Daddy wanted it, and, though he didn't even have a driver's license at the time, for a couple of years he used it regularly to haul vegetables to Eutaw, seventeen miles south of us. I was embarrassed to be seen in the car, which the Jenkins kids dubbed Albert's Tat Tat, because, lacking a muffler, it could be heard a long distance off—tat, tat, tat, tat.

Occasionally I would swallow my embarrassment and go to Eutaw with Daddy to sell watermelons out of the trunk of the Tat Tat. We set up in a parking lot next to Tarr's Place, a bar for black people. Because Eutaw's county was 83% black, naturally most of our customers would be black, and we wanted to park at a place to attract them. But I began to think we had made a mistake parking there because quite often when they came by they would look down at our watermelons and then up at a huge sign which had a frosty bottle of Pabst Blue Ribbon beer on it and then walk on by. We decided to relocate to a place where the competition was not so keen.

Overall, our best customer for produce in Eutaw was Brown Brothers Grocery Store, a black-owned business. It was run by Mrs. Brown, a light-skinned woman with long glistening straightened hair. She seemed quite exotic to me. Quite courteous and soft spoken, she always paid in cash she got out of a huge safe behind the counter. Other stores in the area became regular customers too, and we seemed to be doing well. A wide-mouthed gallon jar on the mantel in Daddy and Mama's bedroom held the silver, and one time it had over $400 in coins in it. And Daddy's billfold bulged with bills. The main concern he had was to save enough to get us through the winter.

Summers meant lots of food. We didn't think about it that way, but we were more or less vegetarians. During the summer when we were at home, each lunch table was filled with seven or eight bowls every day. Pans of golden cornbread or plates of thick biscuits accompanied the vegetables. Except for white meat, which was used to season the vegetables, we saw little meat at all. Occasionally Daddy would bring steak home, and after pounding it with the side of a saucer he would fry it and make gravy. At times we raised a few chickens, and we also ate squirrel and rabbit in the winter, and sometimes even possum and coon. I never liked the game very much at all, and I was particularly revolted when Daddy cracked the squirrels' heads open and ate their brains.

Food during the winter was a problem. Despite the plenty of the summer, Mama did not can food, for what reason I don't know. Once Miss Maurine said in my earshot, I expect for my benefit, that she did not can, but if she had children to feed she would. That sort of burned me. In winter our diet consisted mainly of dried peas we saved, collards, which could bear up under freezing temperatures, sweet potatoes and Irish potatoes we stored up under the house, and cornbread made from meal which Mr. Lacey Lott ground for us from our own corn.

We picked wild fruits in season, mainly black berries and huckleberries, muscadines, fox grapes, plums, and persimmons, and we gathered large quantities of hickory nuts and picked their meat out with hair pins. When we studied the history of Alabama Indians at school, I was struck by the similarity of our diet and that of the Creeks and Chickasaws that had lived in our area before the white man arrived. Their pattern of feast and famine was also exactly like ours, I thought—feast in summer and famine in winter.

One change for the boys in the family that occurred in the summer while we were making money was that we could get our hair cut at the barbershop in Eutaw. During the rest of the year, Mama provided most of our haircuts, and we did not like the job she did at all. She was a one-handed hair cutter, whacking off big hunks until she judged your hair sufficiently short. Nobody but the Jenkins kids had haircuts that looked anything like ours.

When we were able to scrape up fifty cents, we would walk a mile over to Farley Grimes's house early on Sunday morning and let him shear us. He was a county road worker who cut hair on the side, and his equipment was not the best. His old electric clippers would run so hot that he'd have to stop and let them cool off two or three times before he finished to keep from burning your scalp. Even so, I much preferred his haircuts to Mama's.

I liked to get my hair cut in Eutaw, where the barbers actually knew what they were doing, and they dusted your neck when they finished with good-smelling talcum powder. One day when Kenneth and I had gone in for a haircut, I looked up and saw Daddy go by delivering a huge basket of red peppers to a customer.

"Good God A'mighty," my barber said to his partner working on Kenneth, "did you see that? That man had enough hot peppers to burn down Eutaw." I didn't let on that I knew the man, and I was glad because a little later Daddy came back down the street, this time carrying a paper sack in his hand. My barber said, "That man's got whiskey in that sack."

"How you know that?" the other barber asked.

"Look how carefully he's carrying that sack. That man doesn't want to drop that whiskey. No, sir."

The two barbers laughed, and I cringed a little.

Our nearest neighbors at Ralph were a splendid old widow named Miss Ola Robinson and her brother Mr. Cosper and his wife. Miss Ola welcomed our company and immediately instructed us to call her Momola like her grandchildren did. We spent a great deal of time in her little tarpaper house.

Momola tried to maintain the kind of life she had known going back into the nineteenth century. Always dressed in sturdy lace-up shoes and a full apron, her hair plaited and pinned up, she worked constantly—digging in her garden, milking her cow, or slopping her hogs. She had numerous day lilies and jonquils in her yard, and she grew sultana in syrup buckets on the front porch. Several pomegranate bushes and a number of fig trees grew in the front yard, and behind her house was a small apple orchard. She butchered a hog when the weather turned cold enough in the fall, and she made her own sausage, which was spicy and rich. She churned milk and made her own butter.

We bought butter from her for a dime a cake, but it was not very good. It had a sort of chalky consistency because, according to Daddy, she didn't have the strength in her hands to press all the milk out of it. And during the summers until we got a refrigerator we'd go at noon everyday to get a bucket of ice from her. That cost a nickel.

Momola's brother Mr. Cosper was a tall, slim man with clacking false teeth. He fascinated me because I had heard the story of his past from the Jenkins children, whose grandmother he had married in his old age. They said that when he was a young man in Greene County he had killed a man in self defense, and to avoid standing trial he had fled to the Pacific Northwest, settling in Walla Walla, Washington, and living there for many years. In his old age, he began to hanker for home, and he decided that enough time had passed that it would be safe to return.

Mr. Cosper liked his drink, and he took to making homebrew down at their spring. Once Donald and I slipped off down there and inspected his operation. We were impressed. He even had a hand-operated machine to cap his bottles with. Once somebody came down and stole a batch of his home brew, and suspecting some teenagers from the neighborhood, he put out the word that he had a shotgun rigged up down there, and anyone who came near the place would have his head blown off. That was enough to quell any interest I had previously had in Mr. Cosper's homebrew.

When he returned from the west, Mr. Cosper married a Mrs. Minnie Tyree, a sad old woman whose first husband had been drug to death by mules. In her aprons, heavy stockings, and high top shoes, she, like Momola, looked like someone out of a long gone era. The front room of the house was long and narrow, with a dining area at the far end. While Momola and Mr. Cosper sat up in the living room part, Mrs. Cosper occupied a rocking chair in the farthest corner of the dining area. I never heard her utter anything except hello and goodbye, but sometimes when we were there she would get up and go to the safe and pull out a plate of large chewy teacakes she had made and give us one apiece, a slight smile of pride on her face.

Momola had been given a television by a well-off son in Tennessee, and we spent as much time as we could watching our favorite programs. Amazingly, every afternoon Momola and the Cospers watched with us *The Circle Six Ranch*, an afternoon show from Birmingham with a live audience of boys and girls. My greatest ambition for a while was to go to Birmingham and be on the show, and I envied the children who got to. One day when the host Bennie Carl, a dark-complexioned man with slanted eyes, was talking to the children, this one boy mumbled something to him.

"Speak up, son. Bennie Carl likes boys that speak up."

The little boy mumbled something again.

"Say it loud enough for Bennie Carl to hear. Try once more."

The little boy shouted loudly this time: "Bubba pooted. That loud enough?"

I was embarrassed for that boy not knowing any better, but when Momola laughed I felt relieved and I laughed along with everybody else.

We also walked down there at night to see our favorite programs. We never missed *The Millionaire*, and like millions of Americans of the time, I used to dream about John Beresford Tipton delivering me a check. We also loved *Robin Hood, December Bride, The Life of Riley,* and *The Milton Berle Show*. If we got there early, we would sit through the news, and I remember distinctly once when Herbert Hoover came on the program Mr. Cosper got up and went outside. In a little while he came back to the door and asked, "Is he off yet?" We waved him back in. "I can't stay in the same room with that S. O. B.," he said. "He did more to hurt this country than any other president."

I didn't know at the time what had Mr. Cosper so upset, but I did know that he and I agreed on one thing: the Gillette prizefight on Friday nights was the best show on television. My heart always revved up when I heard the theme song come on:

To look sharp
And to feel sharp too
Get the razor
That is made for you.
Light, regular, heavy—hey!
Great shaves for every beard all day.

We'd always agree in advance on which boxer we'd root for. "Hit him, hit him," we'd holler. Somehow it never quite occurred to me that a boxer could actually get hurt, and even the blood, which we would occasionally see, seemed no more than part of the staging.

Another bonus of living next to Momola was that she had many grandchildren, and when they visited we would play with them. Her grandson, Johnny Vance, came from Eutaw every summer to spend a couple of weeks with her. He and I were the same age, and though Johnny had a heart condition, he seemed to have plenty of energy. We dug a cave in the red clay bank behind Momola's house, and there we established a club with just us two as members. And we'd go swimming in a nearby branch.

When we were around ten, Johnny and I had gotten bored and were sitting around on the front steps at our house with Julia and Kenneth, trying to think of something to do. We were sick of playing Blind Man Bluff and Sling a Statue. Suddenly Johnny said, "I tell you what, Norman. You get up on my shoulders, and I'll see how long I can turn round and round before I get dizzy." That I said yes is an indication of how desperate we were for something to do.

I climbed up on his back and he began spinning. It was fun, and I waved an arm in the air as he moved faster and faster. I shouted, "Ride 'em, cowboy," and he whooped loudly. Then suddenly I was falling, hard and fast. I felt my head bang hard against the concrete doorstep. The blow knocked me out for a little because the next thing I remember was seeing Mama standing over me. My head was hurting bad and I began to scream. When she saw my bleeding, cracked head, she shook her own head and said, "This is the last straw."

She took me to the faucet in the back yard and flooded the cut with water. I jumped and hollered because it stung. Kenneth and Julia stood there wide-eyed as Mama pulled back my hair and looked at the wound. "That's not so bad as I thought," she said. "You'll be all right."

Almost all at once we realized that Johnny was nowhere to be seen.

"He ran down the road. I saw him," said Kenneth.

"It's almost dark," Mama said. "I assume he went home."

"No, he went the other way," Kenneth said.

Then we saw Momola coming up our drive. We ran out and told her that Johnny was missing.

"Oh, no," she said. "It's time for him to take his digitalis. He has to have his digitalis every day."

Even Daddy joined us in our search. We went down the road, with me in the lead calling, "Johnny, Johnny. Where are you, Johnny?"

Upon hearing my voice Johnny emerged slowly from a culvert. He looked relieved, but he was still shaking a little. "I was scared I had killed you," he said. "You were laying there so still. I was afraid I'd have to go to prison or get the electric chair."

I laughed at him. By now everybody was surrounding him. Momola hugged him and said, "You almost scared the life out of my body, boy." Daddy asked if he was all right, and Mama patted him and consoled him. They all seemed to forget that I was the injured party.

Momola would sometimes say that she had a good son and she had a sorry son, and she was none too excited when she came up to our house one day and said that her sorry son Rufus P., who was living in Texas, wanted to come back to Alabama and wondered if he could rent our tenant house until he could get on his feet. Up to that point we had not rented the house, but Daddy thought we could use the money so he said he could have it for ten dollars a month.

Shortly thereafter, Rufus P. Robinson, a short, stocky fellow with unmanageable red hair, moved in with Myrtle, his grim-faced wife, and their five children. Bonita, a large bovine girl, was the oldest, and Rufus P., Jr., called Sonny, was my age. The three youngest, named Catherine, Pearly Sue, and Bradford, were all sort of wormy looking. This assortment had to fit into one big room, a small shed room off the front porch, and a kitchen in a separate building across an open yard.

Almost immediately Rufus P. and Myrtle got jobs at the box factory in Tuscaloosa. "We could afford to get a better place than this," Myrtle said, "but we are saving our money. I got my heart set on going back to Galveston, Texas." I noticed that she pronounced Galveston with an accent on the second syllable. GalVESTon.

I thought the Robinsons were rich. Albert's Tat Tat was broken down for good, and I was envious when they drove home one day in a

'47 Pontiac. Its paint job was bad enough to begin with, but when Rufus P. and Daddy finished painting it red, using a fly spray can, it looked hideous. The paint blistered, and the blisters popped open, making it look like a rolling leper. But it ran as quietly as a sewing machine.

On Friday nights after they were paid, the Robinsons would have a feast. My mouth would water when Sonny would say, "Lemme see. We had fried pork chops, potato salad, pork and beans, and doughnuts. And it was sure enough good."

Rufus P. went to the Western Auto store in Tuscaloosa and got Sonny a brand-new red and white, twenty-six-inch Western Flyer bicycle, on which the weekly payment was $2. Sonny was so generous with the bicycle that I rode it almost as much as he did. I was shocked by his generosity because Donald, who had bought himself a used bicycle, wouldn't let us ride it unless we paid him a nickel. He kept it locked up with a combination lock on the chain. But Sonny didn't have a stingy bone in his body.

The problem with Sonny's bicycle was that Rufus P. didn't keep up the payments. The store finally sent someone out to repossess it, but Sonny saw them coming in time to lower the bicycle into the well. But they came back a few days later, and he didn't have time to hide it. I saw it sitting up on the back of the truck as it came slowly by our house, and I grieved for its loss. I assumed Sonny was grieving too, but when I saw him coming up the hill a little later he certainly wasn't grieving. He was grinning.

"Well, they got it this time," he said happily. "But we really got a lot of good riding out of it before they did, didn't we?" I was unable to find the consolation he did.

One thing I noticed about people early on was that those who were happy most of the time, like Sonny, could turn out to be the most vicious when pushed. One day when Sonny, Donald, and I were in the back yard, Sonny was complaining about a huge throbbing carbuncle on his upper arm. I had seen it earlier. It was swollen and red and full of pus, and he held his arm stiff when he walked because any movement seemed to be a torture to him.

"Come here and let me see that," Donald said, pretending to be concerned. Sonny obeyed.

"I can take care of that for you," Donald said, and he drew back his fist and smashed the carbuncle as hard as he could. The core few over the smokehouse, and Sonny collapsed on the ground, holding his arm and writhing.

"Cut that out," Donald said spitefully. "You don't have a carbuncle any more, now do you?" Sonny, still on the ground and crying hard, didn't answer him so Donald walked off, real unconcerned. In a little bit Sonny lifted himself up and headed home, holding his aching arm and crying. I felt sorry for him and hated Donald for his cruelty.

When the pain subsided Sonny obviously began to feel a strong irresistible compulsion to get revenge. His only problem was that he dared not mess with Donald, who was four years older and dangerous. Like Satan getting revenge on God by attacking puny mankind, Sonny began to plot a surrogate revenge through either me or Kenneth. Little did he know that Donald would be pleased at any damage he could do us.

Sonny's first good chance for revenge was with Kenneth, who was seven at the time. Sonny found some stinging nettles, and he held Kenneth by the hand and whipped his bare legs repeatedly with them. Even when huge welts arose and when Kenneth howled in pain, Sonny wouldn't stop. When he finally relented, Kenneth ran home screaming, his legs now almost a solid welt of vibrating whiteness.

"What in the world?" Mama asked, and through his screams he made her understand. She applied calamine lotion, but it did no good. The poison was working so thoroughly by now that Kenneth said he couldn't even walk. Mama got a neighbor to take him to the emergency room in Tuscaloosa where the doctor worried for a while about polio, but, after giving Kenneth a benadryl shot and observing him for a while, pronounced him out of danger.

I more or less stayed out of Sonny's way after that, and he wouldn't come around our house at all because Daddy told Rufus P. to keep him away, he didn't want him near his children. I wasn't really sorry at all when we looked up one day and they were pulling out. As it turned out, they were moving back to GalVESTon.

At Ralph, Daddy continued his periodic binges, and the longer he continued, the less tolerant I became of him. I did not want anyone—particularly my friends—to see him in that condition, and because of his drinking and the general filthiness of the house I seldom invited friends over. The Jenkins kids were in and out, but they didn't count because their daddy not only drank but had been in prison. When Daddy was passed out, they found it amusing, and they would lean over and point at him and laugh out loud.

The most embarrassed I ever was over Daddy's drunkenness was when he announced one morning that he was going to ride the school bus down to the store. "Don't you do that, Albert," Mama said, and we all begged him not to. But there was no stopping him. When the bus stopped, we kids jumped on and ran to the back, but we could hear him tell the driver in his drunken voice that he needed a ride, and then we saw somebody get up and let him have the front seat. He plopped down, and then he immediately turned around to face the bus full of curious students. Smiling idiotically, he asked, "And how are you little children?" I cringed.

Not a soul answered. I was mortified. Everybody looked embarrassed except for Johnny Ray Stoneman, who was now a high school student and certainly wasn't anybody's little child. He turned and looked directly at me, raised his eyebrows, and flashed a sardonic smile. It seared right through me, and I wanted for a moment to die.

When Daddy was on one of his binges, he often got sick and would have to go to the doctor. Once when Sarah and Howard were visiting, he said that he thought he was dying and we had to get him to a doctor. It was night time, and we knew no doctor was in his office, but Donald and I helped Howard put him in the car and we took out to Tuscaloosa. Luckily Daddy passed out in no time.

"What in the hell are we going to do?" Howard asked us.

"Why don't we go to the drugstore and get some pills over the counter and tell him the doctor prescribed them," Donald suggested.

"That's real good Donald. Fast thinking. What kind shall we get?"

The first thing I could think of was NoDoze and without thinking I blurted out, "We could get him some NoDoze."

"NoDoze hell," Howard answered. "We'll get him some Sominex."

We got the Sominex and put it in an old prescription bottle when we got home. Daddy, who never knew what had happened, slept quite well for a few days.

Another time, after a heavy bout of drinking, Daddy woke up with his pillow covered with blood. "Lucille, look here," he said, shaking Mama awake. "Something's wrong."

When Mama saw the blood, she said, "Albert, this is the last straw. I've been expecting something like this to happen." She went and got Donald up and said, "Go get Mr. Herrin to take your daddy to the emergency room."

At Druid City Hospital they discovered that Daddy had a bad case of bleeding ulcers, so bad they said that they had to operate and remove a portion of his stomach. "They put a sheep's stomach in place of his ulcerated one," Donald said to me, but I never got that confirmed.

When Daddy returned home after a week in the hospital, he was in a highly agitated state. We had hoped he might be nice to us for a while, but he began cursing wildly almost immediately. From his bed he would scream at us, "Quit making that goddamn noise. Don't you know I'm hurting?"

I didn't really care that he was hurting. I would have if he had been a little nicer, but I wasn't going to waste any sympathy on a raving maniac. I had begun to think of him as a sort of monster, unlike normal human beings. The feeling had been building for some time, but it was best confirmed when I was about eleven.

It was just before lunch on a hot day in July. Daddy told me to go to Momola's and get the ice for our iced tea. I didn't want to go because Julia was due back at any moment from 4-H camp, and I knew my friend Randy Harris's parents were bringing her and that Randy was almost sure to be in the car. "Not now. Please. I want to see Randy when he comes," I said.

"I don't care who you want to see," Daddy said. "I'm ready for lunch, and I mean for you to get that ice right now."

I decided to pretend to have left on my mission, but instead I went out back and hid to watch for the car. I knew I was taking a chance, but

I didn't care. It was unfair for Daddy to mess up my plans. When I saw the car coming up the drive, I tore out front to meet them.

Just as the Harrises were helping Julia get her things out of the car and Randy walked over to see me, Daddy spotted me. "What in the hell do you think you are doing?" he hollered, grinding his jaw. "I told you to go get that goddamn ice and I meant it." Then he grabbed me and began to whip me with his bare hands, right in from of everybody.

I could not look in their direction. I knew they would be embarrassed. I broke loose from Daddy finally, and I ran in horror down into the woods where I lay on the ground crying. I wished fiercely that the son-of-a-bitch was dead so I would never have to see his sorry ass again.

My resentments were constantly reinforced. "Why can't he take responsibility?" I'd ask myself. When something broke down, it would go unfixed for months. When the electric pump, which pumped our water about a quarter of a mile up hill from a spring, stopped working, there was no money to repair it so we toted our water in galvanized buckets for three or four months. Daddy didn't seem to think there was anything particularly strange about that and was in no hurry at all to have the pump repaired. He seemed to downright enjoy the adversity.

Daddy wanted to make little Spartans out of us, and one way he did it was to be niggardly with fires. Because the house was not well-sealed, a draft blew through it constantly, and during the winter we always wore our coats inside. Except for rare occasions, Daddy would allow only a small fire in the living room fireplace, and we would all huddle around it.

Daddy had a rule that unless the mercury fell to zero we had to have our meals in the unheated dining room, and that made us the world's fastest eaters. In the winter there was no table conversation at all.

Before he went to bed at eight o'clock, Daddy would bank the fire, so we would have to go to bed pretty soon ourselves, jumping into beds that never had enough cover. In the coldest weather we added coats to the cover, and we fought over a heavy army overcoat which must have weighed twenty pounds. In the mornings we hated to put our feet on the freezing floor.

We had plenty of oak and hickory logs lining our driveway. There was so much of it that somebody once asked me if it was a fence. But Daddy wanted that wood to last, so hard had it been to come by. He made us boys help him cut it with a crosscut saw and split it with a maul and a wedge, but we weren't much willing. We fought constantly, accusing each other of riding the saw and complaining that the saw needed sharpening or that it needed to have rosin cleaned from it with kerosene.

I resented more and more the pleasure Daddy took in adversity. One spring our mule Mary got sick after sticking her head through the crib door and eating a large amount of dried peas. When she swelled up to an immense size, Daddy got worried and sent Donald to get Mr. Cosper, who was considered an expert on mules in general. When he saw Mary, he said, "That mule's got the colic it looks like to me. What you need to do is drench her with turpentine." We got the turpentine for him, and he put it in a Seven Up bottle, tying Mary's head straight up to a limb of a tree so he could force her to swallow it.

When he had succeeded in getting the turpentine down Mary's throat, he said, "That should fix her." Thereupon, Mary fell over with her legs up in the air and died. Mr. Cosper looked surprised and said, "I guess there wasn't anything that would've saved that animal."

We had to get Mr. Charley Vance to come with his tractor and drag Mary off.

Daddy was halfway through jo-harrowing a field when Mary died, and he came to Donald and me and said, "I can't afford to buy another mule until the crops come in and I don't know where to borrow one right now. But the rest of the field has got be jo-harrowed. So let's get going. I don't lack much."

"Get going where?" I asked.

"To finish the jo-harrowing."

I was incredulous. "You mean you want *me* to pull a plow?"

"That's what I said. You and Donald."

"This is just too much," I said, looking over to Donald for support, but I could tell I wasn't going to get any out of him. There was nothing to do but to go to the field and pick up one side of the single tree. Under my voice I said to Donald as we went out there, "If he says giddyup, I'm gonna clobber the son-of-a-bitch."

That hot afternoon of pulling a plow was about as low as it ever got, I think. Daddy seemed to be taking immense pleasure in the whole thing, not so much perhaps at witnessing my humiliation as in thinking how resourceful a family we were. But he probably did think that it would toughen me up and do me some good by curbing my pride, which was getting a little out of hand.

This episode did not curb my pride. My martyr's pride only increased, and I became more determined than ever to escape that damned place. My resentment of Daddy seemed to increase rapidly from that time. I would get incensed especially when he would recall his own privileged youth. He would talk about how he and his sister Elizabeth would ride their horses around the countryside when a horse was as out of the question for us as a MG sports car would have been. And he would talk about the wonderful stews their cook would simmer over the fire all morning when we were on a steady diet of collards and dried peas. "He can just cut that shit," I'd complain to Julia and Kenneth. "I'm sick of hearing it."

I was also upset to see how Daddy was letting the house at Ralph go down so quickly. It got shabbier and shabbier. The glass in the chandeliers got broken, and thereafter naked bulbs hung from the ceiling. When the porch screens rotted, they were patched, and then the patching rotted. Windows, broken out and not replaced, were stuffed with old rags when winter came.

The house got in such bad need of a paint job that finally Daddy broke down and bought some paint. Before he began painting, though, he took down the green shutters, and they were never put back up as long as we lived there. Unfortunately, Daddy's ladder was not tall enough to paint all the way to the top, so he painted as high as he could all the way around the house, saying he would borrow a ladder to paint the rest. He never did, and the top few planks were left unpainted for over a decade.

The house also became infested with rats, and Daddy put out giant-sized traps, warning us not to go near them. "You could get a finger broke if you set off that spring," he said. The traps were so big that you could hear them go off in the middle of the night, and you knew that the next morning you'd find a big fat field rat with his neck broke in the kitchen.

One day after we had been living in the house a few years, a nice white Buick drove up. Out of the passenger side emerged a bent old lady with a cane. She looked all around her, and then she headed for the front porch, where Mama was sitting with Julia, Kenneth, and me.

"Hello," the well-dressed lady said, "I'm Margaret Simpson. I used to live in this house. I live in Maggie Valley, North Carolina now. My nephew—he's sitting out there in the car—is driving me down to Laurel, Mississippi, and I just couldn't go by without stopping."

I knew who this was from the love letters Donald and I had got a peek at.

"Do you mind if I look through the house?" she asked politely. Uh-oh, I thought, thinking of the piles of clutter everywhere.

"Why, sure," Mama said, "but you'll have to excuse how everything is. I haven't done any cleaning today."

Or yesterday or the day before either, I thought.

The old lady already seemed confused as she looked at the screen with holes in it and the gap where one of the fleur de lis balusters had broken out. Inside she seemed incapable of taking in what she saw. Standing in the living room, she said, "I was wondering whether you still use the painted window props. My husband made those props, and I always loved them." If she looked, she could plainly see in the window nearest to her a split stick of stove wood holding up the window.

"I don't know what happened to those," Mama said. "You know how children are about losing things."

The old lady walked with her cane from room to room, glancing at unmade beds and piles of clothes and junk. She seemed to have given out of questions, and I was glad to see she had leaving on her mind because my embarrassment had been increasing with every room she went through.

"You must come back again, Mrs. Simpson," Mama said to her. "I wish we'd been a little better prepared for your visit, but you know how things are."

"Yes, ma'am, I do," the lady said, her voice trembling a little. She carefully went down the front steps and to the car, and as she and her nephew drove away I figured she was either crying or laughing before they got out of sight.

The older I got, the more bored I became with my life at Ralph. We never seemed to have any good sports equipment to play with so we had to improvise constantly. We usually played baseball in the back yard with a tin can and a two by four, but once we did make a ball by unravelling a sweater and winding it around a rock. It didn't last out one game. We made bows and arrows from vines and fashioned kites from brown sacks and twigs. Once Evelyn did give us a basketball and a goal, which we nailed to the side of the smokehouse, and Donald, Julia, Kenneth, and I played the game 21 for hours on end until the ball went flat.

Evelyn observed to Mama one time that we were all like a character she had read about in a Willa Cather novel. Nothing ever happened to him but weather, she said. And she wasn't far from right about us. When it hailed we would scoop up the pieces and put them in jelly glasses and fix ourselves ice water, when it snowed we'd beg Mama to make snow ice cream with Pet milk, and when we could get away with it we'd cavort in the rain. If it rained when the sun was shining we said that the devil was beating his wife, and if it snowed we said Aunt Dinah was picking her goose.

We took our fun where we could get it, catching June bugs colored with the turquoise, black, and blue of peacock feathers and tying string to their legs and flying them like airplanes. We caught fireflies at dusk and made a lantern by putting them, vibrating with yellowish-green light, into a pint jar, or we made rings for our fingers by pinching off their phosphorescent tails. We observed the tumble bugs pushing pieces of excrement far too large for them and wondered at their persistence. We coaxed the doodle bugs out of the ground by saying

Doodlebug, doodlebug,
You'd better go home.

Your house is on fire
And your children alone.

We buried sticks in the ground and conducted funeral services, taking turns preaching the funeral sermon. If the stick were long, we said we were burying Longfellow; if it were short, Longfellow's baby. It didn't take much to keep us occupied.

We were never much for pets. From time to time we had cats, which Donald and I would take up in the attic and fling out the window to see if they would land on their feet. They always did. Sometimes we would tie small paper sacks around their feet and laugh as they walked, lifting their legs very high and looking confused. For a while we had a dog named Missy, a very intelligent little feist, but Daddy got tired of her and gave her away. He said he was tired of paying for rabies shots.

We stayed in the woods a great deal, swimming in creeks and in neighbors' lakes. In the Tyler's lake I learned to swim, even though I had seen water moccasins slip into the water on numerous occasions. After getting my confidence up, I decided I could swim all the way across the lake, but when I got three-quarters of the way my confidence left me. I panicked, turned around, and swam back, only to have Donald and a couple of his friends laugh at me and call me stupid. Upon thinking about it, I had to admit to myself that they were right.

At home, we fought boredom by listening to the little Silvertone radio Sarah and Howard gave us the first Christmas we were at Ralph. We ran an antenna wire out the side window of the living room and attached it to the clothes line, and even distant radio stations came in loud and clear.

Our favorite station was W-R-A-G, a low frequency AM station out of nearby Pickens County. It was home of Carl Saucemen and the Green Valley Boys, and we were awakened every morning about six o'clock just as their theme song came on the air. Mama would come dancing into our bedrooms singing

Give me rural rhythm
Let me sway right with 'em,
Played by a real hillbilly band.

I would jump up and run to the living room because I didn't want to miss hearing Bennie Paul Hubbard, a thirteen-year-old boy who got to sing a couple of songs every morning on the show. Never did the sin of envy work more strongly in me than when I heard Carl Saucemen say, "Let's all give a big welcome to Bennie Paul Hubbard, the next big star to come out of Pickens County." I wanted to be Bennie Paul. As I listened to him intone the lyrics to "Your Cheatin' Heart" or "I'm Movin' On" and visualized Bennie Paul in his cowboy outfit with beads sewed on it and his white ten-gallon hat, I dreamed of traveling myself with Carl Sauceman and the Green Valley Boys. I could sing too. I just needed a break.

During the summers we listened to W-R-A-G all day. In the morning the dee-jay did a hillbilly show, and we learned all the words to the hit songs by Hank Williams, Hank Snow, Ernest Tubb, and Kitty Wells, our favorite, who answered Ernest Tubb with "It Wasn't God Who Made Honky Tonk Angels." In the afternoon, the same dee-jay adopted Negro dialect and became the Boogie Man, broadcasting a rhythm and blues show intended for the black listeners they had. But these white children listened religiously. On the show, sponsored by a black funeral home with the slogan, "Often imitated, but never duplicated," we heard songs by Howlin' Wolf, Willie Dixon, and our favorite, Muddy Waters, who sang "I'm Your Hoochie Coochie Man" and "Got My Mojo Working." We memorized all the words. Later, when I was in junior high school, I sang "Got My Mojo Working" in a talent show when everybody else was doing songs like "Davy Crockett."

During the school year, Donald, Julia, Kenneth, and I would come in every afternoon eager to listen to the cowboy shows. From "The William Tell Overture" to "Who was that masked man?" we listened hungrily to *The Lone Ranger*, and on alternate days we listened to *The Cisco Kid.* Cisco was a cowboy with a horse named Diablo and a Mexican sidekick named Pancho, and we loved it best of all when Pancho would say in a sing-song way, "Ceesco, the sheriff—he is getting closer."

In a strange way my favorite time to listen to the radio was on Sunday nights. I liked school, but as we listened to the radio shows that marked the closing hours of the week-end I would feel a strong melancholy sweep over me, much like it did in the fall when I would look at the last of the summer garden, with its dried purple hull peas, now black and rattling on the vines, and its tomato vines with their brown leaves folding down exposing a few tiny scorched tomatoes. This Sunday night bittersweetness was almost more than I could bear. I loved to smell the warm, oily odor emitted from the radio tubes, and when no one was looking I would press my nose to the back of the radio and inhale deeply.

We listened to an evangelist named Wayne Rainey from W-C-K-Y in Cincinnati, Ohio, and after that to one named Brother Hector Ramon on X-E-R-F, Del Rio, Texas, broadcasting with more watts than any other station in America. "Send in only one dollar and fifty cents, dear friends," Brother Ramon would say, "and I will send you a bottle of water from the River Jordan. Put it on anywhere that hurts you and the pain will go away, praise the Lord."

I was not much tempted to part with $1. 50 for the Jordan water, mainly I guess because nothing hurt me. But I did want me one of those prayer cloths he had. "Send in only one dollar and ninety eight cents with your name and address, and we will rush you one of our genuine, personally-blessed prayer cloths, guaranteed to answer your every prayer. Need that new winter coat or that medicine for your sick mother? Just spread that prayer cloth over your radio while I am on and pray for your blessing. If you don't get it in a reasonable amount of time, send the cloth back and we will cheerfully return your money."

Once I saved up my money and came within an inch of ordering one of those cloths, but in the end I resisted the temptation, knowing that Mama would say that the whole idea was common and that my brothers and sisters would laugh at me.

Despite listening to the radio, reading, and watching television, and the other things we would dream up to do, I continued to be bored much of the time. I came to believe that all my problems would be solved if I could just live in town. I wanted to live on a street with lots of other people, preferably in a ranch house. A small house would not get so cluttered, I thought, and I wouldn't be so cut off from everything. I would dream of escape repeatedly.

Except for the two years we had Albert's Tat Tat, we never had a car, and we had to rely on others for our transportation. If we wanted to go

Donald and me

to town, we just stood by the roadside until somebody would stop and pick us up. Even Mama seemed to think of this dependence as normal, and she never appeared to be embarrassed about it at all.

Once I saw Mama catch a ride to Tuscaloosa with a man driving a cattle truck. "The cab's full, Mrs. McMillan," the driver said, "but you are welcome to ride in the back."

"Thank you, sir," Mama said, and she climbed gingerly over the cattle gate and took her seat on the wheel well, never giving the slightest indication that she thought this unbecoming of a lady. She sat there as coolly as the Duchess of Windsor, and as the truck pulled away I saw her reach in her handbag and pull out a pair of sunshades, which she calmly put on.

Sometimes on Saturdays I would catch rides to Tuscaloosa with Donald, even though I knew he would torment me some way before the day was over. We had lots of time on our hands because we would arrive in Tuscaloosa around 8:00 A. M. and would not catch our ride home until 5:00 in the afternoon. Donald always had some money, but he would never part with a cent of it. If I was lucky I'd have enough money in my pocket for a hamburger at lunch time and maybe even a ticket to the matinee at one of the movie theaters.

The rest of the time we just hung out. We discovered that the McLester Hotel had an elevator, on which we would ride up and down at various times during the day. Or we would lounge on their leather sofas. Nobody ever asked us to leave. We would survey all the toys at W. T. Grant's and Woolworth's, we would read the magazines at H and W Drugstore, or we would sit around the Greyhound Bus Station and use the rest rooms there. If we had one to spare, we would put a penny in the scales and weigh ourselves.

We stood on the streets and watched people walk by, and we were especially interested in an old greasy man with a brace on his leg who parched peanuts and sold them in front of Brown's Department Store. "Peanuts, peanuts," he would yell loudly, and Donald and I got where we could mimic him perfectly. There was also a toothless retarded woman named Gladys who walked around in all weather wearing a heavy wool coat and carrying two shopping bags filled with candy and chewing gum. She made her rounds of the stores and also sold to people she passed on the street. "I ain't got no mama and daddy," she would always announce. "Chewing gum? Juicyfruit? Doublemint? Candy?"

Donald would say, "That woman is making a killing. I'm going to buy me some candy and become her competition." Then he would pull his lips down over his teeth, mocking Gladys, and practice his approach to customers: "I ain't got no mama and daddy. All I got is one retarded brother."

Often Donald would act as if he did not know me. If I tried to say something to him, he would ignore me totally, staring straight through me. Once he even went up to a policeman and said, "I don't know who this kid is, but I'm tired of him following me around. Could you take him to jail or something?"

The cop looked at Donald, sort of amused, and answered, "The way I got it figured, boy, is that you're way bigger than he is, and how you get rid of him is your own business. I don't think the Tuscaloosa Police Department will get involved in this one."

Donald just sauntered off down the street without a word, and I followed, a few paces behind. I knew what would happen next. He started to act like he was blind, making his eyes go out of focus, raring his head back, and swaying it from side to side. He pitched his body at a forward angle and moved his hands back and forth as if to feel his way. A couple of people passed by, but didn't pay much attention.

"You gonna get yourself arrested," I said, but he ignored me. I ran down the street so nobody would think I was with him.

At home, Donald constantly looked for ways to make my life miserable. A hoarder of possessions, which he bought with money he earned working at the cotton gin in Ralph, he kept his stuff chained in the corner cupboard in our bedroom. Every once and a while he would open the cupboard and take an inventory of its contents, mainly all kinds of fishing gear—monofilament line, hooks of all sizes, quills and corks, a variety of leads—making sure that I got a glimpse of what he had and would envy him. He almost never used anything from the cabinet; it was the having it and my not having it that mattered.

When the rolling store came on Thursdays, Donald would buy all sorts of foods, not only the Zagnut bars and Baby Ruths that Julia, Kenneth, and I did, but things like baloney and light bread, which he would eat slowly in our presence, unwilling to part with a single bite but commenting repeatedly about how good it was. Anything you wanted from him, you'd better be willing to pay for. Long after he had passed the age to play with one, he kept a cap pistol for which he had a ready supply of caps, and he would charge us a penny a shot to use it. We'd refuse to begin with, but after a while the desire would overcome us and we'd pay to fire off a few shots.

Donald was not a great student, but certain pieces of literature he studied made a big impression on him, notably Oliver Wendell Holmes's "Old Ironsides," and he would come up to me and say, "Boy, I'm gonna tear your tattered ensign down." I thought tatteredensign was one word, and while I wasn't sure what it meant, I was quite sure I didn't want mine torn down.

In the summers, things drug along in Ralph so much that Julia, Kenneth, and I were anxious to make the one-mile trek to the post office every morning to get the mail. We were on the rural route, but it was fifty miles long and we were box 100, almost at the tail end of it, and we could get our mail much quicker this way. Miss Alma Brown, the post mistress, was quite indulgent, and we would sit with her and wait on the HPO—the highway post office—to arrive.

Our mail carrier, Mr. Perkins, didn't seem to be able to figure us out. He seldom spoke as he sat in the corner next to his pigeonholes reading hunting magazines, but once he wondered aloud how anybody could be that anxious to get mail if there was no money in it.

At the time we had taken to buying Ludens Cough Drops and eating them as candy because we thought they were an excellent bargain for a nickel and they left your mouth just the right amount of cool—not too cool, the way Vicks did. "Good night," Mr. Perkins finally said, "Why in God's name would anybody take medicine for a cough you don't have in the heat of summer? It beats me." But we didn't think it was a real question and we'd just smile at him and shake out another cough drop from the box. Miss Alma would say nothing either, but just smile and wink at us.

Mr. Perkins probably could never understand what mail meant to us. It was our transport to the larger world, and even if we were trapped in Ralph, our older brothers and sisters were not, and if they could get out we could too. We regularly received letters from Evelyn, Sarah, and Bill, and later occasionally from Donald after he left home. Plus there were prosaic letters to Mama from an acquaintance we hardy knew, and we devoured them as if they had been written by Chekhov. There were letters from Aunt Elizabeth occasionally and some from a niece of Mama's in Miami. We read them all over and over.

The main problem with Evelyn's letters was that she was bad about outstripping our cheap little dictionary with her vocabulary. Once when teaching on the coast of Oregon, she took a Christmas trip to British Columbia, and on a picture post card she sent from Vancouver Island she wrote, "I am enjoying my peregrinations in Canada this holiday." We all looked at each other in confusion when we read it. Even Mama, who prided herself on her vocabulary, was stumped. What had Evelyn been doing up in Canada? Daddy was so bothered that he didn't rest until someone went to the county library to look up the word.

Later after she had given up high school teaching and had returned to the University of Alabama for a Ph. D. , Evelyn obtained a grant in the late fifties to study at the Shakespeare Institute in Stratford-upon-Avon, where her most eminent professor was the noted Shakespearean, Alladyce Nicol. Once, after being driven to London by Professor Nicol and his wife, she wrote us, "It is indeed ironic that this exalted professor is the most uxorious man I have ever seen." It was back to the county library.

Bill's letters were full of wild stories, in which he was always the protagonist. He decided to make a career in the Air Force, and was stationed in Texas and Maine and England. As one who had missed a lot in his teen-age years, it seemed as if he was going to make up for it by having a prolonged adolescence. His sagas were always wonderfully told—about crashing a Dallas 500 Ball by strapping on a guitar (which he couldn't play) and pretending to be the entertainment for the evening. About pretending to be a reporter so he could see Nikita Kruschev up close. About breaking into an antique car race on the Dal-Worth Turnpike in his 1921 Rolls Royce he had acquired in England and being covered in the news as the "winner."

One feature of Bill's letters always bothered me. His return address always had his name spelled M-C-M-I-L-L-I-A-N because when he entered the Air Force they took his name down wrong, and like the immigrants at Ellis Island he seemed to feel stuck with it. I thought if you were a McMillan you ought to spell it right.

Often the mail we got at Ralph contained money. Evelyn, Sarah, and Bill often included a few dollars in their letters, and often the money went for groceries or clothes. We came to rely on it for survival.

As time went on I became more and more curious about sex. As scant and faulty as the information I was given on the subject was, it's a pure wonder that I survived childhood and adolescence. Donald would tell me nothing explicit, because, he said, "You ain't ever caught a rabbit," and therefore wouldn't understand. My friend Randy told me that you made a woman have a baby by peeing inside her. Daddy, of course, never once uttered a single word on the subject, and Mama broached the subject only once when she caught me by surprise.

Somewhere I discovered that there was something called masturbation, and one day at about the age of ten when I was taking a bath in a galvanized tub in the back yard I began to follow the instructions I had heard. I was having no success and was about to give up when Mama rounded the corner of the house and saw what I was doing.

"Norman," she shouted in shock. "Don't *do* that. It's nasty."

I was terribly dismayed and embarrassed to be caught doing something wrong like this, and I began to cry. "I'm sorry, Mama," I said. "I didn't mean to."

"Well, you'd better be, and you'd better never do that again." She got very serious and said, "God doesn't like for little boys to do that, and I heard of a little boy who died from doing it."

I almost fainted. How close had I come to death? It never dawned on me to doubt Mama's word at all, and for years every time I resorted to the activity I assumed I was risking the graveyard and hell.

Not long after this I experienced, quite by accident, something of the purely physical nature of sex. After Ralph School let out, we had to wait on the bus for thirty or so minutes, and we were free to roam the playground. One day I was shinnying up and down the uprights on the swing set when I had the most beautiful feeling down below my waist. I discovered that if my peter were placed just right and if friction were

Uncle Charlie Goodson (left), with my Aunt Dora, Uncle Bill, Aunt Aouda, and Uncle John

added the wonderful feeling could be reproduced, and subsequently I visited the swing set as often as I could. But each time I would think, "God probably doesn't like this either."

About this time I was playing down under the bridge with the Jenkins boys when we found, freshly written in black on a concrete pylon, something that really got my attention. It read, "Pussy is good to boys." Neither of us knew what pussy was exactly, but I made a vow to myself right then and there that I'd find out as much about it as I could.

The person who told me the most the soonest was my mother's brother, Uncle Charlie. He was a very gold mine of information. Uncle Charlie had started out as a pattern maker in a small foundry shop in North Alabama, but when such shops went out of business during the depression he hit the rails as a hobo. Later he moved from rails to the highways, hitchhiking to every state in the nation. Mama said that his wanderlust had begun early. When he was six or seven, he ran away from home because he was mad at his mother. He was gone about thirty minutes, and when he returned he was rather silent for a bit.

Then he looked around the room and said earnestly, "I see you still have the same cat."

Uncle Charlie would just turn up at our house unannounced. Once he was down on Highway 11 about a mile from our house trying to catch a ride. No luck. So he went over to the other side of the road to try his luck that way. Still nothing. So he walked up to our house and stayed for eight months.

When we would see this tall lanky man with a receding hairline shuffling up the drive, carrying all his worldly goods in a paper sack, we would rush out to meet him. Even Daddy would seem happy to see him arrive, though he tired of him pretty quickly. We kids loved him, mainly because he paid us so much attention. Once when somebody had given us some old boxing gloves, Uncle Charlie squared off against us in the front yard and boxed for hours. Daddy, sitting in a straight chair on the front porch, sneered as he watched.

Uncle Charlie took it upon himself to educate us boys. He'd take us into the woods, and he'd sit down under an oak tree with Donald and me next to him. He'd roll himself a Prince Albert cigarette in OCB papers, and sometimes he'd let us roll one too. Then he'd start talking. When I was in my early teens, I got straightened out on pussy real quick.

"Man, there's poontang a plenty in this world if you seriously go after it," he said, "and brother I seriously went after it." He'd take a deep drag off the cigarette so his point could sink in good. "The only problem was that I got so many women I was about to screw myself to death. I'd look in the mirror in the morning, and I'd say to myself, 'Charlie, you are gonna die if you don't leave this town. You have just about screwed yourself to death.'" To hear him tell it, that was the only reason he ever moved on. He also told us gravely, "One more thing I can tell you for a fact about poontang: it ain't ever free."

Uncle Charlie had an opinion on everything. He said if you were away from your woman too long you should masturbate before you had sex so that you wouldn't climax too early and leave her unsatisfied. I figured I could handle the masturbation; it was getting the woman to satisfy I worried about.

Another time he gave us his theory on homosexuality. "I'll tell you why queers are the way they are," he said. "It's because their daddies keep screwing their mothers too late in the pregnancy and those babies get used to that peter."

Deep down I knew that Uncle Charlie's information was suspect, but I loved hearing it, and I'd be upset when I would come in from school and find that he had left abruptly, no doubt because Daddy had run him off. We were never told exactly what brought things to a crisis, but I suspected it was because Uncle Charlie would sleep until noon, after Daddy had been up for eight hours, and Daddy resented it.

Without Uncle Charlie around, I had no one to consult. Daddy paid no attention to me to speak of, and Donald and I didn't talk. Kenneth was still too young for me to talk to much either. Julia and I were close, but we certainly never spoke of sex. Mama always wanted to talk, and we had lots of conversations, but there was too much I couldn't talk to her about. With Uncle Charlie's departure, my further education on poontang suffered a great setback.

During our first years at Ralph when Marcille was in high school and Elizabeth was in college, but living at home, we younger ones monitored their courtships carefully. After I ran a hat pin into Elizabeth's breast—actually a falsie—right in front of her boyfriend, we were always locked out of the living room when they were entertaining. But we would get in the adjacent kitchen and make loud belching and farting sounds, intended to embarrass them all.

For a while Elizabeth and Marcille dated the two ugliest men I had ever seen, the McGee brothers from Greene County. Elizabeth had Johnny and Marcille had Jimmy. Their faces were covered with moist red acne, and their eyes bugged and their teeth bucked. Elizabeth and Marcille were not really wild about dating them, but they had a good Ford car and enough money to take them to the movies and to buy them small presents.

I once overheard Elizabeth and Marcille discussing an upcoming date. “Ooh, I hope we go to the movies tomorrow night,” Marcille said. “It’s dark in there, and it’ll be hard to see us with them.”

“I hope we go to a drive-in,” Elizabeth said. “Let’s try to talk them into a drive-in because if we sit down low in the seats nobody has to see us.”

The worst was to be taken to a football game where they couldn’t help but be on display to everybody. Once at a County High game, Marcille wound up sitting between the two of them. She said that when she looked at Jimmy she thought Johnny was better looking, and she would get up close to him and act like he was her date. Then when she looked at Johnny she decided that Jimmy was better looking and would move back over toward him. She spent the entire evening shifting back and forth.

Marcille was more of a flirt than Elizabeth. Once when she was in high school she visited Evelyn, who was in graduate school at the University in Tuscaloosa. Evelyn had to go to class, so she left Marcille at Pug’s restaurant on the edge of the campus to have a coke. The young waiter, a college student, started flirting with Marcille, and she flirted back. She eyed him adoringly as she leaned over to take a coy sip of her coke. To her horror the straw went up her nose. She became flustered. Unable to stand the idea of reaching up and removing it in front of the guy, she decided to slowly move the glass away from her. But when she did, the straw stayed up her nose. Her face turned red as she removed the straw, and the boy’s turned crimson as well. She paid hurriedly and went out on the street to wait for Evelyn, anxious to tell her the story even though it was on her.

When Marcille started college she had already met her future husband Bobby, a Greene county boy who had also grown up hard, his father having died when he was young. Elizabeth met a guy named Bernie who delivered fish to Woolworth’s where she worked, and like Marcille she fell deeply in love. Marriage and a new life for both followed soon. Marcille went on and finished college, but Elizabeth quit to become a full-time wife and mother.

Elizabeth and Marcille lived in Tuscaloosa, and when we needed to be in town for something we often spent the night with them. And they made trips home at least once a week, but because they were so routine

Marcille and Bobby Cockrell

Elizabeth, Bernie, and Mary Ann Yon

we failed to appreciate them sufficiently. We could hardly contain ourselves, however, when Bill or Sarah and Howard or Evelyn would come for a visit.

Of all the visits we had at Ralph, none excited us more than those of Sarah and Howard. They would often leave south Alabama after work on Friday, arriving around midnight. We would stay up for them, and the minute we would see their car lights turning up the drive, we would rush out to meet them. Howard always said there was nowhere on earth he felt more welcomed and appreciated than he did at Ralph, and with good reason.

Mama and Daddy would get up, and Sarah would make coffee and cut a cake she had brought. We would talk for a couple of hours, after which Mama and Daddy would turn their bed over to Sarah and Howard. They would sleep far later than we wanted them to the next morning, to eight or nine o'clock, and we'd be waiting on them when they got up. We'd plan the day together. Sometimes we'd go on a picnic to Mound State Park, sometimes we went to the Sipsy River to swim, and some nights we packed into their car and went to a drive-in movie up towards Tuscaloosa.

Sarah I thought to be the prettiest of my sisters. Her hair was naturally blond, her cheek bones were high, and she carried herself like Mama, with the greatest self-confidence and self-respect. She had taken to smoking in college, and she must have smoked three packs a day. I thought it made her look quite sophisticated. Nothing pleased me more than for my friends to see her when she was there on a visit and we went down to the store together.

Sarah and Howard would invite me down to their house every summer for a week or ten days, and that was the only vacation I remember having as a kid. Never did our whole family go anywhere together. The trips to Sarah and Howard's began in the summer after the fourth grade and they continued on through high school. The reason for them was that Howard had a nephew named Skip in Mobile whose mother was divorced, and they would keep him while she took her vacation. I was to be his playmate. That all sounded fine to me until I met Skip.

Skip was a fat insolent boy who was always dressed, to his mother's specifications, in matching shirts, shorts, and underwear. She packed

Sarah, Howard, and Roger Vise

them in sets. The first thing he did when he saw me was to say in utter disgust, "What a scrawny kid." For the whole time we were there he liberally supplied me with punches when no one was looking, and he said to me right off, "If you tell on me I'll give you a lot worse than I have already." I didn't doubt him one bit.

As the week drew on I hated Skip more and more. When we went places he would go up to strangers, point at me, and say, "That boy's a country yokel. I'm a city slicker." He was actually from a suburb of Mobile called Prichard, and when I finally saw it, it didn't look much like a city to me.

Our visit finally ended with the understanding that Skip and I would return the following summer, and for an entire year I lay on the bed at night plotting my revenge. In all my scenarios, Skip lay flat on the ground and I stood over him daring him to get up. When the next year came around I was primed.

Shortly after Skip arrived, we went into our bedroom. He looked at me with an arrogant sneer, called me a scrawny yokel, and popped me one on my arm. Without even thinking, I tore into him, making loud feral noises. I pummeled him in his flabby stomach and I gave him several jabs to his arms, then moved on to an uppercut to his jaw. Skip was so stunned he couldn't defend himself and fell to the floor, balling up in a knot. He began to laugh wildly, and I dropped to the floor and began to laugh too. We hooted maniacally. We became friends at that point, and for the most part he quit mistreating me.

Occasionally, he would backslide. One day on our second visit we were sitting out in Sarah and Howard's Chevrolet, sweltering in the heat. We had removed our shirts to get some relief. Sitting in the driver's seat, Skip began to push the cigarette lighter in and pull it out repeatedly, taking it up and looking at its glowing coils each time. Then suddenly he announced, "I am going to vaccinate you," and he stamped my upper arm hard with the lighter. I screamed and jumped up and down in the seat. "What'd you do that for, you crazy thing?" I asked.

"I didn't mean to," he answered. "I just couldn't help myself. You're not going to tell, are you?"

"No, I won't tell, if you'll promise never to do anything like that again."

"Promise," he said, and I decided to bear my pain like a martyr. In a short time the blisters arose in a perfect set of concentric circles. I put my shirt back on and concealed the wound.

Sarah and Howard were away at work during the day, and we were left to our own designs most of the time. One day some neighbor children lent us their bicycles and we decided to pedal downtown. I hadn't had much experience bicycling because Donald charged us a nickel to ride his, and as were tooling along in front of the post office my bike hit a hole in the sidewalk and began skidding. I struck the sidewalk face first. As I got up whimpering, I could feel with my tongue that the bottom part of my front tooth had been knocked off. I looked up to see four old loafers on a bench in front of the post office laughing, hooting, and pointing. One off them hollered in a red-neck drawl, "Hey, Sonny, did you hurt your bike?"

My first impulse was to shoot him a two-handed bird like Donald had taught me or to holler back at him, "Shut up, you old shitass," but I thought better of it, picked up my bike, and rolled it down to where Skip waited. For years, every time I opened my mouth, the first thing anybody saw was my broken tooth.

Our visits to Sarah and Howard passed quickly. We felt like kings. They took us to drive-in movies and to restaurants, took us swimming at Choctohatchee Wells, and on one Sunday they told us that we would leave after Sunday School to go to a restaurant in a nearby town, but they only said that because they wanted to surprise me with my first trip to the Gulf of Mexico, a little over an hour away. I had no preparation as we drove up to the beach in Panama City. Gasping in amazement, I said to Skip, "Wow, Skip, look at all that water."

"Yep, I know," he said flatly. "I've seen it a million times." He didn't call me a country yokel this time, but I strongly suspected it was on his mind.

One downside of visiting Sarah and Howard was putting our lives in danger by having to ride with Sarah, who easily could have won an award for the world's worst driver. She more or less aimed the car where she wanted to go, and Skip and I would sit in the back seat white-knuckled, holding on to the door handles in case we had to jump out. Sarah's real problem was vanity. She would not wear her glasses, and without them she couldn't half see.

Once we were with her when she sideswiped an old man she met on a narrow street. He got out and surveyed the damage. "Let's see," he said, looking at a piece of chrome lying on the ground, "is that yours or mine?"

"Oh, it has to be yours," Sarah said blithely. "I haven't had any chrome left on this car for years."

The old man frowned his face up and said, "Young lady, this is no time for levity." Sarah couldn't wait to get home and tell Howard what he said.

Another time Sarah pulled into a parking place and knocked over a no-parking sign. When she started getting out of the car, I asked,

"Aren't you going to move to another parking space?"

"Oh, no," she answered. "That's entirely unnecessary. There isn't a no-parking sign there anymore."

Another downside to going to visit Sarah and Howard was getting there on the Greyhound bus, a ride which in those days was always crowded and stuffy. Windows usually were not open, and there always seemed to be someone wearing too much Blue Waltz or Evening in Paris perfume. Inevitably, I got sick, and before the bus got twenty miles down the Montgomery highway I would have to take out the paper bag I had packed for that purpose and throw up into it. I would put the bag under the seat, and its sweet sourness permeated the atmosphere of the bus. People would have about equal portions of sympathy and revulsion in their looks, but I had to abide them. At the first rest stop I would take the bag and throw it in a garbage can. Then I would walk to the counter and order an Alka Seltzer, sipping from the fizzing glass dejectedly.

But by far the biggest downside of the visits to Sarah and Howard was having to go home, leaving the good fun and the good food for the hum-drum existence at Ralph—the dull days, the work in the fields, the coarse country food. I was made for something better. My trips to Sarah and Howard confirmed that.

The dullness at Ralph was intermittently interrupted when Bill would arrive, usually from Texas, with all his high spirits and money jingling in his pockets. Sometimes he would pull out coins and scatter them on the ground so he could see us little ones scramble for them. He would always be driving an interesting car, a 1948 Studebaker that looked like a rocket, a 1954 bronze-colored Chevrolet convertible, a 1923 thirteen-passenger Rolls Royce with the steering on the right. He loved driving us around in these cars as much as we liked being driven.

Somewhere around 1953 he brought his first wife home, a divorcee named Emmalu, who already had a pretty little girl. As it turned out,

Emmalu was more or less a whore, but she was a beautiful one, a dark sultry brunette. The couple's insatiable desire for each other led them to excuse themselves and retire to the back room or go into the woods several times a day while they were visiting us. "What are they doing?" I asked Donald.

"They're screwing, you fool," Donald replied.

The newlyweds left us for an air base in Bangor, Maine, and Emmalu immediately got pregnant. After a son, Roger, was born, Bill began experiencing a variety of anxiety problems, waking up absolutely sure that he was dying. He called ambulances repeatedly to rush him to the hospital. After a few of these episodes, the doctors diagnosed his problem and sent him to a mental hospital in New York, where the psychiatrists told him all his problems resulted from being a boy surrounded by four sisters and an over-bearing mother.

The treatment at the hospital seemed to be working, and he looked forward to the prospect of going home. But there would be no going home. He discovered that Emmalu had run off to Texas with an Air Force officer. Strangely, Bill got better immediately and got himself reassigned to the air base at Fort Worth. He talked Emmalu into giving him custody of the child and, unable to keep a nine-month-old baby, immediately called Sarah and Howard and asked if they would take him. They had no children and thought they could have none, and within hours they were on the road to Fort Worth to get Roger, later adopting him.

After this, Bill was plagued for a while with great depressions, and when he would come home he would complain about terrible headaches and stomach cramps. We kids would go into the bedroom where he lay and rub his head to help him get relief. Before long he would recover and be back at his usual antics. He got transferred to England, where he got married a second time to Vivian, the beautiful blond dancer from Nottingham, who had traveled with a show headed up by the crusty comedienne Tessie O'Shea. He sent us a picture of her in a skimpy spangled outfit and net stockings. I slipped and took the picture to school and told everybody my brother was going to marry a famous actress from England. That really made them sit up and take notice.

Bill and his second wife, Vivian Burnham, at their wedding in Nottingham

Vivian had grown up in a bleak household in Nottingham, and what she knew about America she had learned from American movies. She was anxious to resettle in this country. But Ralph, Alabama, and especially the McMillan household, did not look like the movies.

When Bill and Viv arrived in Ralph, we had a huge receiving committee assembled. Everybody wanted to see this exotic in-law, and we all started speaking to her at once. Mama hugged her and Daddy kissed her, and we all told her our names. She suddenly could not stand it any more, and she bolted back to the car, crying.

"She'll be all right in a little bit. She's just the emotional type," Bill said.

What she experienced with the McMillans in Ralph must have been as strange and frightening to her as if we had been Zulus. Her adjustment to America never got made. She and Bill had two sons and they lived most of the time in the U.S., but she was never altogether happy here.

We also looked forward to Evelyn's visits. She came home to Ralph fairly often when she taught in East Alabama, but for two years when

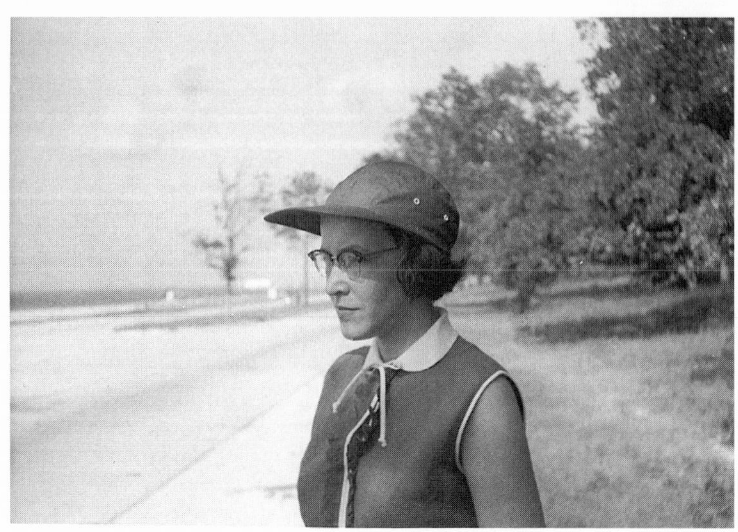

Evelyn

she taught in Oregon we saw her only in the summers, when she came back to Tuscaloosa to attend graduate school. Subsequently, she moved to Tuscaloosa and enrolled in the English doctoral program, teaching classes and receiving the first Ph. D. in English ever awarded at the University of Alabama. While so close by, she could step in when needed at home. Once when Mama made a trip to South Alabama to visit Sarah and Howard for a few days, she came down to Ralph to hold down the fort.

Almost as soon as Evelyn arrived, Daddy got to drinking. She tried to ignore it and proceeded with her work. Though not at all domestic, she decided to fix a good dinner for us one day, even baking a chocolate cake and setting a piece by each of our plates. By the time we got to the table, Daddy was in the vocal, complaining stage that always occurred before he passed out. "I don't want any talking at this table," he said. "My stomach is killing me, and I can't stand it."

"Now, is that reasonable?" Evelyn asked. "I can see why you don't want to hear shouting, but if people talk in moderate voices I don't see how that would hurt you."

"I God," he said, becoming more agitated, "I said there would be no talking at this goddamn table and I meant it."

Evelyn, who was exhausted from all her hard work, was getting enough of him. She stood up and said, "We'll talk if we damn well please, and if I hear one more word out of you I'll hang this chair over your head."

This got Daddy's attention real good. He turned red in the face and stood up himself. "You are not the goddamn say-so around here, and you've got no business talking to me like that." He reached over and picked up his piece of cake and flung it, saucer and all, at Evelyn.

Daddy's aim was perfect. The cake hit her on the head, getting chocolate icing in her hair. She stood there stunned for a moment. Then the leaders on the side of her neck began to stand out, and she held her fists tightly to her sides. Through clenched teeth she snarled, "Goddamn you, don't you ever attempt anything like that again or I'll kill you."

My eyes got wide. The shock to me was not that Evelyn wanted to kill Daddy, who made a hasty departure from the dining room. That seemed perfectly justified. But she had used profanity, and Mama had told us that cursing would land you in hell. Evelyn's "Goddamn you" rung constantly in my head for a few days, and I hoped against hope that it wouldn't land her in hell.

Like most children we knew, we thought Christmas the grandest holiday of the year. Easter never amounted to much, though when we were small we would build nests out of grass and small daisies for the Easter Bunny to leave us something in, but the most we ever got was once when Donald left a little turd in each nest. Birthdays meant nothing but spankings from our brothers and sisters and, if we were lucky, a lopsided caramel cake. Valentines Day meant a pile of silly cards that were to me embarrassingly inane. Thanksgiving, like Christmas, meant great food, and for that reason was greatly anticipated.

But Christmas had everything—food, family, and, even though we could not anticipate having much of a haul, presents. We began gearing up for it a couple of months in advance, poring over the toy circular from the Western Auto Store in Tuscaloosa and looking longingly at the ads in the *Tuscaloosa News.* We got ready to decorate the tree, and we were excited because we knew that for a few days Daddy would shed some of his customary niggardliness and build fires in all of the fireplaces, allowing the entire house to be reasonably warm.

At Ralph School we always had a Christmas play, and in the sixth grade I was thrilled to be cast as the third wise man. Although I had little idea what the words meant, I sang earnestly and loudly the sorrowful words:

Myrrh is mine, its bitter perfume
Breathes a life of gathering gloom;
Sorrowing, sighing, bleeding, dying,
Sealed in a stone cold tomb.

Everybody complimented me on my solo, and I felt proud as I stood there draped in Mr. Luke Rodgers' plaid housecoat Miss Maurine had brought for my costume.

After the annual play in the auditorium, we would go back to the classroom for sugar cookies that had Christmas trees, bells, and Santa Clauses stenciled on them with glittering green and red sugar. There was also red punch that had a metallic taste, as if it had been poured from a can. Then we exchanged gifts. I usually had enough money to get a Scripto lead pencil or a volume of Lifesavers for the person whose name I had drawn, but I was never lucky in the drawing. Every year my present was the same. The box might just as well not been wrapped; I knew that it would be a 1,000-piece jigsaw puzzle, and I would have to act as if I liked it. There would be desert scenes or waterfalls on the cover of the box, and I would say how pretty I thought they were. When I got home, however, I would go out to the barn and smash the puzzles against the side of the barn, saying "shit, shit, shit, shit" between clenched teeth.

Miss Maurine always gave us the same present, a fifty-cent piece taped to a card with a candy cane on it. Naturally, by the time the school

Sarah with Donald, Julia, Kenneth, and me at our first Christmas in Ralph. Julia and I are showing off our new watches and Kenneth his new cowboy suit.

bus arrived, most of us had spent our fifty-cent pieces on candy at Miss Maurine's store, which might have been the idea.

At home the first thing we did was start begging Daddy to cut a tree. "Too early," he'd say. "It'll be dead as a door nail long before Christmas gets here." But we wouldn't let up until he relented, and we'd follow him to the woods to find a fourteen-foot tall cedar, which he would cut down with an ax.

We wanted our tree to go to the living room ceiling, but then we had the problem of finding enough to decorate it with. We had a few fragile balls colored red, blue, and silver that we saved from year to year, and somewhere we has acquired a dozen iridescent icicles that glowed eerily in the dark. And one year I used my fifty cents from Miss Maurine to buy fifty one-cent candy canes to put on the tree, but by the time everybody grabbed one every time they came through the room they didn't last for long.

Mostly we made our own decorations. Using a beer can opener, which Evelyn had taught us to call a church key, we cut many-pointed stars out of tin can lids and tied them on the tree with pieces of string. We cut and glued linked chains made from colorful pages of catalogues, and we painted balls off of sweet gum trees with any left over paint we could find. The tree might have looked like hell to others, but we were proud of it. We would have preferred Christmas tree lights like our friends had, but we didn't dwell on the matter long.

We hung stockings every Christmas, but they were not like the ones made of red felt and trimmed with imitation white fur like most kids had. Our stockings were Mama's discarded nylons, which because of their great elasticity would hold a large amount of oranges, apples, and nuts. Upon seeing our stockings hanging by the fireplace, one of the Jenkins children said, "I wouldn't eat nothin that came out of a old dirty stocking like that," and it was only then that our practice seemed at all strange to me.

Our presents came from Aunt Elizabeth and our older brothers and sisters. Aunt Elizabeth would appear a week before Christmas with large sacks of presents. There were always clothes—jeans and flannel shirts for the boys and sweaters and slips for the girls—but there were toys too. She liked to give kits, and I once received a kit to make cement blocks with. Julia often got baking sets, and once she even got a baking oven with a light bulb in it, which allowed her to bake little pans of gingerbread and a cornbread which must have been created by Yankees because it tasted as sweet as layer cake.

Julia usually got a baby doll with eyes that would open and close, but within a day Donald and I would have convinced her that she should let us crack the doll's head open to see how the eyes worked. After we had done so, we would have a funeral for the doll, with much hymn singing and preaching.

Sarah and Howard, as well as Evelyn, always supplied gifts. They gave me my first wrist watch which ran for a week before it gave up the ghost. As they got more affluent they began to give very nice presents to Mama and Daddy. One Christmas they told us in advance that they were going to give them a deep freeze, but we were not to breathe a word to Mama about it. Although nobody would ever own up to it, somebody swore Mama to secrecy and revealed the secret.

When Sarah arrived on Christmas Eve, she ran in, excited as a child, and said, "Oh, Mama, you can't guess what Howard and I have got you and Daddy for Christmas."

Mama put a puzzled look on her face if she were scouring her mind for a possible guess and answered, "I don't know. It wouldn't be a deep freeze, would it?"

She looked surprised when everybody burst out laughing.

Food was more plentiful at Christmas than any other time of the year. We called the meal in the middle of the day dinner, and Christmas dinner was something else. Family members would bring turkeys and hams, and there would be large bowls of cornbread dressing and cans of shivering cranberry sauce. There would be candied sweet potatoes made by Mama and home-made fourteen day sweet pickles and chili sauce made by Elizabeth's mother-in-law. A tall cake covered with sea foam icing and finely grated coconut would come from the same woman, and Marcille's mother-in-law would send an icebox fruitcake full of raisins, coconut, and pecans. There was so much food left over that we ate it for several days.

Invariably, I was depressed when Christmas was over. There was before me a long stretch, cold and barren, with little to look forward to.

The Bethel Baptist Church was less than a quarter of a mile from us, and we were in and out of it constantly. Mama had quickly assumed her normal role of church leader, being selected to teach the adult Sunday School class and leading the singing. As always, people seemed to defer to her as an authority on the Bible, and she was often called on to settle disputes. Was that really wine at the Marriage at Cana? Was Adam or Eve more at fault for the fall? They wanted her opinion.

Mama with her Bible just before taking us off to Bethel Church.
Evelyn stands behind Julia and Elizabeth behind me.

Mama was missionary-minded, and when there was no money for anything else she would always contribute to the Annie Armstrong Missions Offering and the Lottie Moon Christmas Offering. She once said if she ever lost her mind it would be because of thinking about all the lost souls in the world.

It upset her when her children seemed to stray from the fold, or in Bill's case never got in it in the first place. Evelyn, who had gone into the world and found it quite appealing, especially riled her up. "You're nothing but a freethinker," Mama once said to her.

One day Evelyn and Mama got into a discussion on the nature of faith. "St. Paul says that faith is the substance of things hoped for and the evidence of things not seen," Mama said smugly.

"Well, I can sort of buy that, except I'm not sure about that unseen business," Evelyn responded. "You know, do you not, that there are cultures in which people believe that they actually look on the face of God, right here on earth?"

"I guess," Mama said weakly.

Evelyn's eyes narrowed in wicked pleasure. "You know, I assume, that one Indian tribe in America believed that God was a big old black buzzard." When Mama said nothing, Evelyn added, "And how can anybody sit in judgment and say that they are wrong?"

Mama's eyes began to tear up. "Evelyn," she said, "You know good and well that is a heathen culture. I do hope the Lord can forgive you."

"Forgive me for what, for God's sake?" Evelyn said, feeling herself the victor.

Just to see what reaction he could get from Mama, Donald, then a senior in high school, said, "The Bible says that one of Adam's curses was for a man to earn his living by the sweat of his brow. Now remember, Mama, that's a curse. What that means to me is that people shouldn't enjoy their work and should do as little of it as they can." When he saw that Mama was looking at him like he was a fool, he added, "If you enjoy your work you are acting contrary to God's will and judgment, I think, and, as we all know, that's a sin."

Mama said, "Donald, I never heard you utter such foolishness before. Where did you get such an idea? Don't you know that the curse refers to the loss of the full pleasures of Eden? The curse does not doom us to misery."

Donald didn't see any need in pursuing his idea any further, as he knew Mama would always come up with some answer. I knew she would too, and for many years I preferred her positions to those of her adversaries.

One thing Mama felt most strongly about, not surprisingly, was temperance. Sometime in the fifties Tuscaloosa County had a referendum on the wet and dry issue, and, especially after hearing a Mr. Heiberger from the Temperance Union speak at church, Mama became a vocal supporter of the side that wanted to do away with alcohol sales in the county. "You and all of the bootleggers are working hard to get rid of legalized whiskey," Daddy would say, but Mama would ignore him.

I was on Mama's side. I knew what whiskey could do, and I'd have liked to see it all poured in the Warrior River. Evelyn, though, decidedly did not agree. She liked to drink, and Mama knew it, but since Evelyn was an adult and away from home, she had no intention of complaining to her about it. Evelyn never drank when she was in Mama's house, of course. She knew that would not do.

Evelyn decided to confront Mama on the wet/dry issue, beginning her argument with a question: "Mama, doesn't it worry you that if Tuscaloosa County goes dry lots of people—including young University students—will head south to Greene County and drink in the taverns there?"

Mama started to speak, but Evelyn said, "Wait just a minute. Let me finish my point. Those young people coming down to Greene County have to drive back up to Tuscaloosa on Highway 11 after they have been drinking, and one of them might get killed. Worse yet, some innocent people might be killed. Your own family travels that road often, you know."

Mama looked at Evelyn square in the eye and said unflinchingly, "If I knew that one of my own children would get killed in a wreck caused by people going to Greene County to drink, I would still vote dry. We have to consider the larger good."

"That's bullshit," Evelyn said, but she knew there was no use to try to change Mama. Once that mind was made up, it was made up for good.

Mama

Mama had ideas on everything, and she pronounced them with such conviction that she had a powerful effect both in the family circle and outside it. If Daddy wanted to make us Spartans, she wanted to make us stoics. She taught us that we were to accept whatever came with the greatest equanimity, and we were to feign happiness, even when we were most unhappy. We were never to let anyone think we thought ourselves inferior in any way, she said, and for the time being we were to ignore all deprivations. Godliness and poverty had strong connections, she thought. Our birthright, she seemed to think, was to lead prosperous, satisfying lives, but not right now. That would all come in the sweet bye-and-bye—in heaven, for sure, but also here on earth.

I bought Mama's philosophy, and it gave me a great deal of comfort to look on my adversities as temporary. I was not quite as sure about heaven and that thing called salvation that she said would be crucial to my eternal happiness. While most of the kids my age were joining the church when they were nine and ten, I held out. I wanted to make sure that I understood fully what I was doing, and I didn't think I was ready to make the public profession, which was required by the Baptist Church as the sign of salvation. At the same time, I struggled from time to time with the possibility of going to hell because Mama and my Sunday School teachers had convinced me that I had surely reached the age of accountability, that time when I could no longer claim to have an excuse. For the time being, though, Mama did not get upset with me, although lingering in her mind must have been the case of Bill who wouldn't join the church and now wandered the world as a sinner.

Mama spent a lot of time reading religious books, especially the book called the homiletics, which she used for preparing lessons and study courses. At study courses, members of the church would come together six or so times to study some church-related topic. Once Mama taught a course on missions in Africa, and on the last night she told the class that they were going to discuss race relations in Alabama because she thought that maybe we should treat black people better at home before we started trying to help them in their own countries. Apparently she was met with stony silence and had to lecture for the entire hour. Even though this was after *Brown vs. Education,* people in Ralph could not conceive of a time that schools would be integrated, and to most people racial superiority was an obvious fact.

When Daddy learned what had happened at church, he got quite upset and asked, "Lucille, are you trying to get us run out of the county? I mean this is serious. Some of those people might go and talk to some other people and the next thing you know somebody'll burn our house down."

"Oh, Albert, calm down. They aren't going to do a thing. They'll fume for a while, but it'll do them good to be shaken out of their complacency."

"Well let somebody else do the shaking next time," he said.

When it came to race, Mama was a paradox. She was well out ahead of the community in some ways, speaking out against racial violence, which wasn't rare in our part of the world. She despised racial epithets and taught us never to say nigger. She also thought blacks deserved equal access to restaurants and hotels. Yet she herself could not imagine sitting down to a meal with a black person. She was appalled once when she visited a neighbor and found her having lunch at the table with a black woman. Such behavior, she said, was *common.*

I was greatly confused one day when a black man who lived up the road brought Mama some cushaws, a type of gourd she liked but Daddy wouldn't grow. When she thanked him, he said, "You're welcome, Lucille."

She said nothing to the man, but after he left she was incensed that he had called her by her first name. "Nobody but my closest friends calls me Lucille," she said, suggesting that he had been too familiar. While many other white women in the neighborhood were Miss whatever their first names were—Miss Maurine, Miss Ruth—everyone called her Mrs. McMillan. But despite this, I thought there seemed some odor of racism in what she did.

I did not know many black people. Just up the road lived a powerfully-built teen-aged boy named Coochie who walked by our house often. Sometimes late at night we could hear him come by singing mournfully a slow version of "Down By the Riverside." Once Donald asked him about the singing at night and he said, "They be haints out at night, and just past your house they be that grave yard, and long as I sing real loud ain't no haint gonna mess with me."

Lizzie was an ancient black woman who came by to visit us from time to time, sitting for several hours on the front porch. Her eyes had a cloudy, milky look, and she held her head cocked when she wanted to see something real well.

"You got me a fag?" she would ask us, and if Daddy had a pack we'd run get a cigarette just to see her smoke. "Get it going for me, if you don't mind," she'd say, and one of us would light it up. Once Lizzie held the cigarette to her mouth, it never left there. She puffed frantically, never inhaling in the least and producing a great volume of smoke. She liked it when we laughed at her.

Once a young black man and woman came to our place to pull corn and cut fodder, and I was intrigued by them, following them up and down the rows and hanging on their every word. They didn't seem to mind. There was some kind of sexual banter going on between them that I couldn't understand. He said something about "riding the groove," and the woman laughed and adjusted the scarf tied on her head. "Shee-it, man," she said. "I ain't studying you."

In the early afternoon, I looked up and saw Lizzie walking up the drive to our house, and I asked them, "Do y'all know that nigrah lady there?"

Looking faintly amused, the woman said, "Yeah, we know that cracker lover."

The young man, towering high above me and holding a scythe in his hand, didn't look amused at all. With nostrils dilated in anger, he said, "What did I hear you say, boy?"

I didn't know what he meant. As I was thinking what to say to him, he shook the scythe at me and said, "Boy, did you say nigger?"

"Oh, no," I said. "I never say that."

"Good," he said, "because we cut little white boys' dicks off that calls us niggers. We can call each other niggers, mind you, but we ain't gonna have no crackers calling us that."

"I didn't mean anything," I stammered.

"Just leave him alone, nigger," the young woman said, laughing.

I was too scared to run, but I managed to get out of the field. It hurt my feelings that these people would think I would use such a word. I was too embarrassed to show my face when they came by to get their pay at the end of the day.

The only blacks my age I knew at all lived on my friend Randy Harris's farm. There were two boys, and I would see them when I went home with Randy on Sundays after church. Randy played with them more than anyone else, and he was crazy about them, but naturally, I noticed, he was always the boss. One time this white boy that lived near Randy called them niggers, and Randy tore into him and beat him up good. "They are not niggers," he said. "They are darkies."

I would see other black children at the store in Ralph, and anytime when Miss Maurine was working in the store and a black kid about my age came in she would say, "Norman, just take a look at that. That's what they want to go to school with you. Can you imagine going to school with something like that?"

I was embarrassed, but I would answer, "No ma'am," looking over for a moment at the black kid, who looked embarrassed, but not mad. I knew something was unfair in all this, but the truth was I never much questioned school segregation. Separate but equal was fine with me, and I was like Bull Conner in Birmingham, who said, "I don't believe in white folks and black folks segregating together."

When I went home and said I didn't think Miss Maurine had treated the black boy right, Daddy said, "I'm going to put you in a vat of black dye if you're so damned sympathetic with them." Daddy took for granted the natural superiority of whites, but he was far from being a rabid racist. Having been raised on a brand of honor that such organizations would have offended, he would have never joined the Ku Klux Klan or even the White Citizen's Council. He would have been appalled, however, had anyone told him that his rhetoric encouraged the activities of such organizations.

When I was in the fifth grade, Kenneth started school at Ralph. He might have been the baby of the family, but he was as scrappy as a baby pit bull. He already had a black mark against him because he had gotten in trouble on Visitation Day the previous year when all the prospective first graders were invited to attend school one day. A fat boy named Earl Junior, who was a grade ahead of Kenneth, had parents who were quite well off, and his mother drove Earl Junior around in their black Chrysler sedan with him sitting in the back seat like a potentate. After witnessing that several times, Kenneth got it in for him, and he told us before Visitation Day, "I'm gonna beat Earl Junior Pickett's ass."

We really didn't believe him, but sure enough he was laying for Earl Junior when play period came and without warning went up and started punching. Earl Junior was unable to use his weight or his age to any advantage, so surprised he was, and he ran off crying to Miss Snow, the teacher, who came out with her paddle and gave Kenneth a few licks right there on the playground. "Just wait until your mother hears about this," she said, and she went back in and lettered a note to Mama, which she made Kenneth take to her. He threw it away on the way home, but after school the whole playground had been abuzz about what had happened so Julia and I told Mama what he had done.

"Come here and take your medicine," Mama called to Kenneth. "But first, please tell me why you did something like that."

"I just don't like his looks," was all Mama could get out of him.

When I was in the sixth grade Julia moved up into Miss Maurine's room, and it was sort of weird being in the same room with your sister. Each year the whole room together would have a unit on diet where we studied the various food groups and what we needed in the way of vitamins, minerals, and so forth. We were supposed to keep a record of our breakfasts everyday for a week so Miss Maurine could determine whether we were eating a balanced diet or not. I knew what a balanced diet called for, even though we did not eat it at home, and I would just fill out the menus accordingly.

When Julia was in the room, we had to coordinate our menus since Miss Maurine was not going to believe that Mama fixed us separate breakfasts. As we stood waiting for the bus, we worked our menu for that morning: waffles, sausage, fruit cup, orange juice, and sweet milk. We had to get it memorized because we didn't want to be caught in our lie. Miss Maurine never let on that she suspected anything.

Actually Miss Maurine sort of let a lot of things slide with us. We took our meals in the school cafeteria, and she participated in the illusion that we actually paid for them. Mama would send a little money every once and a while to apply to our bill, but our balance was always immense. Miss Maurine would often hound other children about being in arrears on their bills, but never us.

Miss Ruth Davidson, who was in charge of the lunchroom, cooked marvelous meals, often using surplus government foods. Sometimes there would be contests for the lunchrooms in the county to encourage the cooks to use over-abundant government foods, and once Miss Ruth served us a dish that incorporated rice, canned tomatoes, and peanut butter. We never batted an eye, but wolfed it down as eagerly as had it been pheasant under glass.

Whatever deficiencies our diet at home may have had, we were, overall, a healthy group. But once when I was in the fifth grade I missed an entire month of school. I was never sure what was wrong with me, but I was taken to Dr. Joe P. Perry in Eutaw a couple of times, and he gave me two bottles of vile tasting brown medicine. One of the bottles was so awful I threw it in the trash three times, but it was always retrieved and I finally gave up and took it all. I was also forced to swallow tablespoonfuls of cod liver oil, which tasted more rotten than the medicine.

I could have gone back to school earlier than I did, but I liked being the only child at home. Shortly after the school bus left every morning I'd get better, but by late afternoon all my symptoms would return—mainly a sort of enervated listlessness—and I'd be unable to go the next day.

My classmates wrote me letters saying how much they missed me and how much they hoped I'd get well soon, and Miss Ruth Davidson came to see me and brought me some individual cups of vanilla ice cream. Miss Ruth had taken a liking to me, and almost every Sunday at church she would slip a coin in my pocket, usually a quarter but sometimes a half dollar. Kenneth was as envious as he could be, and later when there was a funeral at Bethel Church he helped Miss Ruth up the gravel path to the grave yard. When the interment was over, he took off immediately. We asked him why he hadn't brought Miss Ruth back down. "I meant to leave her up there high and dry," he said. "I was getting even with her. "

At Ralph School I was a member of the 4-H Club, and each month I would solemnly pledge my head to clearer thinking, my heart to greater loyalty, my health to better living, and my hands to larger service for my club, my community, and my country. In the first meeting of the year, our leader Mr. Holstun, who had a speech impediment which caused a great volume of air to rush out of his mouth along with his words, asked us to declare a project for the year. Most every other boy was raising some kind of livestock, but we didn't have any livestock. So for three years I chose thrift for my project. I was supposed to have a plan for saving money, and for a while I'd resist a candy bar when I had a nickel, but after a while I said to hell with it, and when Mr. Holstun asked for a report on my progress, I'd make up an answer. How was he going to know the difference, I thought.

At school we had various projects for making money to supplement what we got from the state. The most profitable thing we did was to have cakewalks. For a nickel you could walk around a circle painted on the floor while someone played the piano. When the piano stopped, if you were on the square whose number was called you won the cake.

One night I surveyed the cakes. There were about thirty, the very best one being Miss Hettie Tyler's tall chocolate cake decorated with yellow roses. The worst looking cake, by far, was the lopsided caramel cake Mama had contributed. At church suppers Mama could always win the prize for the ugliest dish, I thought, and this was just as bad as ever.

When Mama's cake came up, I was humiliated because very few people wanted to walk for it. Several numbers had to be called before they could get anyone to stop on the winning square. Finally one of the Cobb boys won it, and he immediately took out his pocketknife and cut into it. When he lifted the knife, every bit of the icing, dark and chewy, came off the cake. It looked like a little crumpled pillbox hat. Everybody laughed, and I was further humiliated.

In the fall every year students at Ralph School were also taken to the West Alabama State Fair at Alberta City. The idea was that we were to look at all the exhibits, but most of us gave them only a cursory glance. Who was interested in livestock and handicrafts? I did like the industrial tent better because you were given things there, like miniature loaves of bread from Hardin's Bakery, a yard stick from Allen and Jemison Hardware, and a key ring with a little white-sidewalled tire on it from B. F. Goodrich.

We all wanted to get to the midway as soon as we could, but I couldn't take the rides. I steered clear of them after getting dizzy and nauseated on the tilt-a-whirl the first year I went and having to run over behind a tent and throw up. After that, I lay on the ground for several hours wishing I were dead or at home.

What I liked most were the sideshows. I loved to see freaks, like the hermaphroditic goat named Willy Nan, a three-headed chicken, a pair of husband and wife dwarves who sat on tiny chairs in their own little living room, and a woman with a thick black mustache. Once they had a real hermaphrodite, but you had to be twenty-one to see it. Ralph

Harris said his uncle, who went to see it, said, "The dick on that morphodite wasn't any bigger than a good-sized wart."

One year we could pay a nickel and see a woman in an iron lung. A pinched, pained face peeked out the window at the top, and I felt very sorry for her as I listened to the machine making its loud, pumping sounds. Several hours later I saw the same woman walking around just as normal as you please with another carnival worker, and I overhead her say to the other woman, "I am about wore out. I been in that goddamn iron lung all day."

When I left Ralph School for Tuscaloosa County High in the fall of 1954, Miss Maurine, unbeknownst to me, wrote a letter to Mrs. Bronson, my seventh grade teacher there. By accident I saw the big, fat letter on Mrs. Bronsons's desk when I was feeling bad and did not go out for play period, and I slipped and read every word of it. I knew Miss Maurine meant well because basically she was telling Mrs. Bronson that I was worth giving attention to. She told her I was very sensitive and, as she put it, should be handled with kid gloves on. Then she went on with the tale of my family, especially stressing Daddy's shortcomings and Mama's strengths. All this upset me somewhat because I would as soon have started Tuscaloosa County High School with a *tabula rasa*. But that was not to be.

Tuscaloosa County High School

PART 5

High School

In 1954, when I started seventh grade at Tuscaloosa County High School in Northport, I began a double life that lasted more or less until I graduated in 1960. I had one set of friends I saw almost exclusively at school and another set at Ralph. My friends at school, who were very important to me, hardly knew where Ralph was and certainly never set foot in it. For the most part, my friends from Ralph and I had little to do with each other at school, and some of them, from the nearby community of Knoxville, went to a different school in Eutaw, about twenty miles to the south. This double life I led did not seem at all strange to me at the time.

I took the daily journey of about fifty miles roundtrip from Ralph to Northport on Schoolbus 14 which, because a governor had been installed to insure our safety, chugged along at a maximum speed of forty-five miles per hour, stopping often to take on or let off students. There was very little socializing on the school bus. Usually we looked like fifty zombies sitting two and three to a seat, staring straight ahead and thinking our private thoughts. Only occasionally would there be excitement, like when a couple of guys would get into a fight and you'd have to try to get out of their way as they tumbled up and down the aisles.

One day there was a bit of excitement I could have done without when Donald got in a fight with Mr. Sparks, the bus driver. He had brought home a pig's heart, preserved by his biology class in a gallon jar, and when the elementary school students got on at Ralph School they were especially curious about it. "What is that?" asked a little third grader Anita Sterrett, her eyes widened in fear.

Donald shook the jar in her face so that the heart whirled around in its preserving fluid, and he said in a voice one would use to tell ghost stories, "It's a human heart. I took it out of a little girl about your size."

Anita began to cry, and when Mr. Sparks realized what was happening, his normal placid demeanor changed immediately. He stopped the bus on the side of the road and ran back to where Donald was sitting, his face reddened with anger. He snatched the jar from Donald's hands and put it down in the aisle, then grabbed Donald by the collar and screamed in his face, "If I ever hear of you doing anything so stupid as that again, I'll throw you off this bus."

Donald, who was a good six inches taller than Mr. Sparks, didn't flinch one iota, but merely reached out with both hands and put them under Mr. Sparks' arms, lifting him and carrying him out in front of him like he was a wet puppy, depositing him gently back in the drivers' seat. Then he went back slowly and picked up the jar from the floor, calmly sitting down and looking rather proud of himself. For his part, Mr. Sparks didn't even look back, but started the engine and drove off.

It was in the natural order of things on the bus for older students to boss the younger ones around. Myrtle Crenshaw, a constantly disgruntled senior with a pock-marked and florid face, spent a great deal of time combing and fluffing her auburn hair, which was her only good feature, and she was obsessed with keeping it from being blown. Even in the hottest weather she would go up and down the aisles of the bus when she got on, flailing her arms up and down and saying, "Up, up, up with the windows. Up, up, up with the windows." Although we badly wanted fresh air, we would dutifully close the windows. Even Johnny Ray Stoneman, the toughest guy on the bus, would cower before her and sit and smolder.

My own tormentor when I was in the seventh grade was a senior strong man named Aubrey Perkins, son of our mailman. The only reason I can think of for being chosen his victim was that I was smaller by far than any other seventh grade boy. I certainly never did anything to provoke him. But for a couple of weeks not a day went past without Aubrey ordering whoever was sitting next to me to vacate his seat and then easing in beside me, a look of the purest sadism entering his face. "Is the candidate ready for initiation?" he would ask solemnly.

"No, Aubrey. Please," I would whine, knowing all the while that he would have no mercy.

"The candidate will prepare himself for initiation," he would say. Other riders on the bus would by now have turned in their seats to witness the event.

I prepared myself for initiation by setting my jaw.

"I hereby initiate you into the P. T. A.," Aubrey said gravely, thereupon grabbing one of my tits and grinding it around in one excruciating circle. The pain was so unbearable that as much as I fought it, tears would enter my eyes. Aubrey would look pleased then and would say, "You are now a full-fledged member of the Purple Tittie Association with all the rights and privileges thereunto appertaining." A couple of the observers would clap, and I'd seethe in hate for them as well as Aubrey.

I would never have complained to Mr. Sparks, who apparently was unaware of my plight. Aubrey had whispered to me the first day he initiated me, "If you complain about this to anyone, in your next initiation I won't limit myself to one tittie. I'll have to do a double initiation." Because I was fairly sure he would, I bore the pain and humiliation in silence, knowing that there was nothing to do but let Aubrey get bored with the proceeding, which he did after a while.

Despite the unpleasantness of getting to and from Tuscaloosa County High School, I liked being there very much. Having come from a school with three grades to a room and six people in my class, I was now in one of three seventh-grade classrooms with around twenty-five students each. And the students were from all over the county. Although

My seventh-grade class. I'm fifth from the right on first row.

we were housed in an annex to the main building and didn't change classes like the older students did, I felt very grown up being there.

Mrs. Bronson, my teacher, really took to me. Whether Miss Maurine's big fat letter had prepared the way for me or not I didn't know, but I became the teacher's pet. She always called on me first when we did our lessons, gave me special tasks to do, like cataloguing the books on the shelves in the corner of the room, and sent me on important errands for her. Her son also taught seventh grade, and one day she said to me, "Norman, go down to Mr. Bronson's room and get me the *Iliad* and the *Odyssey*."

I had no idea what the *Iliad* and *Odyssey* were. But somehow images of furniture appeared in my head and I asked, "Can I tote them by myself?"

Mrs. Bronson laughed gently and said, "Yes, Norman, I think you can handle them by yourself."

I was amazed when Mr. Bronson handed me the two leather-bound, much-read books, *The Iliad for Young Readers* and *The Odyssey for Young Readers*. When I returned to my room, Mrs. Bronson introduced us to Homer, reading aloud the tale of the Cyclops, which I thought was about the best thing I had ever heard. She allowed me to take the books home, and I read them hungrily, concluding that the *Odyssey* was far superior to the *Iliad*.

We got to go to the library once a week for an hour. The librarian was a lethargic woman, whose swimming eyes betrayed a mild derangement. She had been librarian since the 1930s, but she still didn't know where the books were or what was in them. One day I said, "Mrs. Shortley, I want a book on the Crusades."

"I'll tell you what, Sonny," she said. "You just go and find yourself a book on the Crusades."

That was about all you'd get out of Mrs. Shortley, but the trips to that library became my life's blood. We could check out two books a week, and I would select books in a sort of wonderful ignorance. I even read *Quentin Durwood*. My favorite discovery was *Of Mice and Men*, which I would reread periodically throughout high school.

At the end of the day, it was back on the bus and back to Ralph. Mama was eager for our return because she wanted us to tell her about what we had done during the day. If we were too short in our summaries, she would complain. What she really wanted to know most was how we had distinguished ourselves in some activity that day and what approving comments we had received from our teachers. Success to Mama was always in the academic sphere; athletics mattered not one whit to her. Daddy never seemed to pay much attention to either academics or athletics.

After starting to Tuscaloosa County High, I became even more aware of our poverty. It seemed as if everybody else in the fifties was getting more prosperous while we were getting harder and harder up. Many of the older students drove their own cars to school, and we didn't even have a family car. When the conversation worked around to cars, if no one from Ralph was around I would say we had a gray Plymouth station wagon with eight cylinders, feeling sure that they would never find out any different.

Though I was desperate for money, there was very little opportunity to get any of it. In the summers I made a good bit of change picking vegetables at home, but I never saved any of it. For a while I also sold

Grit newspapers, keeping two cents out of every dime I collected per issue. My marketing scheme was to hook the patrons, mostly housewives, by reading the serialized stories and then discussing them with them, but my clientele was so far flung that I couldn't get around to many customers on foot, and I wound up spending all my earnings at Luke Rodgers' store on ChoChos, Orange Crushes, Stage Planks, B-B Bats, and fireballs.

My most ambitious undertaking to make money was a joint project with Julia when I was fourteen and she was twelve. We had copies of the Avery and McMillan coats of arms, and Julia found that she could paint very good copies of them. Our plan was to market these all over America and get rich, and we decided to start with the McMillans, since we thought there would be more of them. We didn't care whether there was any connection with our line of McMillans or not. The name alone was all we cared about.

We carefully composed our letter:

Route One, Box 100
Ralph, Alabama

Dear McMillan Family Member,

Like you, we are very proud to be McMillans. We are a brother and sister from Ralph, Alabama, and we want to make you an offer you can't refuse.

We will paint for you your own personal copy of the authentic McMillan coat of arms for the low price of $5. Yes, you can enjoy this artistic masterpiece in your own home for the bargain price of only $5. Order your copy today.

Yours most sincerely,
Norman and Julia McMillan

Mama suggested the "yours most sincerely," and the rest of our wording was inspired by the evangelists we had heard on X-E-R-F and W-C-K-Y.

We borrowed a defective manual typewriter from our post mistress,

Miss Alma, who followed our project with amused interest. We began our typing, for which we had no training, and after many false starts we had a stack of thirty-two letters, all going to McMillans from the Mobile area, whose addresses we had taken from the pages of a telephone directory which my friend Skip provided us. Every letter had several ugly erasures, but we mailed them anyway. Then we waited. And waited.

Several weeks later a letter finally arrived, and our hearts were thumping as we opened it. With disappointment we noticed that no five dollar bill fluttered out, but there was a hand-written note on lined tablet paper from a widower named Hulett McMillan, who said that he was not interested in a copy of the coat of arms, but that he was greatly interested in Julia, as he was a very lonely widower in great need of female companionship.

"If you can get to Mobile, Miss Julia," he wrote, "I would be glad for you to stay at my house. Just let me know when." After that, if she got out of line, we would threaten to send Julia to Mr. McMillan in Mobile. No other reply ever came, and we had to scrap our sure-fire money-making scheme.

When I was about twelve I began to do yard work for the two best-off citizens of Ralph, both of whom had large places with acres of mowed lawns and flower beds. I commanded forty cents an hour, and that seemed pretty good, considering what I had made selling *Grits*.

Mrs. Rosalinde Chancey was my main employer. A small, intelligent woman with weather-beaten skin and gray hair pinned into a bun, she spoke very deliberately in a measured cadence. She was the widow of a physician, and though she seemed to have plenty of money she lived rather simply in a neat, sparsely-furnished cottage. Across the highway from her house was a clapboard grocery store, once a flourishing business but now barely stocked at all. Mrs. Chancey said she kept the store open because she needed a place other than her own home for the riff-raff who borrowed money from her to come to make their payments.

Mrs. Chancey's only real indulgence seemed to be the grounds on her place. They were spectacular, covered with azaleas, dogwoods, red buds, and rhododendron and great stands of day lilies of numerous varieties. She pored over day lily ads in various publications, and she delighted in finding a new variety she didn't have. Sometimes she would pay as much as ten dollars for a bulb, and I would think, "What a waste."

In the early spring the Chancey place would be yellow with jonquils, and in the fall blazing beds of chrysanthemums brightened the place. There was a small lake on the grounds, and there were a number of stone terraces and footpaths. Almost every year some group would include Mrs. Chancey's place on its garden tour, especially during azalea season.

The work on Mrs. Chancey's place always had a carefully prescribed routine. The mowers had to be serviced every time I used them. I had to check the oil and add some if needed, and before every use I had to grease the large self-propelled mower. She intended for her equipment to last. Before I would do any new job, she would demonstrate exactly how she wanted it done. She was especially particular about the mowing, demonstrating precisely how to mow right down to the water at the lake without tearing up the sod and how to mow so as to throw the grass in the direction she wanted it to go. She instructed me about the "obnoxious weeds" in the flower beds that had to be destroyed. She showed me how to apply blue stone to the lake to kill algae. Everything had its own method.

Mrs. Chancey would instruct me to come to the store at 7:00 A. M., and when I arrived she would invariably say, "Norman, the dew is still on the grass. You can't start mowing yet so have a seat here until it dries." Then she would begin talking, and I would listen at a rate of forty cents an hour. She spoke sometimes about her two children. Of her son Tom, a medical doctor in Florida, she said, "I knew he would do important things one day. That's why I taught him at home until he was old enough to go to the Catholic schools in Tuscaloosa, which were the best schools at the time. I think the public schools may be better now, but they left much to be desired in those days." Then she would add proudly, "Tom, you know, was the first person to massage a human heart and bring it back to life." That was one of the claims to fame of our community, and we would often boast about this accomplishment when people would want to know about Ralph, a place whose name reduced most people to giggles.

She also told me about the death of her daughter. "Laura had gone over to Atlanta for a wedding, and the out-of-town guests were all staying at the Winecoff Hotel," she said. "She was most likely asleep in her room when the fire broke out. There was naturally a general panic, but I was told that the managers of the hotel were trying to help get the people to safety in an orderly way. Laura had started down the fire escape, and as she made her way to safety a man went berserk and shoved her." She paused a moment, then said, "She landed on the pavement below." Mrs. Chancey told her story very objectively, showing very little emotion, but because she referred to it fairly often I knew she wasn't over it. "I didn't look at the body when it was returned home," she said. "I preferred to think of Laura as she was when she was alive."

After Mrs. Chancey had talked a while, she would always go to the door and look out at the lawn. "No, not ready yet. Still wet," she would say. Mrs. Chancey lived alone, and I think she longed for somebody to talk to who appreciated what she had to say. I was happy to listen because I enjoyed her stories, but making forty cents per hour at the same time was fine too.

More than once Mrs. Chancey told me about how she became an FBI informant. "One day I was sitting here in the store reading, and this short, balding man walked in and said he wanted to get a soft drink. I pointed to the drink box"—she gestured to the corner where she still kept the drinks—"and as he walked over to it I noticed he had one hand in his coat pocket. He never removed that hand the whole time he was here, and that struck me as very strange indeed. In a moment, Norman, it came clear to me: 'That man is going to rob me,' I thought. But strangely I wasn't frightened one bit. I knew being scared wouldn't do me any good." I didn't doubt a word Mrs. Chancey said. She was always as cool as an icebox.

"I decided I needed to look him over very carefully. I made a mental list of eye color, estimated height and weight, and I specially noted a hair-line scar on his upper lip. He brought the coke over and placed it on the counter, and I thought, 'This is it.' He looked at me very closely as he took the coins from his pocket with his free hand, and I returned his gaze with full measure. He stood there a minute like he was puzzling over his next move, but finally he picked up his coke and walked out, got in his car, and drove away.

"Three weeks later a black sedan drove up, and two well-dressed men got out and came in. I knew they were FBI before they even showed me their badges. 'You're here to ask me about a man who came in my store a few weeks back, aren't you?' I asked. I think I surprised them. When they answered in the affirmative, I gave them a full description. They said they were looking for a man who had robbed stores and killed the proprietors starting out in Akron, Ohio, and coming south. They were trying to find any lead. They informed me that the man's last hit had been in the panhandle of Florida, where he had shot an old lady running a store about like mine. I told them he had been in my store and described the man in detail. They told me the information was very useful and left, and naturally I felt very grateful to be alive after what they told me.

"Some time later, the same two FBI men came back. They told me the criminal had been apprehended in Miami just before sailing to Cuba and that he was convicted largely on the strength of my accurate description." Her face beamed with pride as she acknowledged her importance in the search for the criminal. "He admitted that he had his hand on the pistol in the coat pocket the whole time he was in my store and had come in with every intention of robbing and killing me. They asked him why he didn't, and he told them, 'That woman looked at me too hard.'"

Many of Mrs. Chancey's tales ended the same way: "Ralph may be small and out of the way, but we've had our excitement through the years." I couldn't help but notice that all of the excitement at Ralph seemed to pass me by. But I listened on as she told more and more stories, earning about as much listening as doing yard work.

My other employer at Ralph was Miss Hettie Tyler, a woman Mama once called the dowager queen of Ralph—and not without reason. More well-to-do than Mrs. Chancey, who was her next door neighbor, Miss Hettie and her bashful husband Andrew owned veneer mills in Demopolis and the cotton gin in Ralph as well as citrus groves in Texas and pecan orchards in Marengo County. Miss Hettie and Mr. Andrew lived with their extremely intelligent son Andrew Waters in a large house in the English manor style, and they pretty much dictated what projects the community would take on and how the Baptist church would be run and decorated.

Miss Hettie had read somewhere about Russia's Five-year Plans, and though she took a dim view of the communists, she determined that they had at least one good idea. She started her own five-year plan to turn her place into the Garden of Eden. She picked out an undeveloped plot covering about an acre next to her lake, and often she would accompany me down to the spot and work right beside me, which surprised me at first because she was a lady of soft features and great refinement. She could use a slingblade quite expertly and was not at all averse to using an ax. We'd slowly cut a swath through the undergrowth and dig up the roots thoroughly. Once I mentioned that the place looked awfully snaky, and Miss Hettie said, "My theory is that snakes will not bother you if you don't bother them." She waded right into the densest patch and started hacking bushes. A little embarrassed, I waded in too.

The best thing about working for Miss Hettie was that she served a wonderful lunch prepared by Babe, her half-black and half-Indian cook. With hair plaited and tied behind her head and a great number of gold teeth, Babe–to me–was quite handsome. She cooked a full meal every day, with fried chicken or pork chops or beef roast and gravy or pork roast, platters of boiled and fried vegetables, and always a dessert like lemon icebox pie.

Babe was much prized by the Tylers, but one day as we were finishing lunch I saw Miss Hettie get real put out with her. Marian Anderson was appearing on television, and Babe made the mistake of bragging on her singing. "She does not know her place," Miss Hettie said shortly and then got up and left the room. Miss Hettie had still not gotten over the big flap at Constitution Hall in Washington D. C., and she hated Marian Anderson about as much as she hated Eleanor Roosevelt.

Miss Hettie had extremely poor vision, the lenses on her eyeglasses as thick as the bottoms of a coke bottle and marked with concentric circles. I first learned how blind she was one day when I was around twelve as I was walking home from the store wearing a long coat that belonged to some grown relative and a county cap from Ireland that Bill had left at home. Miss Hettie pulled up beside me in her blue Packard and stopped. Leaning over and rolling down the window, she said, "Would you like a ride, little lady?"

Poor eyesight or no, she drove all over the place, endangering the lives of her fellow citizens, both vehicular and pedestrian.

When I was fifteen, Miss Hettie became embroiled in a great controversy with the Tuscaloosa County Commission because they would not agree to paint a dividing line on the short stretch of crooked road that ran between her house and Bethel Baptist Church, the route she most often took. She maintained that public safety demanded that the divider line be painted, and I thought she had a point, given the fact that she used the road so often.

Finally Miss Hettie, realizing that the Commission was not going to do anything about the problem, took matters into her own hand. She enlisted me and her son Andrew Waters to help her. Andrew Waters, who wore glasses and always had his hair freshly cut, was known by all to be a genius. He had earned two engineering degrees from the University of Alabama and also had a Ph. D. in chemistry. During cotton ginning season, he kept the old gin running with his expertise, and Miss Hettie knew she could count on him to come up with the best way to paint the stripe down the center of the road.

When we were ready to start the job, Andrew Waters opened the trunk of his mother's car and took out some bailing wire and a block of wood he had rigged up. "The width of this wire," he said in his high voice, laying it out flat, "is precisely the width of the road. And the width of this block, which I have placed in the exact center of the wire, is the width we want to stripe to be painted. That will serve as your guide, Norman." His plan seemed imminently reasonable to me, even if a bit crude for a civil engineer.

"Norman," Miss Hettie said, "open up your paint," and after I had done so she and Andrew Waters each took an end of the wire and began to move slowly along the road. "If we go too fast for you, you just let us know," she said back over her shoulder.

As they started walking and I started painting, I recognized Andrew Waters's mistake almost immediately. He had assumed that the sides of the road were exactly parallel to each other. They decidedly were not because when I looked back over my shoulder after we had painted about fifty feet I was aghast to see that the white line slithered crookedly out behind me like a pit adder. My mouth flew open, and just as I drew a breath to tell them, I noticed Andrew Waters had turned around and was shaking his head and making a *shh* sign. What he knew, of course, was that Miss Hettie would never be able to see that the line was crooked, and we'd save ourselves a whole lot of trouble by keeping our mouths shut. I was glad to have been thwarted.

I went on painting my crooked line, never looking back again. When we finally finished, Miss Hettie turned back to survey our work. "Wonderful," she said, her face glowing. Proudly she announced, "Well, we have certainly shown the County Commission what positive results can come from good vigilante action."

A few years later the County Commission painted its own line down the road, but for many years Miss Hettie's faint crooked line danced visual obbligatos around the Commission's perfectly straight line, a monument to Miss Hettie's resourcefulness.

About the time I graduated from high school, Miss Hettie's resourcefulness got her into some hot water. For years she had funded the upkeep of the church cemetery, hiring me and other boys and even doing some of the easier work herself. Thinking, I suppose, that all this gave her the right to make decisions unilaterally, she decided that the graves in one section of the cemetery were scattered about with no sense of order whatsoever so she had the tomb stones pulled up and rearranged in neat, straight rows.

Miss Virgie Franklin, a widow who had been bringing flowers to her husband's grave and having a little talk with him every Sunday morning ever since he died, got so hysterical when she couldn't find him in his usual place that her daughter had to take her home and put her to bed. Others were so unhappy when they didn't find their loved ones' graves where they were supposed to be that they threatened to sue Miss Hettie. "I want Ernestine's grave put back exactly where it was," Homer Snipes said. "The dead may not care, but I sure as hell do."

Miss Hettie stonewalled, and she seemed genuinely puzzled at why they were unhappy. She told me, "Why should they care? The cemetery looks much better and it's not as if we exhumed any bodies or anything." The graves were never returned to their original places, and people adjusted to the change.

The cemetery at Ralph was adjacent to Bethel Baptist Church, which was about a quarter of a mile from our house. The church sat on a beautiful spot atop Bethel Hill, the highest place in Ralph, and, compared to most country churches at the time, it was a splendid edifice, painted gleaming white with high front steps made of brick leading to a deeply raked sanctuary. Miss Hettie, who had overseen the decoration, had contributed rich cherry paneling for the choir loft and pulpit, and there were stained glass windows, bearing the names of those they memorialized written in an old-fashioned fraktur script. When the sun was right, the glass cast muted tones of wines and purples across the pews and floor.

Miss Hettie wanted things tastefully done, and that extended beyond church décor. No longer were there all day singings with dinners on the ground, as we had been accustomed to in Bucksnort. The singing of gospel quartets was grating and disorderly, she said, so all we could hope for in the way of special music at Bethel Church was a poorly sung Easter cantata every year.

A few miles up the road from us was Shiloh Baptist Church, and I went up there as often as I could for revivals and other special events. I quickly observed that the Shiloh Baptists weren't nearly so concerned with taste as Miss Hettie was. They had red carpet up around the pulpit, and on the wall there was a garish picture of Jesus with a lamb in his arms. Their preacher was a fat, greasy-faced guy who hollered when he delivered his sermons, and I heard that he'd often get so worked up when he preached that he would wind up crying. But I envied the Shiloh kids because they had singings and dinners on the ground two or three times a year, and their revivals were much more spirited than ours.

Once when I was taken to a revival at Shiloh, the visiting evangelist was a totally bald man with large red ears who preached in his shirtsleeves. His text was the end of time, and as he warmed to his topic he looked sternly toward the back of the church where I was sitting with the other teenagers. He got a real serious look on his face and said, "I want to address the following to you young people out there in the congregation. I know how it is. I was young once, believe it or not." I had a hard time imagining it.

He walked to the side of the pulpit and stared at us, his voice becoming hushed. "Now listen good to what I'm saying to you," he said. "At the end of time you each and every one are going to be called before the seat of judgment to give an account of yourselves. Everyone of you. And you know what Jesus is going to do?" He paused dramatically, his voice rising in pitch and volume. "Jesus is going to erect a giant movie screen, and ever last thing you ever done in all your life is going to be projected right up there on that screen in graphic detail for the whole world to see." He paused for effect. "Now do you want the world to know what you are secretly doing, I ask you? Oh, my young friends, do not be found wanting."

Ordinarily I would have thought "Bull shit," but I was suddenly terrified by the image. When I came home I couldn't get it off my mind, and for many years I could be in the midst of some particularly pleasurable sin, and I would think of that projector running.

Bethel Baptist Church, although a little dull compared to Shiloh, was the center of my social life. We had what we called socials pretty often. We'd start out playing silly games like gossip and rhythm, but at some point in the evening we'd sneak around and play post office or spin the bottle, and I kissed more girls at church socials than anywhere else. We'd make freezers of home-made vanilla ice cream and roast wieners and marshmallows, and we'd chug down gallons of Kool-Aid.

Once when we had a social at Miss Hettie's lake, Donald ate fourteen hot dogs and went swimming immediately afterwards. He got the cramps out in the middle of the lake, and somehow managed to holler that he was drowning. Temple Robertson had to swim out and drag him in. I thought it served him right for making such a pig of himself. I had only had one hot dog and five icy uncooked wieners myself.

Although I liked the socials, I continued to have difficulty with the religious part of church. Something just wasn't clicking. Sunday School confused me. My teachers could never resolve for me whether King Solomon and Queen Esther were real people, and Jesus himself was more or less an abstraction. It was as if everything in the Bible had happened in a little bubble outside time and space. All the lessons in the Sunday School books bored me. I did not care for their little stories with the moral tacked on nicely to the end in case you missed the point.

Also, I wasn't much edified by the sermons preached by our minister Dr. Stroud, a white-headed and shiny-skinned man who was pushing eighty. He came down from Tuscaloosa on the first and third Sundays, driving up in a two-toned Buick Roadmaster, sometimes accompanied by his second wife, who would take over the piano when she came.

Dr. Stroud was not popular with most of the congregation because, they said, he used words that flew over their heads. "I catch about every fifth word," Clarence Bowling said. "I need me a interpreter." But Miss Hettie adored Dr. Stroud, and because she and her husband footed most of the bills around there we had him for years.

Dr. Stroud was somewhat ethereal, but after I walked in on him in the church library one Sunday and heard him fart I knew he had feet—or maybe an ass—of clay. He could be in the midst of the most complicated sermon, and I'd look up at him and think, "That man farts too."

The thing that continued to baffle me the most at church was the business about being saved. Unlike most boys, who made their professions by ten years of age, I had reached thirteen without making my public profession of faith. I wanted to be sure of what I was doing, and the more I heard salvation explained the more confused I got. I just couldn't take such a serious step without certainty, I thought.

Before long I sensed that there was a campaign being waged to save my soul. Old ladies would take my hand in theirs and tell me in earnest voices that they were praying for me, and one Sunday after church while everybody was standing around outside a crusty old man named Mr. Horace Rice came up and faced me. I could tell something was coming because of the look of scorn on his face. He looked hard into my eyes and said fiercely, "Boy, if you ain't got Jesus Christ in your heart, you ain't got a shittin' ass thing." Luckily he didn't wait around for a response, but walked away agitatedly. I was speechless.

The leader of the campaign for my salvation was, of course, Mama. She had begun to dwell on what would happen to me if I should die unsaved, and I began to dread more and more the flames of hell. "They go on forever and forever and forever. They never let up," she said. "I cannot stand to think of your enduring that, Norman. I love you too much." Until then I had thought of death very little, but about that time a man I hardly knew was buried in the cemetery at Bethel, and all I could think about for days was his body decomposing underground, rotting a little more every day. "That will happen to me and all my family one day," I would think, and I would wish to be delivered from my fear. But I just couldn't quite figure out what to do.

In the midst of my resistance, a well-known evangelist named Eddie Jackson came to Denny Stadium at the University of Alabama for a series of revival meetings, and I knew what the church members had in mind when we got into cars and went in a caravan to one of the meetings. Julia, Kenneth, and I rode in the back seat of Miss Hettie's Packard, and it seemed to me she wasn't too excited about going. I myself was excited, as I'd never seen Denny Stadium. I had heard an old man down at the store say that the evangelist Eddie Jackson and the Alabama coach, J. B. "Ears" Whitworth, who had begun his famous 0–10 season, had one thing in common. "They can both fill Denny Stadium and have everybody saying 'Jesus Christ,'" he said, and though I knew he was being sacrilegious I laughed along with everyone else.

When we got to the stadium, I was amazed by its enormity. We took our seats on the forty-yard line and listened to a man and woman in matching royal blue suits singing "How Great Thou Art," accompanied energetically by a gray-haired woman at a baby grand piano. She, it turned out, was the evangelist's mother, who later got up and told us how Jesus had saved her from a life of playing piano in honky-tonks and houses of ill repute.

Eddie Jackson I immediately took a disliking to. Wearing a shiny silver suit and a red tie, he ran onto the stage to various flourishes on the piano by his mother. Holding a microphone in his hand, he stood in a spotlight, his plastered hair shining. "There is only one reason, dear children," he said to us, "that I'm in Tuscaloosa, Alabama tonight. One reason. I am here to snatch as many souls away from the devil as I can before it's too late. And as we all know, the time is short. He will come in the twinkling of an eye. Are you ready out there? Or will you die in sin?"

I could feel several sets of eyes on me as he asked the question, but I returned no gazes. I occupied myself with looking at the people down the row in front of me, settling on one old lady who held on tightly to a giant black purse on her lap and nodded to everything Eddie said. Occasionally someone in the stands would shout out, "Yes, Jesus." That was new to me. We didn't allow any shouting at Bethel Baptist Church.

"We got the Holy Ghost here in Tuscaloosa for just three days," Eddie said, "and I plead with you to let him have his way with you during this service here tonight. After three days he'll be gone to Birmingham. Let him have his way tonight while he's still here in Tuscaloosa."

Eddie Jackson's passions crescendoed as he proceeded through the message, and by the time he got to the invitation to all the lost souls there to come forward, he was crying. "Oh people, I love you, I love you, I love you." Sob, sob, sob. "And God loves you too. He doesn't want to see you spend eternity in hell," he said. Then he paused and put his hand to his ear, stopping his sobbing immediately. "What is that I hear off in the distance?" he asked the crowd. "Could that be the chariot of the Lord? Is that the Lord returning right now to Tuscaloosa, Alabama? What is that sound?"

I could hear the rumble off in the distance as he spoke, and it was slowly getting louder. "Hurry, hurry, hurry, dear children," he pleaded. "It's coming. I can hear it. It's the chariot of the Lord coming. Come on down and give your life to Jesus before it's too late. Come down and give the preacher your hand. Save yourself from hell right now. Hurry, or it'll be too late." His mother played the hymn, "Oh, Why Not Tonight," and the mass choir on the stage sang urgently.

People all over the place were jumping up and running down wildly as the sound got louder and the chariot neared us. I felt someone sitting behind me poking me in the back, but I sat there stock still. I had seen through that fake. When I looked up and saw the single-engine Cessna fly by overhead, there was no doubt. I could not help smirking as I looked down at all the saved souls milling around down on the football field.

As we walked back to the cars, I could tell that many of the church members were disappointed that I had passed up another chance to get saved. I did take some comfort, however, when Miss Hettie said, "I have to admit that I don't like that kind of service. I prefer quietness and dignity. I don't think the Holy Spirit flourishes in that kind of racket."

Miss Gertrude Skelton looked at Miss Hettie like she was crazy and said, "Well, God works in mysterious ways his wonders to perform, and what speaks to one don't speak to another."

I thought, "And this'n sure don't speak to me."

Finally the pressure to be saved built up beyond my endurance, and I knew there was no way out but to go on and profess my faith in front of the congregation, which I was determined to do the next Sunday. Most of all I wanted no more to be an object of concern to others. I wanted them off my back too, and that was much more on my mind than the theological niceties of what I would be doing.

When Sunday arrived, I got up early, washed carefully, and put on my white shirt. At Sunday School I didn't hear a word the teacher said nor did I really hear any of the sermon. "You gotta go through with this," I kept saying to myself over and over. When Mrs. Stroud started playing "Pass Me Not Oh Gentle Savior" and when Dr. Stroud said, "The doors to the Church are open," I jumped up and flew down the aisle. Dr. Stroud took my hand and whispered a few questions about my intentions, then presented me to the congregation as the church's newest brother in Christ. The people came streaming forward, clasping my hands and hugging me, and I was sure that I had never felt any better in my life. I knew, I thought, what it meant to be saved. I was free. I was one with the body of believers, and I was as ecstatic as if I had been snatched from the gallows. I no longer had to worry about frying in hell. On Mama's face, I detected tremendous joy, and I knew from now on she could spend all of her concern on Bill again. No one would have to worry about me any longer.

I was baptized in Tuscaloosa at the First Baptist Church because there was no baptistery at Bethel Baptist Church, and Miss Hettie thought it unseemly to baptize in the creek, the way the black Baptists did. She drove Mama, me, Julia, and Kenneth to the service. Dr. Stroud was waiting when we arrived, and he took me back to a small room to get ready. As he put on what looked like waders to me, he said in his shaky, infirm voice, "Norman, understand that being baptized is like being buried in a watery grave." His metaphor was a little close to the prospect of reality for me to take much comfort, given his feebleness, but I tried to quell my nervousness as I listened to him continue. "The old life will be washed away. You will die from the old life and be born into a new. You will be reborn into the kingdom of heaven. Do you understand?" he whispered.

"Yes, sir," I said, as we moved toward the baptistery and waded into it. My mind was more on physical things than spiritual ones, but I survived the sacrament and I was resolved to be a good Christian for the rest of my life. I was so utterly relieved not to be hounded either by my own conscience or well-meaning adults that I felt the glow of salvation bright and strong, at least for a while. But puberty was doing its work quite well, and I didn't seem to be able to stay very long away from impure thoughts. It seemed that the message I read on the pylon several years before—"pussy is good to boys"—would pop into my mind entirely too often. A neighbor woman tousled my hair at Luke Rodgers's store and said, "You're growing into a man, Norman," and wham: "Pussy is good to boys." A girl at a church social would sit next to me and take my hand, and bam: "Pussy is good to boys." I had a better notion of what pussy was, but no idea how I would ever be lucky enough to get any of it.

And my penis went into steady revolt. The least thing would evoke its attention. It seemed I went around with a constant erection. The summer before the ninth grade it was a constant source of embarrassment to me, and I couldn't stand to think of how awful it would be to have to start school that fall with the problem. I decided that there was nothing to do but invent a contraption to keep the member in place. I took an old leather belt and made a hole in the right place and lashed my penis to my leg, but my plan was faulty because it did not accommodate both excitement and rest. I would just have to face the humiliation of walking the halls of County High with my books held awkwardly in front of me.

When I was around fourteen, I fell for my first girl, Sarah Beth Owens, who was a couple of years younger than me and attended school in Greene County. My desire for her swung about evenly between utter idealism and base carnality. At church she sometimes played the piano, sitting blond and radiant on the piano bench, her light colored dresses tucked tightly under her rounded butt.

Sarah Beth's brother Richard was my age, and for a couple of years I would frequently go home with him after church and spend the afternoons. While his mother would finish the lunch, Richard and I would sit in the living room waiting, joined by Sarah Beth, changed now into pedal pushers and matching top. She would sit by me and smile, and I would get dizzy. It seemed she didn't have any idea what she was doing to me. I felt sure that the idea of pussy had never crossed her mind, and the closest I ever got with her was a few chaste kisses at church socials.

It was not long before I realized that Richard was outstripping me in his knowledge of the world. He never seemed to be afflicted with a tender conscience, and by the time he was fourteen he was drinking beer with some regularity. I knew that was the devil's drink, and the thought that my friend was downing it regularly shocked me, repulsed me, and thrilled me all at the same time.

And he got some first hand knowledge of poontang while it was still an abstract concept to me. He and I and two other boys our age, both of whom were as inexperienced at sex as I was, were selected by the church to go to the Baptist camp, called Shocco Springs, and because Richard's parents could not take us over on Monday, when the camp opened, the officials agreed for us to come on Sunday and stay in the bunk house over night, unsupervised as it turned out. Almost immediately Richard began telling us about all of the girls he had tapped, and all he planned to tap, and where he bought his rubbers, and why lubricated rubbers were better than regular. He told us there was a place in Tuscaloosa you could get Spanish Fly for two dollars and a half and how if you slipped it into a girl's coke she'd have her panties off in five minutes. We sat there with our mouths open. This information coming so fast and hot was about more than I could take, and I was shocked that Richard would talk this way at a religious camp.

But the most shocking thing of all was when Richard knelt on the top bunk and started whacking away for everyone to see. I just about fainted over that, turning my head away in horror. He didn't even stop talking while he was doing it.

We had an entire week of hymn singing and preaching at Shocco Springs, and on the last night there was a grand service in which singers and preachers were brought in from all over the state. Although I was a recently-professed Christian, when they called for all those who had done wrong and had thought impure thoughts to come down and rededicate their lives to Jesus, I found myself jumping up and going down. To my great surprise, there was Richard, right behind me. The other two guys from Ralph followed suit.

We were to return to Ralph on the Greyhound bus, so the four of us rededicated Christians went into the station in Talladega and bought our tickets. Suddenly we realized that Richard was nowhere to be seen, but in a few minutes he returned with a *Playboy* magazine he had bought at a drugstore down the street. It was the first *Playboy* I had ever laid eyes on, and I almost fainted. The girls were buck-naked, but anything between their legs had been airbrushed away. That didn't matter much to me though. I was seeing more than I had ever seen before, and I had trouble keeping my eyes off the page. Finally, I turned from the magazine and closed my eyes and prayed silently, "Dear God, help me resist this temptation. I know I rededicated my life last night and I meant it, and I'll try. But you got to help me. Amen." I looked up and the other three guys were looking furtively at the pictures. It was at that point I knew it was no use. Call me a hypocrite if you want, I thought; I was going to look at every picture in the book and read as much as I could. And I knew all the while that I would feel guilty as hell.

When we returned to Bethel Baptist Church, our Sunday School teacher, a well-meaning woman who plaited her hair and wound it around into a bun and had a faint mustache, asked us to report on our trip to Shocco Springs, and Richard took the lead. "It was a great blessing to me, and I believe that I can speak for the others. The Lord moved among us all, and, praise His name, we all rededicated our lives to him. We promised to lead good clean Christian lives from now on."

When he finished, the teacher asked, "Do any of you other boys have anything to add?"

We all three shook our heads and said, "No, ma'am."

The biggest deprivation I felt during high school came from my lack of transportation. Except for part of my junior year when I had a car, I had to rely on friends, neighbors, and strangers to go anywhere. I often walked down to Highway 11 and hitchhiked to Tuscaloosa. One Saturday I had to get into town because the high school choral club was performing the next day at Calvary Baptist Church in Tuscaloosa. As I walked by a neighbor's house on my way to the highway, holding a brown paper sack with a white shirt in it for the next day, I was feeling happy for a chance to go to town. I had walked by the house numerous times before without incident, but on this day the Herrins' bird dog, Buster, took a great interest in the paper bag and bounded out and ripped it from my hands. He shook the sack back and forth until the shirt fell out on the muddy ground. He sniffed of it a second, lost interest, and went back toward the house. In the process of getting the sack, he had scratched my hand, but when I looked down there was hardly any blood at all.

It turned out that Miss Rina Herrin, a large, unmarried woman of fifty who had been dating the same man for thirty-five years, had witnessed the entire proceeding. Running out to the road flailing her arms, she called, "Are you all right, Norman?" I nodded as she approached me, but she made me hold out my hand for her to see anyway. After looking at the bite, she seemed to decide I was all right. "Buster's had his shot," she said. "Don't worry. "

Then Miss Rina looked over at the shirt, picking it up and shaking her head as she looked at the red smears of mud. She quizzed me about what I was carrying the shirt for, and when I told her she said, "Wait here." She ran to the house, returning with four crisp dollar bills she held out to me. "Go to Sears Roebuck when you get to town and get you a new shirt," she said.

"Oh, no ma'am," I said, at the same time reaching for the bills.

I made a handsome profit that day because when I got to Elizabeth's, where I was spending the night, she laundered the shirt for me and I was able to pocket the money and buy lunches and snacks with it for a few days. When I told what happened to Kenneth, who was still too young to get many chances to make much money working, he was put out. "Why do you have to have all the luck?" he said, and he later told me that for weeks he tried to lure Buster into biting him, but with no success.

My transportation was not always by hitchhiking. I had a number of friends who took me places. A guy named David Jinks from down the road in Greene County took a liking to Julia, and he would take her and me and his sister Stella in his pickup truck to movies, church socials, and Eutaw football games. We'd squeeze into the cab of the truck—the two girls between us—and we'd sail off down the road, always greatly exceeding the speed limit.

When we were riding home in the dark, I would begin to make my subtle moves on Stella. I had a slow hand, and I would move in imperceptible increments from her shoulder downwards until I had eased my hand over her bra cup. I would hold it there real still. She never once let on that I was doing anything, but she never removed my hand either, and that was about as much as I could hope for, I supposed. Our eyes never met.

For a year or two we were also taken places by a young married couple who moved into a nearby house. Arthur and Flossie Drummond, in their early twenties but more children than adults, were two of the most unsightly people I ever knew, but that didn't keep us from going places with them whenever asked. Flossie, a short, overweight, acne-faced woman who had nerve trouble, admitted that while they were living in Ralph she had twice gone to the smoke house and tried to get up her courage to hang herself. But she just couldn't go through with it.

Arthur was a red-faced three-hundred pounder who was real hard on furniture, once riding a wrought iron barstool at a neighbor's house right down to the floor. He always wore blue jeans and penny loafers with dimes in the slots. He made a good living at the rubber plant in Tuscaloosa, and as near as I could tell most of his earnings went into groceries. They were always wanting us to eat when we went to their house, and we happily accommodated them. They fried huge pieces of kielbasa, they opened oversized cans of pork and beans to which they added redhots, and they opened cellophane packages of cinnamon rolls and jelly doughnuts. They made numerous sandwiches with thick slices of souse meat or several layers of liver cheese. They sautéed onions and chili peppers in lard and added them, with canned tomatoes, cheese, and chili peppers to scrambled eggs. They had large hoops of rat cheese and bought five-gallon cans of meat skins. We loved it all.

In the summer, Arthur and Flossie took us several times a week to swim in the Sipsey River. We'd climb onto the back of their International pickup and ride the seven miles with the air blowing hard in our faces. The truck lacked a muffler so everybody, inside the cab or on the back, had to scream to be heard. When we went by, people on their porches or in the fields must have thought we were crazy.

When we got to the river, the girls would head in one direction and the guys in another to change into our suits. As we disrobed, I would think that for a three hundred pound man Arthur Drummond had the littlest peter I ever saw, emerging only slightly from the rolls of fat. "Can he really satisfy Flossie?" I wondered, imagining him struggling to get close enough to her to penetrate.

The Drummonds often drove to Pickens County for country music shows in Carrollton, and though I floated great hints they never took me there. But once they brought a country singer, Rita Balls, home with them, and she stayed two weeks. "I been needing a hiatus," she told us. "The country music field is very demanding."

While Rita was there, she wanted to have a party at which she would be the live entertainment, and because Arthur and Flossie didn't have many adult friends they mainly invited us and some other kids. After we had eaten all the pimento cheese sandwiches and Ritz crackers with peanut butter we could hold and had washed down several slices of store-bought orange-coconut cake with icy Upper Tens, we went out to the front porch to listen to Rita. She was sitting on a stool wearing what looked like a square dancing outfit, a guitar strapped over her shoulder. Clear plastic glasses encrusted with various colored jewels sparkled under the porch light, and she squinted as she began to pick the guitar.

I was standing right next to her, staring at her hands and thinking to myself, "She is damn good." But the way she got into the music so heavy, never changing her expression, spooked me a little bit.

"Y'all know 'Blue Moon of Kentucky?" she asked and everybody nodded. She started us off:

Blue moon of Kentucky keep on shining,
Shine on the one that's gone and left me blue.

As we sang, Rita kept looking over at me real hard, and that made me nervous. When we finished, she said, "Boy, come here a minute." I went over reluctantly.

"Hey," she said, "you got a good voice. What's your name, anyway?"

"Norman."

"Well, Norman, you might very well have a career in country music ahead of you. Did you ever think about that?"

I did not tell her that when I was younger and had listened to Carl Sauceman and the Greene Valley Boys, I had been envious of the young singer on the show named Bennie Paul Hubbard and had longed to get me a cowboy suit and travel with them. That was all in the past, I thought, so I just said, "Nome."

"Well, you ought to. It's a hard life, but it's sure been good to me. "

I was torn between being flattered by her attentions and allowing my cynical side to kick in. My cynical side had been kicking in more and more lately, and all I could really think was, "If country music has been so good to you, what are you still doing in Pickens County?" But I didn't say anything. I merely thanked her. I was too well-trained by Mama to say anything truly scathing to anybody's face.

Often lacking anything else to do during my high school years, I continued to hang around Luke Rodgers's store a lot. In the afternoons, a number of older men congregated there, and they seemed to think that they should teach a lesson or two about life to whatever young boys were standing around. Daddy was never among these men, and he would have been extremely embarrassed because they talked about poontang fairly often.

Mr. Andrew Jenkins, a pillar of Bethel Baptist Church, was always there. His face interested me, as his false teeth were so large that his lips could close only in the middle, making his mouth shaped like a sideways figure eight.

"Godamighty," Mr. Andrew said one day when my friend, Randy Harris, and I were hanging out, "did y'all see that calendar picture of Marilyn Monroe? She was as nekkid as a jay bird. My son-in-law wrote off for a copy and he showed it to me. That is one more good looking woman."

"A little bit on the skinny side, if you ask me," Mr. Luke said.

"You just too picky," Mr. Andrew said.

Old Man McCullough, who had the reputation for being a tough old bird, prepared to speak on the topic. He always talked slow and soft, and everybody always stopped talking to hear what he had to say. "Shee-it, fellows. I could look at a nekkid woman all day and never feel a thing. But show me a good looking woman with a little bit of red petticoat showing under her dress and I get hot as a fire cracker." Everybody laughed, including me and Randy, but I didn't really think there was anything funny about what he had said.

Figuring he had closed out that part of the conversation, Mr. McCullough turned to me and said, "Boy, did you ever fart under the covers and then put your head up under there to see how it smelled?"

I had never heard of such a thing. "No, sir," I said.

"He's lying," Mr. McCullough said. Then he turned to Randy. "I bet you have, ain't you?"

Randy grinned sheepishly and didn't say anything.

"See, I told you he had done it, and that other one has too. He just won't admit it."

I grinned sheepishly too, not wanting to be thought an odd ball.

Mr. Andrew said to Randy, "Y'all getting you up a community ball team again, ain't you?"

"Yes, sir, we practiced last Saturday."

"What position you play?"

"First base, and I pitch sometime," he answered,

"What about you?" Mr. Andrew said to me.

There was really no answer to his question because I played whatever was left over, that is if I even went to practice. I did anything

I could to miss practice, but if I couldn't find an excuse to miss I was usually put out in right field. As I stood there, I hoped against hope that no one would hit in my direction. I didn't have an arm at all, and when I had to throw in, the ball would go a short distance, roll along the ground until the second baseman or short stop would run out and scoop it up. I just didn't get the game, and I hated it. But all the boys my age played, and I knew I was expected to as well.

I realized I had to say something in answer to Mr. McCullough's question, but before I could, Bobby said to Mr. Andrew, "Norman keeps score," and all the men laughed a little. With that, the topic of sports had been covered for that day.

By the time I was a junior in high school, I began to take every opportunity I found for staying away from Ralph, and I spent many nights with my sisters in Tuscaloosa and with my friend Henry Lowery in Northport. Because we didn't have a telephone, there was no way to let Mama and Daddy know my plans, but that did not seem to matter a bit to them. If I showed up, fine; if not, no need to worry.

I liked staying with Henry. An only child, he had parents who were, if not rich, quite well-off. No matter how much I stayed at their house, Mr. and Mrs. Lowery always seemed to welcome me, having the misguided opinion that I was a good influence on their son. I didn't use slang and bad grammar or profanity—especially where they could hear it, and I was a member of the National Honor Society. "Good boys like you are a rarity in this world today," Mrs. Lowery once said to me.

"Thank you," I said seriously. "I just try to do my best." Henry, standing where his mother couldn't see him but I could, spread a sneering smile over his face.

Henry had the reputation for being a screw off. His description in the school annual read, "He wouldn't walk around the corner to watch the world blow up." But I knew better. He was smart in science and math, and he wasn't lazy at all. We'd spend hours in his room with him sitting at his desk drafting airplane designs, which he intended to do for a living one day. I'd prop up on his bed reading novels.

Sometimes we talked about how horny we were and the prospects of doing something about it. "You reckon Betty'd let you or me in her pants?" Henry asked me one day, not even turning from his drawing.

"Not a chance," I answered, closing my copy of *The Great Gatsby*. "Bunky told me he tried and she slapped the hell out of him."

"Aw, no. You're kidding? You know she didn't do that to Bunky."

"That's what my sources say," I answered. My source was Bunky Wilcox himself, a running back for the County High Wildcats. He had taken me into his confidence one day before assembly after I swore I wouldn't tell a soul. The way I figured it, something that unflattering had to be true.

Henry pushed his chair away from the big oak desk his parents had had built for him and folded his arms. He got a real serious look on his face. "What our school needs," he said "is another nymphomaniac or two. You know, like Carmel. There's just too many guys in Tuscaloosa County High School for her to service everybody."

"I'm turned off by Carmel myself," I said sort of sanctimoniously. "She looks nasty to me. To tell you the truth I don't want to be with any girl who's screwing everybody else. I really want one that just screws me and me alone." I stared off in space and added dolefully, "And so far that hasn't been easy to find."

"I know what you mean. I tell you one thing, I ain't about to participate in any gang bangs," Henry said. "My conscience wouldn't let me."

"Mine either," I said, still feeling sanctimonious.

I thought of Betty Merle Loggins, a classmate I lusted for constantly. "God, I'd never complain again if I could get a piece from Betty Merle."

"Hell, you ain't had a kiss or felt a tit yet," Henry said, quite accurately. The fact was that I despaired of Betty Merle Loggins ever giving me as much as the time of day. She liked me, but she liked me as a brother. She actually said that to me, and I felt nauseated. I had enough sisters already.

When the County Fair came in the fall, Henry and I would hang around the strippers' tent, waiting for them to come out and work up a crowd. We knew that there was no chance of being admitted to the show, but we could at least get a good peek at the women. One night a barker, wearing a powder blue tuxedo, stepped out into the spotlight and began calling in a high, loud voice, "Step right up, gentlemen. We got the most beautiful women in the world. And if you come in this tent for our show, you'll see everything. Let me just give you now just a tiny sample."

A loud throbbing music began to come out of the loud speakers. I recognized the dah-dah, dah-dah, dah-dah, dah-dah; it was "Peter Gunn." Slowly, one by one, the strippers emerged from a flap in the tent. Lining up side by side, they began to gyrate their pelvises to "Peter Gunn" and they made the tassels on the ends of their bras spin like pin wheels. Suddenly, I realized that one of them, the blond one with a diamond tiara, a leopard skin outfit, and backless silver shoes, was making eye contact with me. It scared me half to death, and I tried to tell myself that I was just imagining it. But then there was no doubt. She wiggled her finger right at me and ran her tongue over her lips. I was so much in shock that I said to Henry, who hadn't noticed any of what had just happened, "Let's get the hell out of here."

"No," he said. "It's just getting good."

I ignored him and started to leave. When I looked back at the woman she was still looking at me, and I knew I would have fainted if I had stayed there another minute. I picked my way through the crowd, and then I heard Henry hollering after me, "Wait, Norman, wait. What's the matter with you? You sick or something?" He sounded real irritated.

"Yeah," I said. "I thought I was going to faint."

"Well, all right. Let's get out of here. But, hey," he said, "did you see that one in the leopard skin suit coming on to me? She was making eyes at me like everything. And did you see how she motioned to me with her finger? God a mighty, what a woman."

I started to tell Henry he had it all wrong, that she was looking at me, not him. But what good would it do? Even if he believed me, he'd really think I was crazy for running off. We walked out to the gate and waited silently for his parents to pick us up.

The time I spent with Henry and his family was my first extended view of how middle-classed people lived. They ate well; they had all the appliances. Henry had his flat-top shaped up every Saturday. He even had a standing appointment at the dentist to get his teeth cleaned. As for me, I had made only one trip to the dentist in my entire life, and that was to have two aching jaw teeth pulled when I was thirteen.

I had been in agony for a couple of days, actually moaning for hours with the rotten teeth when late one afternoon Daddy got us a ride to Eutaw to see Doctor Payne. We caught him about closing time, but he agreed to stay. Taking my seat as directed in the tall chair, I was terrified as Doctor Payne cranked me back, flipped on a light, and took a little mirror and inserted it into my mouth. He seemed to be surprised when he saw the shells the teeth were reduced to, because he let out a whistle of disbelief. "Mr. Mc, that's the two worst teeth I ever saw—if you can call what's left teeth. I don't see how the boy stood it."

Dr. Payne reached over and took up a syringe out of a box, and as he attached a needle to it, he said, "This is gonna feel real good—what's your name?"

"His name is Norman," Daddy said.

"You gonna like this, Norman."

I couldn't imagine liking it as he inserted the needle into my mouth, but after the initial sting, which caused tears to rush out of my right eye, I felt the greatest relief I had ever experienced. "That Novocain is a miracle, isn't it?" Doctor Payne said. "It's purely revolutionized dentistry."

I didn't care what it had done for anybody else. It had saved me, and I drifted into a half sleep and was not in the least bothered when Doctor Payne broke my teeth into numerous pieces as he tried to pull them. I didn't care when he dug out the roots with his shiny instruments.

When Doctor Payne finished and I had spit out the blood and debris into the little round bowl running a steady little stream of water, he packed my jaws with gauze. "Now, Norman," he said, "the fun is over. This deadening is gonna wear off in a couple of hours." He turned to Daddy. "Give him three aspirin when he needs them."

When we got home I went to bed immediately, but during the night I woke up with my jaw throbbing and my mouth full of coagulated blood. As I went to Mama and Daddy's room to get my aspirin, I fell out cold in the floor. Somebody heard me and ran and got up Mama and Daddy, but I had come to when they got there.

"Are you all right?" Mama asked.

"No. I'm hurting."

"Take these aspirin and you'll be fine," Daddy said. He handed me a snuff glass of water he had brought in from the kitchen. I swallowed about as much blood as water, but I didn't care. I just wanted relief. Then Daddy took me back to my bed and sat on the side of it and rubbed my back until I could get back to sleep.

It occurred to me one day that if I had had regular checkups like Henry did I could probably have those kept those jaw teeth and wouldn't have had those two big gaps in the back of my mouth. But why worry about it now? Dental care was not something to be taken for granted. The wonder was that I kept any of my teeth. Both Mama and Daddy had lost all of their teeth in their early thirties when they had pyorrhea, and neither wore their bottom dentures, which meant their lower lips were always slightly sunk in.

After Albert's Tat-Tat broke down when I was in the sixth grade, Daddy never had another car until I was in college. For a few years, I lived, drank, and ate cars. I knew all the models and could tell by sound if a car had a glass-pack muffler. I knew how to drive. Sarah Alice had started letting me take the wheel when I was fourteen or fifteen, and my friends with cars would let me drive occasionally. I decided that I should go on and get my license in case I could figure out some way to get me a car, and I began hinting to my brothers-in-law that I wanted to borrow their cars for the drivers' test. They ignored me, but eventually my first cousin's husband offered me his 1955 Chevrolet station wagon. As it turned out, though, I didn't need the wagon the day I went in get my license.

The first thing they did at the licensing office was to test my eyes, and that's where things stalled. Even though I had no idea that anything was wrong with my eyes, I couldn't get past the big E at the top of the eye chart. I was amazed because at school I was always able to see the board, perhaps because I usually sat on the first row.

Miss Hettie Tyler found out about my plight and got me an appointment with her eye doctor. At the end of the examination, he said, "Boy, you got 20/200 vision. You need to get you some glasses in a hurry." Miss Hettie offered to buy me a pair of glasses, and what a revelation it was when I put the mock tortoise shell horned rimmed glasses on for the first time. The textures and details of things came out in startling ways. Trees actually had individual leaves on them, and people who had seemed pretty good looking were suddenly ugly, their faces covered with enlarged pores or zits and acne patches. I was repulsed until my eyes adjusted.

Wearing my new glasses, I went back to the licensing office and passed the eye test easily. I did the same for the written test. Then came the road test.

I had never driven my cousin's station wagon when I started the road test. I found that the car had the stiffest clutch I had ever encountered, and that, coupled with my nervousness, meant for a jerky ride. The officer, wearing sunshades and slouched against the window, kept shooting looks over my way. That further unnerved me, and in the midst of it all I committed the fatal mistake. I ran a stop sign.

The officer sat up straight and said, "Didn't you see that sign, son?"

Fighting back a great impulse to say, "Yes, I saw it, but I decided to ignore it," I said meekly, "No sir."

"Well, if you didn't see that, you got major problems. I can see you gonna have to practice summo before we release you on the roads of Alabama." I thought he sounded sarcastic, but I knew there was nothing to do. "Let's just take her back in," the officer said wearily. "And do watch out for stop signs from now on."

There was no opportunity to practice, but I made arrangements with my cousin to meet him at the license office the next week. Just as I had dreaded, the same officer who had conducted my abbreviated road test the previous week was standing there.

"You been practicing?" he asked.

"Yes, sir."

"Okay. Let's get going," he said, and we got in the wagon.

I took off, but almost immediately I made a bad assumption. I had a good memory, and I assumed that we would follow the same route as the week before. When we came to the first turn we had taken then, I took it again.

"Why in the name of heaven did you turn there?" the officer said, removing his sunshades so he could look disgustedly into my face.

"That's where we turned before, sir," I answered feebly.

"Let me tell you something," he said very slowly and deliberately. "Before ain't got nothing to do with now. I call the shots—right here, right now, right today. You read me?"

I nodded.

"You are to do nothing," he said, "and I mean pure-oh-dee nothing without a direction from me. You got that?"

I nodded as I began to stop so I could back up and undo my error.

"What in God's name are you doing now?"

"I'm gonna back up and go the way you wanted me to."

"In this traffic? For God's sakes drive ahead or you're gonna get us both killed."

I finished the test without a hitch, even parallel parking just fine. When we got back the officer looked at me closely and said, "Boy, I'm gonna give you this license, but do be careful. There are a lot of innocent people you got to share the highways with."

"Yes sir," I said, surprised to be taking the papers from him. I left hurriedly, with the decided opinion that he gave me the license because he didn't ever want to have to get in the car with me again.

So I had the license. Now the car. When Evelyn returned to Tuscaloosa for graduate school, she realized that I was suffering from the lack of wheels, and her first thought was to learn to drive herself and get a car she could lend me when I needed it. But she really had no interest in driving, and eventually when I was a junior in high school she told me she could give me $150 if I could find a used car for that. I jumped at the opportunity, even though I knew that finding a decent car for that amount would be a real challenge. My friend Henry took me around to used car lots.

Most of the salesmen would look sort of surprised when I told them what I could spend, but one finally took me out to the back of the gravel lot where there was a '47 Ford with a stick shift in the floor. "You want to test drive this one?"

I really didn't want to, but I thought that since he had gone to the trouble to come out there that I should try it out. When I mashed the starter button, it wouldn't even turn over. "Hold on. This car hasn't been driven for a while," the salesman said. "I'll jump it off."

While he was gone, Henry said, "Norman, to tell you the truth, I wouldn't have this piece of shit."

"I don't want it either," I said grimly, "but between this and nothing I'd take it."

The man returned and attached the jumper cables and the car sounded off real loud, like it didn't even have a muffler on it."

"These old cars make noise," the salesman said. "But these Fords were well-made automobiles. Cars like this won't set you down on the side of the road." He opened the driver's door. "Get in," he said. "Give it a spin."

I got behind the wheel, and Henry got in the other side. We sprayed gravel everywhere as we left the parking lot, not intentionally but because I was not familiar with the gear shift. We took off down the street, the car making a deafening noise.

"My God," Henry hollered, looking down at his feet. "You can see the frigging road through this floor." He was right. I could see it on my side too. We began to laugh like maniacs.

"Let's take this piece of shit back," he said as carbon monoxide began to drift up heavily into the car.

I stopped the car to turn around, and when I did it went dead. "You think we ought to push it off?" I asked.

"I ain't pushing this piece of shit anywhere," Henry said firmly. "Let's go back to the lot and get my car and tell that bastard he can go get it himself."

"Suits me," I said, and we left that piece of shit on the side of the road.

Our other attempts were getting us nowhere when we remembered that this girl we knew had a daddy in the loan business, and she said that they were always repossessing cars. I went to him, but when I said $150 he scratched his head as if in deep thought and finally said, "I'll tell you what. It's worth more, but because you are a friend of my daughter I can let you have that gray '49 Plymouth out there for $150. It'll be a sacrifice, but I'll do it for you."

The car looked pretty good, and it did not even have to be jump started. After a short drive, I went and got Evelyn, and she came and bought it and got me some liability insurance. I was off to great things, but that car—or I—seemed jinxed from the start. The first thing I did was tear up the driver-side door. Our newspaper, which often arrived after dark, was thrown at the end of a long drive. One night I couldn't find it, so I decided to drive the car down and shine the lights around. As I held the door open so I could look out as I backed up, I unfortunately got too close to a hedge terrace, and when it caught in the hedge the door sprung back, never to work again. I forced it shut and secured it with baling wire.

The lack of a door on the driver's side was more embarrassing than anything else. I tried to make jokes about it, but most people, especially girls, didn't find them funny. If a girl would go with me more than once in a car like that, I took it as a sign of real interest. A pretty girl from Greene County named Violet Summers went out with me a number of times, and I felt sure that meant she was in love with me. Violet had a speech impediment, her *s*'s coming out *th*'s, for example. But the lisp was not pronounced, just bad enough to be detectable.

Everywhere Violet and I went, I'd have to climb in first, and Violet would climb in and get right up next to me. We could have easily had another couple in the front seat, we sat so close together.

Violet and I got into some pretty heavy petting in the Plymouth when I'd bring her home after a date. We'd sit in her driveway and french kiss, and she gave my hands pretty free license except for her breasts and one other place. Any time my hands got too close to either of them, she would grab my hand and say firmly, "Thop. Thop." I always thopped because I knew there was no use. Pussy might be good to boys, but I was pretty sure I wasn't going to find out about it in that Plymouth, and especially with Violet.

But we enjoyed what we did, as far as she would let me go. We knew at some point that a light would come on in her parents' bedroom. Then Violet would give me one more quick french kiss before bolting to the front porch. Only a time or two did she meet her father in the doorway. By then, I was well on my way out of the yard.

Violet had to put up with more than the bad door in the Plymouth. Almost immediately after I got it, the car began to make a loud racket, which a mechanic I knew told me was a loose rod. There was an ominous knocking sound, and I always dreaded throwing the rod while I was out with Violet somewhere and couldn't get her back home.

It was almost a year before the rod was finally thrown. And it at least was not at night, and Violet was not with me. I had taken Daddy to Eutaw to buy groceries, and on the way home as we were coming up Spencer Hill, we heard a loud ker-wham, and the Plymouth breathed its last. We were almost in front of Taggart's store, and the Taggart boy got a chain and towed the car home, where it sat for a couple of years before somebody gave Daddy $20 and hauled it off for parts. "He got a good deal," Daddy said. "Two of those tires didn't even have boots in them."

My sense of deprivation became quite heavy after the Plymouth threw its rod. I found it harder and harder to accept Mama's idea that you had a far greater chance of realizing your dreams for the future if you ignored your present adversity. But I kept trying to believe it. Occasionally, though, something would really get to me so bad that I'd feel terribly victimized by our poverty.

During my junior year in high school I was chosen to be a sponsored delegate to Boys State, a week of activities designed to teach the workings of the three branches of state government to a couple of hundred boys from all over Alabama, most of whom could care less. I was proud to have been chosen, but I worried because in order to go I would have to have a physical exam. I was relieved when Daddy told me to go to his physician, Doctor Wedgeworth, in the First National Bank Building in Tuscaloosa. He would undoubtedly be glad to fill out the required forms, he said.

When I arrived at Dr. Wedgeworth's office after school the next day, I first encountered the receptionist who was named, according to the plaque on her desk, Mrs. Skates. A drawn, hatchet-faced woman with permanently narrowed eyes, she wrote down my name without looking at me directly, then went back to reading a magazine with a title that had *Church of Christ* in it. I took a seat with six or eight others, and after a while a nurse came and took me in to see Doctor Wedgeworth. He was through with me in five minutes, mainly just asking me the questions on the sheet I provided. I walked back out through the waiting room, assuming they would send a bill.

When I had just got past Mrs. Skates, she called out to me in a sarcastic voice so that everyone in the waiting room could hear, "And just where do you think you are going?" As I turned to her, she looked me over with disgust and loathing. "I know what you're doing," she said. "You don't fool me. You're trying to sneak out of here without paying."

"Oh, no ma'am," I said. "I thought you'd just send a bill. My Daddy will pay you."

"Hah," she scoffed, and turned to the decent people in the waiting room. "Tell me, what can you do with people like this?" she asked. I could tell that several people shook their heads, but I thought I got a quick look at a face of a woman who didn't seem to approve.

Looking back at me, Mrs. Skates suddenly dismissed me, saying, "Just go on. Just go on and get out of here." She said it like I was a dog or something.

I left hurriedly, too embarrassed to do anything else. My face was burning and my hands shaking as I walked into the hall and down the stairs. I had never been treated like that before. The shock and hurt were so great I thought I might get sick. But as I walked further down the stairs and into the street I could feel the hurt turning to anger, and for the first time in my life I found myself seriously wanting to commit a homicide. I could see the scene.

I took her by her yellow neck and began to choke her. Her little slits of eyes began to bug out on their stems, and they seemed to beg me to spare her. But I would have nothing of it. "You goddamn bitch," I was saying. "This death is too good for you. Wipe that smug look off your self-righteous Church of Christ face. I hope you burn in hell for all eternity."

I felt better after that, but for days aftershocks of murderous revenge came to me at odd times, and I re-experienced the pleasure of murdering her again and again.

As time went on, Daddy continued his drinking, but his sprees became less frequent. He also became more reclusive and thus did far less to embarrass us. But he acted up big time when a woman named Mrs. Stallworth, a teacher of my niece Mary Ann and an acquaintance of Elizabeth's and her husband Bernie, wanted to interview Daddy for an article she was planning to do on his Aunt Sallie, who had been Miss Julia Tutwiler's protégé at Livingston Normal School. She thought he'd be indispensable because he had spent so much time with her when he was young.

From the first, Daddy did not want to be interviewed, but he finally agreed after Mama had browbeat him sufficiently. Plans were made for Mrs. Stallworth to arrive at our house at 2:00 on a Saturday afternoon, and that morning everybody pitched in and cleaned up the house to make it presentable, paying no attention to Daddy. By 10:00 we discovered that he had been getting into the whiskey.

Mama was livid. When Elizabeth and her husband Bernie and Mary Ann arrived at 1:00, Daddy was sprawled side-ways in the porch swing, his head bowed down. "I wish you'd just look at that," Mama said disgustedly. "I'll tell you one thing. We're not going to let that woman see him in that condition." She turned to Bernie. "We're going to have to get him in your car and haul him off somewhere. Grab his other arm."

I stepped forward and told Mama I'd help. Bernie and I pulled Daddy up out of the swing and pretty much drug him to the car. He did not so much as move a muscle as we stuck him in the back seat, maybe not even knowing where he was as we propped him against the window.

All the others stood in the yard and watched. Bernie, who could always come up with a funny simile, eased the tension a little when he took out his handkerchief and mopped his forehead and said, "That was

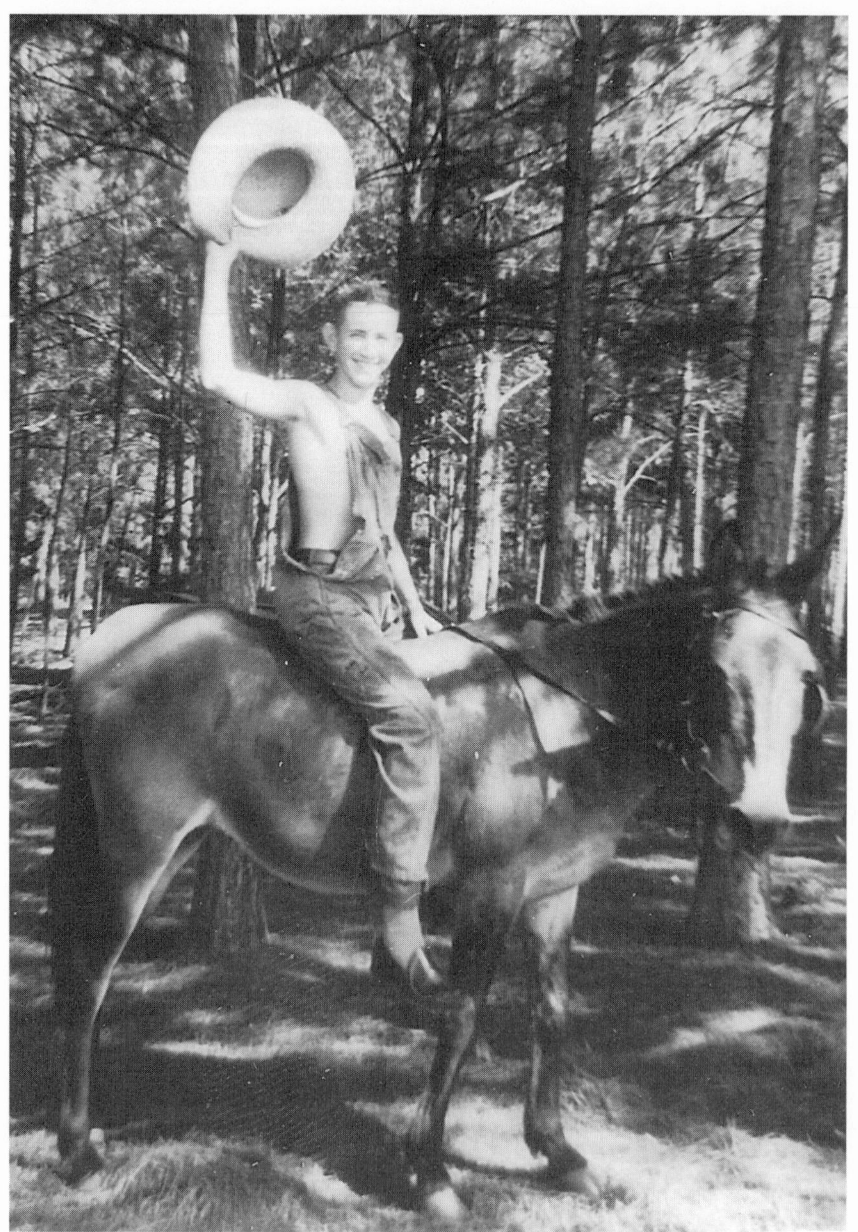

Kenneth

sort of like dragging a beached whale, wasn't it?" Even Mama laughed.

Although I knew the whole situation was pathetic, I continued laughing as I got into the front seat with Bernie. We took off to the Sipsy River, stopping and getting us two Upper Tens at Bowling's Store and driving to the river bank, where we got out to drink them. "I don't drink alcoholic beverages any more," Bernie said, "but this is one time I wish this Upper Ten was a Falstaff beer."

Occasionally we could hear a slight groan coming from Daddy, but we pretty much ignored him. After we had sat on the bank for a while, Bernie asked me whether I thought the woman would be gone by now. "It's 3:00," I said, "and since she hasn't got an interviewee anyway I'd think she'd be back in Tuscaloosa by now."

But Mrs. Stallworth's Chevrolet was still in the driveway when we got back. Kenneth, who had appointed himself sentinel, waved us on. We came back by four more times before the woman finally had left. By then the gas gauge on Bernie's car was indicating empty.

Mama walked out, still angry. Her jaw was set. "I hope he knows this has just about killed me," she said. She snatched opened the back door of the car and said, "Come on. Let's pull him out."

As we walked him to the house, I wondered why Daddy had had to spoil everything. And in just a fleeting moment I wondered if he could have been trying to avoid facing how far he had fallen from his successful forebears. Maybe it was just too painful to talk about his Aunt Sallie. But surely he didn't have to make Mama and the rest of us suffer the way he did.

About this time, Mama's health took a bad turn. Her gallbladder would flare up periodically, but her main illness was rheumatoid arthritis. Although she got some relief from cortisone shots, her joints became inflamed and swollen, her knuckles becoming knobs, her fingers twisting, and her ankles billowing out over her shoes. She didn't complain much, but to avoid the pain she chose inertia, staying in bed most of the time. She had always spent a lot of time in bed reading, and she increased that as her condition worsened. And she took lots of cortisone tablets to supplement the shots.

Mama had never been a good housekeeper, but we began to see what all she did do after she got ill. Julia, as the only daughter at home, had to take over many of the duties, receiving very little help from either me or Kenneth. Daddy praised Julia for her work, and he tried to help out more.

Mama, who almost never did anything to discourage me, was not always understanding of Julia's problems. Once when Julia fell for a McCullough boy who rode Bus 14, she found that she had a rival who began to circulate ugly stories about her. Someone on the bus told her what the girl was saying, whereupon Julia broke into a fit of crying in front of everybody.

The story eventually made its way to Mama, who called Julia to her and said, "I am so disappointed in you. The very idea that you would let those common people on that bus see you cry is shocking. Never *ever* let people see that they have gotten the best of you. Act like you could care less. If you have crying to do, do it in private." There was not a single indication that she had a shred of sympathy for what Julia was feeling. We were not at all surprised at Mama's response. It was totally in character. But I felt a momentary pang of sympathy for Julia.

Daddy became more considerate of Mama after she got sick, I thought. He was more solicitous about her than I had ever seen him. He had always had a sort of romantic side to him, gathering the first violets of the year down at the pump house and presenting her a bouquet along with a kiss on her cheek. Plus he was jealous of any man paying her any attention. Once when Mr. Rufus Chalker, an old man in the Sunday School Class Mama taught, came by for a visit, he gave Mama a chaste kiss when he left. Daddy was furious. "I'd have killed the son-of-a-bitch if he hadn't been so old," he said.

Even if Daddy did ease up some, he and Mama continued to argue regularly. They agreed on hardly anything. When election time came around they usually did not even have to go to the polls because they canceled each other's votes out. Mama tended increasingly to talk for Daddy, and that irritated him. If someone asked Daddy how he was doing, she would literally say, "He's doing just fine." This did not seem strange, or even improper, to me at the time.

Sometimes their disagreements were almost comical. One winter night when we were sitting in the living room, Mama turned to Daddy

Evelyn

and said, "Albert, that wind is really blowing out there." Daddy answered, "Well, Lucille, I can't help it."

I did not cut an imposing figure in the halls of Tuscaloosa County High School. As a senior, I spread a measly 118 pounds over a five foot, seven inch frame. My waist measured twenty-eight inches. I could finally wear a man's size fourteen and a half shirt, which was good because my brother-in-law Howard provided me all the dress shirts

I wanted from the Van Heusen factory he managed. At least I was well-dressed from the waist up.

Throughout high school my eating habits were quite irregular and my caloric intake very small. After the eighth grade I would no longer take my lunch, which invariably was a dry, unwrapped sliced apple sandwich. There was something just too humiliating about sitting among your classmates eating a dry sandwich with warm mayonnaise in it without the benefit of any drink. I decided I would do without, and I got where I didn't even get hungry at lunch time. If I managed to scrape together the thirty-five cents, I would buy a cafeteria meal, which I thought very good and would eat thoroughly. I was completely mystified when the other students said the food was slop, and I looked on in amazement as girls picked at each item on their plates and threw away most of their food.

Things actually began to pick up during my senior year. I didn't have any wheels, but when Evelyn got an apartment near the University of Alabama I was able to spend a good bit of time with her, sleeping on her living room couch. I loved the graduate students and younger faculty members from the University of Alabama who often came to Evelyn's apartment for drinking parties, but Evelyn thought me too young to attend and instructed me to stay back in the only bedroom. As it turned out, that wasn't so bad because everybody had to pass by me to get to the john, and most of them would spend time talking to me. Once Evelyn went into the bathroom and after tinkling for a very long time she announced on her way back through, "They don't call me artesian for nothing."

I would strain to hear what they were talking about in the next room, and I thought them all sophisticated. I began to conceive a plan to become a teacher too because I thought nobody had as much fun as they did.

Evelyn had a friend in the next building named Mary Grace Caughran who taught German at the University. Mary Grace seemed up on everything, including the popular music on the radio and the newest novels, and I thought her the very wittiest person I had ever met. She had a record player, and she and Evelyn introduced me to the Weavers and other folk groups, and I loved an album called *New Faces of 1952* which had Eartha Kitt on it. But my favorite albums were those of Tom Lehrer, and I memorized all his songs and sang them to anyone who would listen. Most people I found didn't give a hoot, but those who appreciated them really appreciated them. I began to imitate his voice as I sang:

About a maid I'll sing a song,
Sing rickety-tickety-tin.
About a maid I'll sing a song
Who did not have her family long.
Not only did she do them wrong.
She did every one of them in, them in,
She did everyone of them in.

Evelyn and Mary Grace would have highballs as they listened to the music, and I told them I thought I could handle one too. Finally, I thought I had arrived when they gave me some sherry in a small glass a shrimp cocktail had originally come in. I nursed the sherry for a good hour, feeling warmer and warmer and rosier and rosier with each sip.

Evelyn gave me a key to her apartment, and when she was away for the week-end I had the place to myself. I'd have my friends, including several girls, over sometimes, and we would slip some of Evelyn's whiskey to drink. One Saturday afternoon when Evelyn was sitting alone in the apartment reading, she heard female voices shouting, "Norman, Norman, where are you." She went to the window and saw a carload of girls trying to find me. She decided to lie low, but she told me I should be careful about having girls over there. Later when she told my brother-in-law Howard about it, he said, "Norman, that apartment doesn't have a back door. Don't ever take a girl into a place that doesn't have a back door. If someone calls the cops, you've got no way out."

I think the time I spent with Evelyn did a great deal to make me see a world much broader and more exciting than I had known of before, and I knew that I would do what it took to claim my own place in that world.

At high school I slowly cultivated the idea of being a bohemian, even though I was not altogether sure what the term meant. I had few of the requisite props, but I did have an opium pipe Donald had brought back from Okinawa. I discovered that a cigarette would fit nicely in its tiny bowl so I began placing my Old Gold Filters in it, the cigarette standing perpendicular to the narrow stem. I also marchanned my hair to a reddish gold, and I read Edgar Cayce, sometimes pretending to be a clairvoyant myself. I tried to be glib and philosophical, telling my classmates such things as that there were no fires in hell, that hell was simply a state of mind, or that Jefferson Davis was a transvestite. I wrote awful poetry, which I passed around, and Miss Beavers, my senior English teacher, seemed fooled. She said I was another Edgar Allen Poe.

One poem, entitled "The Vision," was especially popular with my teachers and classmates. I wrote it after consulting the dictionary for big words that would impress people. The poem had thirty stanzas of four-lines, the first of which went as follows:

'Twas in a vision drempt one night
I saw a tortile river.
Through fructuous forests it did wind
And led to a sea incarnadine.

I felt a thrill when I worked in the word *fructuous*.

I also wrote a poem called "Thanatos of the Enlightened," which I thought had the very best simile I had ever written and maybe seen:

My inner soul was filled to bursting,
Like pus in an angry boil in need of release.

I loved the simile because it captured so well how I felt most of the time, being enlightened myself, of course, but surrounded by insensitive, ignorant dolts.

In class I scribbled notes and drew caricatures, passing them around to keep my fellow students entertained, and I began to write satirical pieces for the *Blue-White*, the school newspaper. When it came time for the senior class prophecy I was drafted to write it, and I thought what I produced was quite witty. Some of my classmates did not.

The *Blue-White* staff

I predicted that Connie Black, a blond who was rumored to have screwed thirteen boys in a row one night, would become an overnight success as a bubble dancer when they gave her a batch of sorry soap. She walked up to me fuming. "That reflects on my good name," she said, not knowing, it seemed, whether to be angry or hurt.

I looked at her squarely in the eye and said as acidly as I could, "That would be impossible, Connie, because you would have had to have a good name to start with." She just walked off, and I went looking for someone to tell what I had said to her.

I wanted to be known as a smart mouth, and I especially liked to make smart remarks to teachers. Once in English class while I was taking a test, the teacher Mrs. Warden was called out of the room, and Steve Grant, whose IQ was in the idiot range, asked if I could supply him with some answers. Not seeing any reason to refuse—he wasn't going to pass anyway—I began to feed the answers to him. It was then that Mrs. Warden suddenly returned to the room and caught us.

Mrs. Warden told Mark and me to remain after class, and we did as told. "I'm surprised at you two," she said. "Aren't you embarrassed?" No answer. "Aren't you sorry?" Mark stood there with a dumb look on his face, and the truth was that I felt neither embarrassment nor sorrow so I didn't say anything either.

"I'm going to teach you two a lesson," she finally said, giving up on trying to get an apology out of us. "Each of your English grades will be lowered by one letter this six weeks."

"Wait," I said. "You can't do that, Mrs. Warden. Steve already has an F so you have no way to lower him."

She looked like she was trying to think what to say. I went on, "And furthermore, I think cheating is a moral failure, Mrs. Warden, not an academic one. Rather than lowering our English grades, you should give each of us an F in deportment for the six weeks. That's what we deserve."

"Oh, no," she said. "That wouldn't hurt you one bit. But lowering your grade in English will."

But she was wrong. I was proud of that B and bragged about what I said to Mrs. Warden to anyone who would listen.

My senior homeroom teacher was a skinny gray-headed woman named Miss Mabel Pyle, a teacher of commercial subjects. When you went down the hall and passed her room, you'd hear her in front of the class screeching out things like a-s-d-f-j-k-l-sem. Miss Pyle did not care for me. Once during lunch period when I remained in the room by myself, I saw an assessment form on her desk in which she had written that she thought I was "somewhat conceited." I had the strongest urge to tell her she had me wrong, that I was *exceedingly* conceited. But I resisted that temptation since I didn't want to admit I had been reading stuff on her desk.

My major confrontation with Miss Pyle came one day when two of my friends and I slipped out of her homeroom early one morning to go to a pep rally. As we hurried down the hall, she came to the door and called out, "You boys get back in this room."

"Let's ignore her," I said, and we began running in different directions. I decided to go into the library, where I crouched down behind the card catalogue. In a moment, in walked Miss Pyle. When she found me, I could see that her face was a cherry red. "Come back down to that classroom this minute," she said, and I walked beside her out of the library into the hall. She was stomping in anger. Finally she asked, "Are you a member of the National Honor Society?"

"Yes I am," I answered, trying to sound indifferent.

"Well, I'm going to do everything I can to have your affiliations cut off."

"Oh, Miss Pyle," I said as seriously as I could sound, "please don't cut my affiliations off. I want to have a family one day."

She made no answer, but rushed ahead of me into the classroom, and I knew I had won that round.

But my greatest glory with a teacher came in journalism class, which was taught by Mrs. Hyche, a blond-headed, innocent-faced girl just out of college, the wife of a Baptist minister. She was exceedingly mealy-mouthed, never for a moment getting control of the class. I was, without shame, one of the ringleaders in making her life miserable.

We never listened to a thing she said, talking to each other and passing notes, doodling in the margins of our textbooks, and sometimes reading magazines we had smuggled in. She kept droning on, no matter what, her voice getting weaker and more morose as the class progressed. At the end of class one day, however, she slapped her book on the podium, and when we looked up we could see she was trembling in rage and near tears. This was a new Mrs. Hyche. "You students don't have any idea how hard it is to stand in front of this durn class day in and day out facing a bunch of rude students who have no idea how to behave. I am sick of it and I'm tired of it," she said, her voice turning whiny, undoing any sympathy she might have earlier garnered.

Then Mrs. Hyche recovered her firmer voice and said, "I have decided it is time to teach you rude people a lesson." She paused, and we waited for what she had in mind. "Norman," she said, looking angrily in my direction, "you can just teach chapter nine tomorrow and see how it feels."

I read chapter nine carefully during lunch period that day, making out a set of questions as I went along, and for the rest of the day when I met my journalism classmates I assigned them questions. I instructed them all to raise their hands eagerly in class the next day every time I asked a question, but of course I would have the list of who was actually responsible for answering each question.

I could not have expected anything to go so well. Mrs. Hyche's mouth fell more and more open as the class proceeded. Her little mind was inadequate to figure out what was happening. For my part, I was quite happy to be talked about for a couple of days all around the school, and my conscience did not bother me a whit.

I sometimes thought I would have made an excellent criminal because I seldom felt regret for any of my wrong doings. My list of crimes was short but sweet. It began when I was in elementary school at Ralph. Donald and I went into the school's kitchen and stole two cans of orange juice concentrate out of the deep freeze. We took them down to Beaver Creek and opened them with our knives, and then we lay on the bank and sucked them slowly, relishing every bit. My conscience never ever said a word, and there was no evidence that Donald's did either.

I did have one habit that bordered on cruelty. I imitated people, often retarded people or rednecks or people I thought dumb. When I was a senior I began to tread on dangerous ground because I started mocking the football players. One day I was standing before a small group of my friends, dangling my arms in a simian swing and mumbling remarks like the one they often made at pep rallies—"Y'all come out and back us up and I think we'll take this one." Just as I got the sentence out of my mouth and just as my friends were beginning to laugh, Rusty Vance, a 250 pounder who had already been signed to play tackle for VPI, walked up.

"What are you doing, you little shit?" he said. I didn't answer. "I said, what the shit do you think you are doing?" I still didn't answer, and he reached out and grabbed me by my shirt and pulled me up to him. Rusty's thigh was the same circumference as my waist. We had measured it one time. He was about six foot-two, and as I looked up into his menacing face I thought, "This guy could kill me if he wanted to."

I had to think fast. I drew myself up in a little bundle and put an exaggerated look of fear on my face and said, "Please, Mr. Rusty, please don't throw me in the briar patch." Rusty began laughing and released me with a push, "Get out of here while the getting's good, you little monkey." I walked off feeling pretty victorious, finding it funny that that orangutan had called me a monkey.

The truth was, of course, that I was not quite as sure of myself as I acted. I constantly felt I had to be clever and entertaining in order to keep from getting run over. I always knew deep down that when all was said and done I was destined to be on the outside of things, at least for the time being. At Tuscaloosa County High, I never went to a sock hop or a prom. I went to very few football games. My sphere was the halls of the school, and I had to make the best I could of it. So I kept telling dirty jokes, acting as irreverent as I possibly could, and pretending to be an intellectual. I wanted to be liked, and whatever it took to achieve that I would do.

No matter how much I told myself I wasn't a nerd, I had to admit that I had many of the markings. I wore horn-rimmed glasses and uncool clothes. Even if I found a way to buy myself a red pair of pants or a pink shirt when they were all the rage, I knew that it was obvious to everyone that they were of the cheapest cut. Wearing them, I felt myself an impostor.

Most guys would not have been caught dead singing in the high school chorus, an organization for nerds and unpopular girls, but I became a member and thoroughly enjoyed singing music by composers that I had never heard of. "Joyful, joyful, we adore Thee, God of glory, Lord of love," I would sing happily, thinking there was no more beautiful tune in the world. Chorus also got me out of PE, which I didn't cotton to much, and the group got to travel around for concerts, competitions, and all-state chorus.

In many ways I would have rather been a member of the band—which was made up of borderline nerds. I would have given anything to play a trumpet and march in all the formations on the football field during the half-time show, but I could not afford a trumpet. The human voice, on the other hand, was free, and in my case my voice was about worth what I paid for it.

I had a nasal baritone, but I was as good as the others, and I had the added advantage of being pretty good at sight reading. When we would go to regional competitions, sight reading was always included, and Mr. Hawkins, our director, would call me aside and say, "Now, Norman, I'm counting on you to carry the baritones." Although I appreciated his confidence in me, I knew it was unwarranted, and invariably I would get real nervous and lose my place. We never scored high on sight reading.

I thought of myself as an arty person so when the senior play try-outs were announced I decided to go for a big role. We did a stupid play entitled *Grammercy Ghost*, but, pushed by a gorgeous student teacher whom we alternately lusted after and hated, we made the most of it. During the second week of rehearsals, she announced that a loving cup would be awarded to the member of the cast named outstanding actor on the night of the main performance but that at the rate we were going the judges would probably vote not to give the award that year. That was all it took for me to decide that I would be the best Thespian of the 1960 senior play, and I worked hard to milk my character, named Parker Burnett, for all he was worth. A sophisticated New Yorker, he was quite a stretch for me.

The night of the final performance of *Grammercy Ghost* Mama was in the audience, having been driven there by a woman from Ralph, and I knew she would be thrilled if I won so I tried especially hard. When Colonel Richardson, our school principal, announced that I was the winner, I walked out and proudly took the golden cup from him. The rest of the cast came onto stage to salute me, as they had been instructed to do.

The thrill of winning the loving cup was short-lived. I had expected one of my fellow cast members to ask me if I would like a ride to the cast party at the home of the female lead, but no one did. I was too proud to ask, and there was nothing for me to do but get myself and my loving cup in the car with Mama and her driver and head home as morose as I could be.

Another thing I did in high school, which some fellow students let me know very bluntly they judged to be nerdish, was mostly an economic matter as far as I was concerned. There were a number of oratorical contests at the time, and students were invited to compete for cash prizes and, in the case of the *Birmingham News* competition, scholarships. I was particularly interested in winning the cash, and I found out I was quite good at giving orations. I could get passionate about anything if there was money in it, and I quickly figured out that it was the passion the judges liked. Substance came in a distant second.

When my elementary teacher Miss Maurine, who always kept up with her former students and obviously felt largely responsible for any successes they had, found out I was interested in competing, she volunteered to help me write my speeches. In fact, she actually wrote them for me completely. Her first composition, called "The Constitution of the United States: A Living Reality," was for the American Legion Oratorical contest. Her speeches were great, with the titles always having classy colons, and I immediately found that they invariably allowed me to get emotional.

The savings bonds, usually given as prizes rather than hard cash, started coming in, and not a one of them, of course, ever matured. I would cash them at the earliest possible date, and a couple of times I would borrow the money from Mr. Luke Rodgers at the store until I was able to cash them.

Near the end of my senior year Miss Maurine wrote what was to be my most lucrative speech for the *Birmingham News* oratorical contest. She entitled it "Jefferson Davis: American Patriot." I won the school and the county contests, and when I moved up to the district contest Miss Maurine told me that I should practice my speech before an ancient woman from a nearby community, a woman who had taught elocution at a female academy before she retired. As I practiced my speech in her dim living room, she would say in a surprisingly loud voice, "Put some real stress on that part about states' rights, Norman" or "Come in loud and clear on that part about federal encroachment." I tried to do what she said, and I continued to win.

I finally made it to the state finals in Birmingham, and, lacking transportation of my own, I was transported by my English teacher, Miss Beavers. This was an all-expense paid trip, and I spent the first two days of my life in a hotel—the fancy Moulton Hotel. I felt quite prosperous as I repeatedly ate New York strip steaks and scalloped potatoes, all of it covered in catsup, while Miss Beavers ate things like Waldorf salad and creamed chicken in a little pie shell.

On the day of the contest Sarah even brought Mama up from Ralph to hear me. For some reason their presence made me feel even surer that I would come out the winner of the first prize, a four-year college scholarship. I gave my speech to a large audience in an auditorium on the campus of Birmingham-Southern, and I vibrated with connection to the crowd. As I let loose the emotion, I knew I was impressing them all. But then things turned bad. I had somehow missed the point that at the state level a second part was added to the competition, an extem-

Winning second place in the *Birmingham News*, oratorical contest

poraneous speech that asked the contestant to enlarge on some point made in the prepared oration. The idea was to see if the contestants could think on their feet, I assumed.

After my prepared speech, I was handed a sheet of paper on which was typed my question for the extemporaneous speech. After someone had taken me to an empty classroom to prepare for it, I eagerly read my question: "In your memorized oration you said the following: 'At the close of his term under Pierce in 1857, Davis again entered the Senate and became one of the strongest defenders of the South in their position on slavery.' Based on your research, explain how Davis did this."

I had not the faintest idea how he did it. I hadn't done any research, and other than what was in my speech I knew next to nothing about him other than he was wearing women's clothes when he was captured. I sat there in the classroom trying to manufacture something to say, but nothing would come. I was beginning to get edgy, and when they called me to come back out I hadn't the foggiest notion what I would do. But for five minutes I let out the biggest spate of bullshit that surely was ever uttered from that stage.

This time, the judges couldn't forgive me, so embarrassingly weak was my extemporaneous speech. After it was all over, one judge whispered to Mama that I had it sewn up until the second part. A fat girl, whose bullshit was not so transparent as mine, took first place for a speech on another Confederate hero, and I had to settle for second place.

When I joined Mama, Sarah, and Miss Beavers after the contest, I felt somewhat sheepish. "I sort of messed up, didn't I?" I asked.

Mama jumped right in. "No, you did not mess up. You won second place, and that is nothing to be ashamed of. And I shouldn't say it, but I thought the question they asked you for the extemporaneous part was not fair. They were asking you to drag us back through the whole slavery question again."

I knew she was wrong about that, but I said nothing. There was Mama, in her usual form, putting the best interpretation on events and being, as she had always been, my greatest supporter. And she had me and Sarah and Miss Beavers both nodding.

I left Birmingham with the one-year scholarship to the University of Alabama. Whatever happened between then and fall, I would have it, puny as it was, to fall back on if nothing else turned up. Birmingham-Southern was where I had wanted to go, and I had gone to the competition for the Phi Beta Kappa Scholarship, expecting to win it just as Evelyn had about twenty years before, but I didn't even receive an honorable mention. The University of Alabama might have to do.

During my senior year, I wanted more than anything to be self-sufficient. I did my best to find part-time work in Tuscaloosa, but such jobs were almost non-existent. I would have loved to work as a salesman in a store, to jerk soda, or to pump gas, but no luck. When I got money from my brothers and sisters, as I did pretty often, or the prize money from the oratorical contests, I didn't throw it away. I'd usually spend it on food and clothes. I finally got desperate enough to take a job selling magazines door to door for National Periodical Enterprises, the last resort for the young and hopeless.

Luckily, another senior who had a car took a job with National Periodical too, and Charley gave me a lift from school to our gathering place, which was the Barbecue Inn on the edge of town. There, ten fidgety guys looked warily at the man who identified himself as our boss, Johnny Dubchek. "Just call me Johnny," the greasy, baby-faced man said. "Nobody can pronounce my last name down here anyway."

"Who says?" I thought, as I looked over at the overweight man who was wearing his shirt and pants at least one size too small. A skinny blue tie with gray stripes hung around his neck, and I noticed that the top button on his shirt was not buttoned. He handed each of us a printed sheet. "This," he said in a Yankee accent, "is what you'll say to the person answering the door. Take a few minutes to look it over and memorize it."

I looked it over, but I sure didn't get it memorized.

Johnny Dubchek went on: "Boys, I want you to know that you've got a first-class opportunity here to make yourselves some darn good money. But there's two things. First, you got to believe in your product, and I can tell you truthfully that National Periodicals has got the best magazines published in America today. Just look at that list I gave you. You won't see any trash here."

He gave us a minute to act like we were scanning the price list before beginning again. "Second," he said in a very serious voice, "you gotta believe in yourselves." I decidedly did not believe in myself when it came to selling magazines, but I needed that darn good money so I listened attentively. "When you knock at that door," he went on, "you speak right up good and loud with real self-confidence, because one thing I know is true: if you don't have confidence in yourselves nobody is going to have confidence in *you*." It struck me that he thought he was the first human being to say such a thing, and I caught myself grinning a little bit.

Johnny Dubchek continued, "In a good loud voice, now, you tell that housewife or man, such as the case may be, what a savings you have to offer. Say it like it's written on that sheet I gave you. Tell them that if they buy a package of any five magazines, they'll save eighty percent off cover prices. Tell them that. That'll get their attention."

Then he looked closely at each of the nervous and unenthusiastic faces before him and said with a knowing grin on his face, "Now I know what you're thinking. You're thinking, 'What's in it for me?' Well, what is in it for you is twenty percent of everything you sell. We estimate an average sell of forty dollars per household, and if my arithmetic's right, you just made yourself eight dollars. And that's just one sale. You may have as many as five or ten sales a night."

I was pretty skeptical as he handed us out the order forms, but I tried to be positive as we fanned out into the streets we had been assigned. For two hours I walked around the affluent neighborhood we started in, half-heartedly knocking on doors, and I didn't get anywhere. They could obviously tell I lacked self confidence. When we met back up with Johnny, only one boy—Horace Stamps—had sold a thing. He was proud to have sold $40 worth to an invalid woman.

"That is really good. Horace made a sale, everybody," Johnny said. "But I don't want the rest of you to be discouraged. This is your first night, and you haven't really gotten the things you're supposed to say memorized very well. That's understandable. Work on it at home tonight, I'd say in front of a mirror, and I'll guarantee you you'll do better tomorrow. I never expect too much the first night."

As we left, I told Charley that I'd give it one more night, and when I got to Evelyn's apartment I told her I didn't have much hope of selling anything. As she left to work on her dissertation in the library, she suggested that I might come up with my own spiel, that the one they suggested seemed too stiff and not very convincing. So I did that, deciding that my approach would be like this: "Ma'am (or sir), I represent National Periodical Enterprises. My company has become seriously committed to raising the reading standards of the South, and therefore we have special bargains not available anywhere else in America. If you'll just look at these prices, ma'am (or sir), I believe that you'll admit you've never seen magazines so inexpensive." I even practiced in front of the mirror.

As Charley and I went to work the next day I felt hopeful. Only six of our original ten showed up, but Johnny said that was no surprise to him. "Some people have it," he said, "and some don't." When we reported at the end of the evening, I had made two sales, one for thirty dollars and one for thirty-five, and in my head I figured my earnings to be over twelve dollars. Johnny beamed. Charley looked depressed, and I could tell that he hadn't sold anything. No one else had either. But Johnny said things would be better the next night.

I was shameless in using my spiel about improving the reading habits of the South and it seemed to be working, not that I had many sales, but I was outselling everybody else. We had started in the more well-to-do parts of the city where people had, it was supposed, disposable income, and we were moving down the economic ladder slowly. That didn't seem to make much difference in the amount of sales, it seemed to me.

One night I knocked at the door of a modest frame house near the University, and I was shocked when Dr. Ernest van Tuyll, an English professor at Alabama whom I had met one time through Evelyn, came to the door. Although I was unnerved, there was nothing to do but go on with my sales pitch. When I finished, he asked in a rather weary voice, "And just what magazines are going to raise the reading standards of Southerners?"

Nobody had ever asked me such a question, but I stammered out an answer, "*Field and Stream, Ladies' Home Journal, Time, Argosy. . . .*"

A slight sardonic smile came to Dr. van Tuyll's lips, and he said flatly, "Those magazines aren't going to raise the reading standards anywhere."

He had me, so I left in a hurry.

The job was becoming more and more of a drag. Charley and I both grew to hate it so much that the only way we could stand to report to duty was to go by Evelyn's apartment first to get a snort of her bourbon. The neighborhoods were getting worse and worse. We had worked our way down to Kaulton, a rough part of town that was so bad that Mama refused to ride through it, even with car doors locked. The houses were cheap bungalows, and some were tar-paper shacks.

One night I knocked at a bungalow door, and after a while a middle-aged man wearing a denim railroad cap, a denim shirt, and blue jeans appeared before me. He was extremely neat, but there was a wildness in his eyes that was off putting. When he invited me in, I walked into the living room where I saw another man dressed exactly like him cleaning his nails with a pocket knife and an old woman with yellowish gray hair sitting in the corner with her hands in her lap. The man who answered the door invited me to have a seat in a vacant rocking chair.

As I sat down, I began to tell them that the company I worked for wanted to raise the reading standards of the South, but before I could finish, the man came over to the rocker, stood by it, and began to rock me back and forth. "Say," he said, "do you think it's smart for a boy like you to walk into people's houses you don't know. That sounds dangerous to me. Don't it sound dangerous to you, Wert?" he asked the other man.

"It sure do," he said, not looking up from his fingernails.

"You never know what you'll find inside, now do you?" he asked me.

Then I saw the madness in his eyes more clearly than I had before. "No, sir," I said weakly. He kept on rocking my chair and didn't say anything.

The silence was unbearable so I volunteered, "I can go, if you want me to."

He leaned over near my face and grinned enormously. "You're not going any goddamn where. You'll do what I say. Do you understand that?"

The other man came over on the other side of my chair, and standing in front of me he shook the knife toward me. "You ain't going nowhere until we've finished with you." He seemed to be holding his groin with the hand that was not holding the knife.

I had no idea what to do. One salesman had got propositioned by a housewife, but there had been no threat there. Then the old lady sitting in the corner alarmed me terribly when she started crying and whining. I looked over and could see she was trying to get up out of her chair. I heard her say, "Now y'all quit that, boys. Leave him alone. He ain't done anything. Y'all better not do him like y'all done that other one. I'll call the law."

"Shut, up, Mama," the first man said, "You ain't got nothing to do with this."

I was shocked to see her go over to the guy with the knife, draw back her arm, and smack him hard in the face.

Donald

He stepped backward, screaming, "Stop that, Mama, or, God as my witness, I'll brain you." But I was a little relieved to note that he looked pretty much cowed by the old woman.

I began to get out of the rocking chair, and as I did so she grabbed the other man by his collar and snatched him around. "Run," she said to me.

I ran to the front door, and I could hear the first man yelling at me, "Yeah, why don't you just get your little goddamned ass out of here right now?"

As I pulled the front door open to get out, I fully expected to feel a knife in my back. Shaking all over, I ran down the steps into the street, and I didn't slow up until my little ass got to Johnny Dubchek's car. "I quit," I said breathlessly, handing him my subscription pad. I didn't wait for an answer. I didn't wait for the other salesmen to return. I walked the two miles back to Evelyn's apartment and poured me out a glass of her bourbon, which I drank neat.

I quit my job for National Periodical Enterprises about a month before graduation, and that gave me more time to think about life after high school. I wasn't sure at all what the future held. I had the scholarship to the University for the fall, but I didn't know whether I'd use it or not because I had decided to go to Fort Worth, Texas, for the summer at least. My two older brothers had gone to Fort Worth after high school, had joined the Air Force, and had never moved back to Alabama. Donald was stationed at Carswell Air Force Base, and he said that I should come on out, that I could use his Fiat 600 for transportation when I needed it and stay in the same rooming house he had stayed in when he first moved there. That settled it. I would go. Texas to me was spelled f-r-e-e-d-o-m and o-p-p-o-r-t-u-n-i-t-y, and I was anxious for a new life.

Dimming my excitement about finishing school was an announcement that came over the intercom the week before graduation. The school secretary's voice read the message: "Attention all seniors. Attention all seniors. Some of you are in arrears with your school fees. These must be paid before graduation if you intend to graduate. I repeat. These MUST be paid before you are allowed to graduate."

School fees were only $10 per year, but I had never paid a cent, and I had a whopping bill of $60. I concluded that there was no way that I could part with the money I had been given for graduation, it being necessary for settling in Texas. I thought for a moment of going to the principal, Colonel Richardson, and telling him I wasn't able to swing it now. Colonel Richardson, who was fond of saying that he didn't care whether he was loved or not, but he intended to be respected, and who effected a gruff, military demeanor which even his bright colored bow ties and love of Broadway musicals could not totally undermine, was really a very nice man. On a couple of occasions when he had driven me to oratorical contests he had gotten downright chatty, and he'd been nice to me on a one occasion when his son, who was also a senior, had invited me to their house to hear music. I really had no reason, then, to fear talking to Colonel Richardson, nor did I have any reason to think that he would withhold my diploma. But that is exactly the idea that formed in my mind. I convinced myself that when I took the diploma in on the morning after graduation to get him to sign it, as we were required to do, he would refuse because I had not paid my fees.

Despite this cloud hanging over me, my buddy Henry and I made our plans for graduation night. I mentioned nothing to him or anyone else about my worries. There was to be a party down in Greene County at a place called the Cotton Patch, and Henry and I told those planning it that we would be there. In preparation, we went over and stood in front of the state liquor store in Tuscaloosa, waiting for someone we thought we could approach about buying us a bottle of vodka. When we saw a skinny derelict slowly making his way toward us, we knew we had our man. After looking all around to make sure we weren't being observed, I told the man we'd give him a tip if he's get some vodka for us, and he agreed, taking the ten dollar bill Henry held out and entering the store. When he came back out, he had a bottle of Hannah and Hogg vodka in a paper sack, and we felt greatly relieved to see it. "Keep the change," Henry said. Then we went to the grocery store and bought a half-gallon can of Donald Duck orange juice to mix the vodka with.

Henry did not have a car of his own so we would have to go to the Cotton Patch in his family car that night, and because his family had to use the car to go to graduation we had to hide the vodka. Like Mama, the Lowerys were tee-totalers, and they would have been shocked to know that Henry and I drank. So we took the bottle to Northwood Lake and hid it under a tree we thought we would easily find that night.

An hour or two before the graduation ceremony started, it began to rain. The exercises had to be moved from the stadium to the gym so it was just as well that none of my family had planned to come anyway. The seating was greatly restricted. I won the Woodman of the World Prize in American History, and as I got it I thought, "Surely they won't hold me back for not paying my fees now that I have won this." I also had the glancing idea that I might give the school the solid gold pin I received in lieu of the cash I owed.

After the ceremony, Henry and I took his parents home and headed to Northwood Lake, where Henry pulled out a flashlight he had hidden in the trunk. It had stopped raining, but as we walked into the woods to retrieve the vodka I could tell that my new suit that Evelyn had bought me at W. T Grant Company was getting quite soggy from the rising damp. "Wasn't it over here?" Henry said, shining the light toward a tall oak tree.

I realized at that moment that I had no idea where we had hid the vodka. "I think so," I said.

He went over and looked, but no Hannah and Hogg. We repeated that scene for over an hour. "Let's just go, dammit," I suggested just as Henry stumbled up on the right tree and reached down and lifted up the wet sack. By then, our suit pants were dripping, but we had nothing to change into. We headed toward Greene County anyway. After we had driven a few miles in silence, Henry said, "You know what, Norman. I'm not going into any party looking like this."

"I know what you mean, but what the hell do you want to do?"

"Let's find somewhere to drink this frigging vodka," he said, turning off a side road. We parked the car and sat there dourly, mixing ourselves drink after drink of vodka and the metallic-tasting Donald Duck orange juice.

"This is so goshdarned good," I said, but my heart wasn't really in it. This was not my idea of a celebration. But it was better than nothing. We sat on the side of the road until we could drink no more, and then we just sat there, waiting for daylight. I'd doze a little, and I knew Henry was sleeping a little because he was snoring.

About six o'clock, Henry suggested that we head back to the high school and wait in the parking lot until we could get our diplomas signed, and I agreed. Both of us felt lousy. Our heads were aching, our hands were trembling, and I was afraid I was going to throw up any minute. Our suit pants had dried out a little, but after sitting in them all night they were terribly wrinkled and clung to our legs. Henry's heavy beard needed shaving, and neither of us had a comb for our hair. And I worried still about what would happen when I placed my diploma in front of Colonel Richardson.

When the opening bell rang, we got unsteadily out of the car and went in and joined the line of seniors who had come early to get their diplomas signed, most of them so they could take off on their senior trips to Panama City or Gulf Shores. I had earlier envied them, but now I was relieved that I wouldn't be going anywhere today but home.

Colonel Richardson was seated decorously at a table that had been set up in the front of the auditorium, signing the diplomas placed before him with a great flourish of his pen. I tried to read his face. I looked to see if he was consulting a list of those who could not be graduated, and I could not tell that he was. When my time came, I tried to act nonchalant and steady as I placed my diploma before him. Without a moment's hesitation, he placed his name on it, and I felt the greatest relief pass over me. I felt reinvigorated.

"Best wishes, Norman," he said, looking at me sort of hard, I thought. "Remember, I expect to hear good things of you."

"Thank you, sir," I said, and I stood there a minute and watched Colonel Richardson sign Henry's fully-paid-up diploma.

Henry drove me to Ralph after we got our diplomas signed, and I went in and showed Mama the Woodman of the World pin. She said she was real proud, and, though I could tell she was worried about my appearance, she didn't preach me a sermon.

I stumbled off to bed, and when I woke up it was about nightfall. I sat on the edge of the bed and counted my money. I had $190, more than I had ever had in my life. People who were aware that I was leaving for Texas knew I would prefer money, and I was thankful to them all. I packed my striped suitcase and put it in the front hall. Mama and Daddy had already gone to bed by this time, but I talked to Julia and Kenneth for a little, and I could tell that they were envious of my being able to go to Texas the next day. I took a bath in the newly installed bathroom, a gift from Sarah and Howard, and went back to bed, anxious to make my start to Texas, to what might be a new life.

PART 6

New Beginning

On many occasions I had heard the story of my great grandfather David Avery heading out for Alabama from North Carolina, and I was acutely aware that he would have been almost exactly my age when he began his adventure. My trip seemed rather puny by comparison, but I was heading west too and I supposed that what I was feeling, the excitement and fear, he too might have felt over a century earlier.

Fort Worth would be the fartherest I had been from home, and to get there I would be hitchhiking. I couldn't begin to think of using any of my graduation money on a bus ticket. I got up at 4:00 the morning of my departure, and when Mama heard me moving around she got up in the dark and made me some biscuits. Daddy, Julia, and Kenneth got up too and joined us at the breakfast table. We buttered our biscuits in silence. Everything felt awkward so I rushed to leave. Julia and Kenneth just stood there. Mama kissed me on the cheek, and Daddy, standing there stiffly looking embarrassed, took my hand and shook it formally.

But there were no tears on either side when I picked up my suitcase. "Write," Mama said.

"I'll write you as soon as I get settled," I said, and I started walking down the dirt road past the terraces covered with dewberries and past the stands of wild plum trees filled with red and yellow fruit. I found myself looking at everything more closely than I ever had before. I turned back for a moment and looked at the house that had been my home for nine years. The top planks still needed paint. I then walked past the fields of vegetables, mostly still unripe. Afterwards, I passed Bethel Baptist Church cemetery with its straightened graves and then the church itself, standing high and white in the first light of day. For the moment I had no regrets. Although I had no firm idea where I'd end up, I felt somehow confident that I was taking a saved, unburdened soul into the brand new life before me.

AFTERWORD

For those curious about the lives of my family after 1960, the following brief accounts are provided:

Daddy

By the mid-sixties all of the children had left home, but my parents continued to live in the house at Ralph. By the mid-seventies, however, they were not really able to keep the place up any longer, so they moved to Tuscaloosa and lived in a one-bedroom apartment, a place Daddy deplored because, as he said, "There isn't any air that can come in or go out of this place."

Despite his hypochondria, Daddy's health remained pretty good. In the mid-seventies he did, however, have carotid artery surgery that left him unable to focus his eyes properly, and his greatest pastime, reading, was taken from him. He had little use for television, except for *Sanford and Son,* which he watched with great pleasure.

As my mother's health deteriorated, Daddy was less able to take care of her and an apartment, and around 1978 they moved into the Park Manor Nursing Home in Northport. After my mother's death, he remained there, unwilling to participate in any group activities and furtively swigging on pint bottles of Old Crow Kenneth smuggled in for him regularly and deposited in the pocket of his trench coat.

For years, Daddy had been concerned with the function of his greater bowel, but in his last few years he became obsessed. When you visited him he gave you a report on how things were going. On the day he died, according to the people at the nursing home, he got up, had his breakfast, and then went to the toilet and had an excellent session.

Immediately thereafter he had a massive coronary and died before he could get his pants back up. Kenneth said we could all take comfort in the fact that he died happy, and we agreed.

Mama

During the sixties Mama felt more and more the effects of her rheumatoid arthritis, and as the pain grew she became more and more sedentary. By taking big doses of cortisone, she could still get around some, attending weddings and funerals, and she made her only airplane trip in 1971, flying with Sarah to Ann Arbor, Michigan, to see me receive my Ph. D.

Mama's main pleasures were reading and watching television. She prided herself on being up on political matters, and she relished the entire Watergate crisis. She watched every second of the televised Senate Watergate hearings, idolizing Senator Sam Ervin as much as she demonized Nixon and his cronies.

As the seventies wore down, so did she. Her bones had been made so brittle by the cortisone that she could break a bone by merely turning in the bed. As she lay in her hospital bed during her final days, in torment because of pain and sometimes out of her head because of the morphine, one of us children would stay with her. I had duty the day before she died, and at one point she turned to me and said, "Norman, when that male nurse comes in here to turn me over, I want you to run him out. It just hurts too bad. Will you run him out?"

"Yes, ma'am," I said, thinking that she was not really aware of what she was saying.

The nurse came in, and he turned her. The agonized sound that came from her was inhuman, the most horrible I had ever heard. When the nurse left, Mama—always before my greatest booster—turned to me with a look of absolute lucidity and said very deliberately, "You are the stupidest man I ever knew. I always thought your Daddy was stupid, but you are even stupider."

Those were the last words I heard from my mother.

Evelyn

Evelyn began her college teaching career the fall after I graduated from high school, first at Athens State College and then at Jacksonville State University, where she remained until retirement in 1990. Never owning a car or a house and largely uninterested in worldly goods, her only luxuries were books and travel. She lived modestly for many years with Martha Howell in Jacksonville.

Evelyn took students for annual study programs at Stratford-upon-Avon, where she had studied, and she provided all her nieces and nephews a trip to England when they graduated from high school or the equivalent in cash. Her generosity extended to her parents and to her siblings as well.

In the late fall of 1991 Evelyn suddenly became ill, and shortly thereafter she was diagnosed with cancer. By that time it had spread to most of her organs. Ever the stoic, she faced death with grace. She died in February of 1992.

Sarah

Everyone assumed that Sarah and Howard could not have children, but in 1963, a son Avery was born, joining Roger, their adopted son. In the early sixties, Sarah and Howard moved the family to Greensboro, where Howard became manager and part owner of garment factories. Sarah served as bookkeeper for those plants as well as of other businesses owned by Howard's brother. Sarah and Howard were now close enough to Ralph to visit often, looking after my parents' needs.

In 1975 Sarah began to have chronic pains in her shoulder, which she attributed to bursitis, but suddenly she had to be rushed to the hospital in Selma in the middle of the night, where they discovered a collapsed lung. Tests showed immediately that she had lung cancer—unfortunately no great surprise as she had been a heavy smoker since college days. She lived a horrible year with radiation therapy and chemotherapy, but nothing worked. She faced all of it with amazing equanimity, dying at home at the age of forty-six.

Bill

Bill remained in the Air Force until the early seventies, and during the sixties he and his English wife Vivian had two sons, Kevin and Phillip. Vivian was never happy in this country, and occasionally she would go home to Nottingham on a visit and would not return until Bill went over and brought her back. Once, in the mid-seventies she went back without the sons, and when she failed to return he decided not to go get her. A divorce ensued.

Although by this time Bill was an alcoholic, he managed to raise his sons alone, living in various Texas towns and in Alabama for a short while, working mainly for the Veterans Administration after retiring from the military. In time the alcohol took its toll, and finally he checked himself into a detox program in Houston, joining the AA after he got out. He has been sober for over twenty-five years.

After retirement, Bill moved to Galveston. He uses his time traveling (primarily by train) all over the country, actively participating in AA activities, meeting women on the internet (marrying one woman twice), and going around to thrift stores in the Galveston/Houston area, where he buys upscale clothes, selling on eBay what he does not wear or give away to the family. Recently, he has remarried.

Bill has six grandchildren and two great-grandchildren.

Elizabeth

Elizabeth, the most artistic member of the family, and her husband Bernie had three children, Mary Ann, Jamie, and Freddie. They have lived in the same house for over forty years. Elizabeth, who never learned to drive a car, supplemented her children's school education with her own enrichment programs at home, and all developed a love of the arts and were quite creative.

Elizabeth is known for her various charities. She has helped countless people, especially through her church, serving on a committee to seek out and aid people in need. In addition, she has tutored international students in English at the Baptist Student Center on the campus of the University of Alabama.

When our brother-in-law Howard died a year after Sarah did, Elizabeth and Bernie raised their thirteen-year-old son, Avery, and a few years ago, when their son Freddie divorced and obtained custody of his son, they began keeping their grandson Beck in their home. They also have a granddaughter Emily.

Marcille

Marcille and her husband Bobby had two children, Bob and Marcia. Marcille completed her undergraduate degree and a masters in elementary education at the University of Alabama, subsequently teaching fourth and fifth grades at Vestavia Elementary School in Northport for many years. She and Bobby have lived in the same house in Northport for thirty-three years.

As active members of the Air Stream Club, Marcille and Bobby have traveled all over America and Canada in caravans with their many friends. Having retired from teaching, Marcille has an outlet for her creative spirit by writing, producing, and acting in skits for the Air Stream groups and at her church. In addition to traveling with Air Stream, they spend a good bit of time at their beach house in Panama City, Florida.

Marcille and Bobby have three grandsons and one granddaughter.

Donald

After getting out of the Air Force in the early sixties, Donald married an Arkansas girl, Flo Nowlin. He worked in the automobile industry in Texas for a while, painting half of the inside of the trunks day in and day out. Early on, he decided he wanted to be a missionary, and he took courses at a divinity school near Fort Worth, Texas. He and Flo learned Portuguese and went to Belem, Brazil in the mid-seventies, where they still are.

Donald and Flo have six children—Michael, Melissa, Michelle, Mark, Melody, and Mindy—all of whom have the initials MDM. Except for one, all now reside in the U. S. Donald and Flo periodically return on furlough, and they plan to live in the U. S. when they retire. They have three grandchildren.

Norman

In the fall of 1960, Norman returned home from Texas to attend the University of Alabama, from which he graduated with a B. A. in English in 1964. When a freshman, he met Joan Shannon, a business major from Birmingham, and in 1962, at the age of twenty, they were married.

In Tuscaloosa, he and Joan had a daughter Sally, and in 1967 he earned an M. A in English. Subsequently they moved to Ann Arbor, where their son John was born and where he received a Ph. D. in English from the University of Michigan in 1971.

Norman taught English at the University of Montevallo from 1971 to 2000, and now in retirement spends much of his time on writing projects. Joan has been a legal secretary for almost thirty years. Much of Norman and Joan's time is occupied by their three grandchildren, Helen, Marion, and Egan.

Julia

Julia attended the University of Alabama, majoring in Spanish and marrying Jim Cork while an undergraduate. After graduation, she moved to Atlanta, where she taught high school Spanish and had two daughters, Mary Beth and Carolyn. After her marriage ended in divorce, she married Allen Walker and had another daughter, Jessica. She has five grandchildren.

Julia has had numerous interests and shifts in her career. After teaching Spanish, she first changed to English and later to working with at-risk students of junior high school age. At one point she became interested in parapsychology and studied the subject at the University of West Georgia. Her interests in American-Indian culture have led her to study with a shaman, and she has traveled the world as part of a women's peace movement. Most recently she has volunteered with My House, an Atlanta program which takes care of premature babies who have been abused or neglected, primarily the children of drug-addicted mothers.

For the last few years, she has worked for a direct-mail publisher in Peachtree City, Georgia, writing books primarily on health questions for women interested in using preventive and nontraditional measures to maintain good health.

Kenneth

Like his older brothers, Kenneth headed off to Texas after graduation, later joining the Air Force in the mid-sixties. After his stint in the service, he returned to Ralph, living with our parents and attending the University of Alabama. But in the early seventies he dropped out and took a job at B. F. Goodrich in Tuscaloosa. Shortly thereafter he married Brenda Nelson, and they had two girls named Jennifer and Kimberly. They have one granddaughter.

For a number of years Kenneth and family lived in the family house in Ralph, but later they moved to Tuscaloosa. When the B. F. Goodrich plant was bought by Michelin and many of the perks the union had negotiated for the workers were taken away, Kenneth chose to take a buy-out, after which he became a successful real estate salesman and broker.

Kenneth and Brenda often travel abroad, and they spend a great deal of time at their beach house in Panama City, Florida.

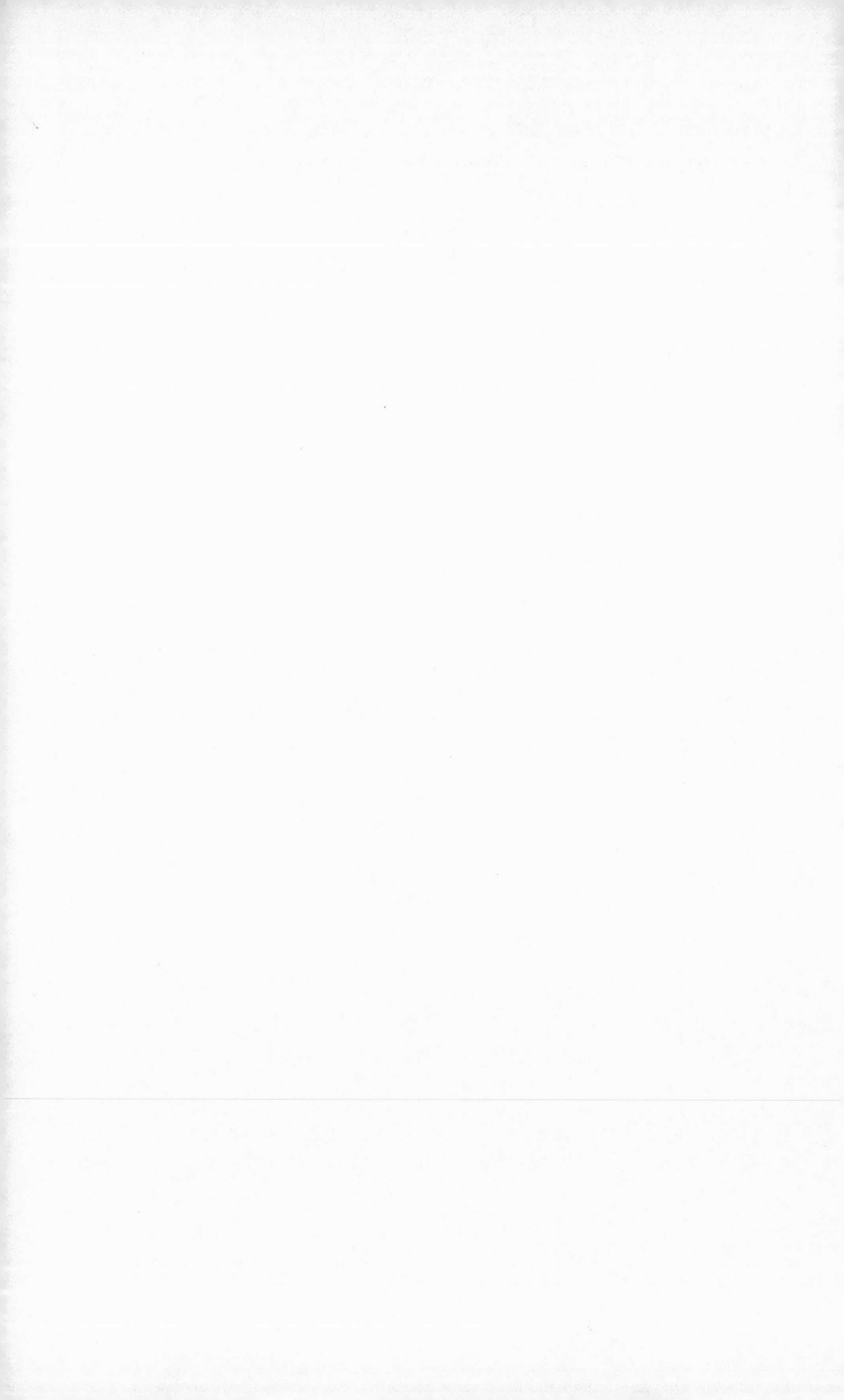